Asian Immigrants in North America with HIV/AIDS

AKM Ahsan Ullah
Universiti Brunei Darussalam (UBD)
Bandar Seri Begawan
Brunei Darussalam

Ahmed Shafiqul Huque
Department of Political Science
McMaster University
Hamilton, ON, Canada

ISBN 978-981-10-1374-4 ISBN 978-981-287-119-0 (eBook)
DOI 10.1007/978-981-287-119-0
Springer Singapore Heidelberg New York Dordrecht London

Printed on acid-free paper

Springer is part of Springer Science+Business Media (www.springer.com)

Preface

Discrimination and stigmatization have had profound impact on the livelihood patterns of the refugee and migrant population living with HIV/AIDS worldwide. The extent to which they suffer and succumb to irrational and risky behaviour is largely unknown. This book intends to reveal the dynamics that influence choice, behaviour and lifestyle of the infected immigrants and refugees. By scholarship, therefore, this book adds to the existing knowledge about refugee and migrants and expands a unified theory of discrimination and stigmatization within the context of human rights.

Refugee and HIV issues have emerged as one of the most important topics in contemporary scholarly discourse on public health and human rights. Refugee populations are the most vulnerable groups due to various reasons. Dislodged from their homeland, they descend into a situation of total uncertainty in terms of financial, physical and health security; resettlement process; and adaptation in a new society. The situation becomes unbearable if they are diagnosed with HIV positive, which places them in extremely precarious conditions as they are in desperate need of shelter, protection, healthcare services and psychosocial counselling. Only a handful of resettlement countries accept them on the basis of their commitment to the 1951 Refugee Convention, and Canada is one of them. The book formulates a number of policy recommendations based on the findings of the empirics with a view to helping reshape polices regarding refugees, HIV/AIDS and the social ramifications. By scholarship, this expands a unified theory of stigma, discrimination, prejudice, xenophobia and human rights through a contemporary perspective.

Several individuals and institutions have contributed to the preparation of this manuscript. First and foremost, we are thankful to the subjects of this research. They were willing to give us time, provided valuable information and trusted us in sharing their experiences. Without their help, it would not be possible to complete this manuscript.

We would like to register our gratitude to the Canadian Institutes of Health Research (CIHR) for the financial support for conducting the research. We are indebted to Ronald Labonte and Kevin Pottie, whose guidance has been invaluable.

A number of Toronto-based organizations for providing services to HIV-positive people from South and Southeast Asia helped establish contact with the subjects of the research.

We thank the University of Ottawa and McMaster University for the support extended towards the completion of this research. We wish to thank various people for their contribution to this research process. Corinne Packer and Jodie Karpf are highly acknowledged for their support in logistics and research.

Although this project resulted from the support and encouragement of many people who cannot be named for lack of space, some must be mentioned. Ainslie Avery helped with editorial support; Mukul Bodiuzzaman gave a constant support through comments and critique. We would also like to acknowledge Amirul Islam and Nermeen Abdel Aziz for assisting with literature search and Md Mizanur Rahman and Maria D'aria for their comments and feedback on the manuscript.

Without the support of our family members, this research could not have been possible to complete. They provided unconditional support, and we would like to register our gratitude to them.

Brunei Darussalam AKM Ahsan Ullah
Hamilton, ON, Canada Ahmed Shafiqul Huque

Contents

Abbreviations

ABS	American Behavioral Scientist
ACCHO	African and Caribbean Council on HIV/AIDS in Ontario
ADR	Alternative dispute resolution
AIDS	Acquired Immune Deficiency Syndrome / Acquired Immunodeficiency Syndrome
APIAHF	Asian and Pacific Islander American Health Forum
ART	Antiretroviral therapy
ARV	Antiretrovirals
ASAAP	Alliance for South Asian AIDS Prevention
ASARC	Australia South Asia Research Centre
BCC	Behaviour change communication
BMC	Boston Medical Center
BSS	Behaviour Surveillance Study
CAC	Citizen's Advisory Committee
CARE	Cooperative for Assistance and Relief Everywhere
CAREC	Caribbean Epidemiology Centre
CARICOM	Caribbean Community
CATIE	Clinical Antipsychotic Trials of Intervention Effectiveness
CBO	Community-based organization
CBSA	Canada Border Services Agency
CCDIC	Centre for Communicable Diseases and Infection Control
CD4	Cluster of Differentiation 4
CDC	Centers for Disease Control
CIC	Citizenship and Immigration Canada/Canada Immigration and Citizenship
CIDA	Canadian International Development Agency
COSATU	Congress of South African Trade Unions
CPHA	Canadian Public Health Association
CPJ	Citizens for Public Justice
CRN+	Caribbean Regional Network of People Living with HIV
CRSF	Caribbean Regional Strategic Framework

CSHA	Canadian Strategy on HIV/AIDS
CSME	CARICOM Single Market and Economy
CSO	Civil Society Organization
DFID	British Department for International Development
DHHS	Department of Health and Human Services
DRO	Dispute Resolution Officer
ECHR	European Court of Human Rights
EU	European Union
FBO	Faith-based organization
FCC	Federal Court of Canada
FINIS	Framework Integrating Normative Influences on Stigma
FSW	Female sex workers
GFATM	Global Fund to Fight AIDS, Tuberculosis and Malaria
GIPA	Greater Involvement of People Living with HIV
GT	Grounded theory
HAART	Highly active antiretroviral therapy
HFLE	Health and Family Life Education
HIV	Human immunodeficiency virus
HSSWG	Health and Society Scholars Working Group
IACHR	Inter-American Commission on Human Rights
IAD	Immigration Appeal Division
ICAD	Interagency Coalition on AIDS and Development
ICASO	International Council of AIDS Service Organisations
ICCPR	International Covenant on Civil and Political Rights
ICEARD	International Convention on the Elimination of All Forms of Racial Discrimination
ICESCR	International Covenant on Economic, Social and Cultural Rights
ID	Immigration Division
IDB	Inter-American Development Bank
IDU	Injecting drug user
IFAD	International Fund for Agricultural Development
IFH	Interim Federal Health
ILO	International Labour Organization
IOM	International Organization for Migration
IRB	Immigration and Refugee Board
IRPA	Immigration and Refugee Protection Act
IZA	Institute for the Study of Labor
JIAPAC	Journal of the International Association of Physicians in AIDS Care
KAP	Key affected population
LGBTI	Lesbian, gay, bisexual, transgender and intersex persons
LISR	Library and Information Science Research
LTTE	Liberation Tigers of Tamil Eelam
MDG	Millennium Development Goals
MSM	Men who have sex with men
NAPO	National Anti-Poverty Organization

NAPs	National AIDS Programs
NAZ	NAZ Foundation (India) Trust
NGO	Nongovernmental organization
OCASI	Ontario Council of Agencies Serving Immigrants
OHCHR	Office of the High Commissioner for Human Rights
OVC	Orphans and Vulnerable Children
PAHO	Pan American Health Organization
PANCAP	Pan-Caribbean Partnership Against HIV/AIDS
PHAP	Public Health Associate Program
PICT	Provider-initiated counselling and testing
PLHIV	People living with HIV
PLWHA	People living with HIV/AIDS
PMTCT	Prevention of mother-to-child transmission
PRRA	Pre-removal risk assessment
RAD	Refugee Appeal Division
RPD	Refugee Protection Division
RPO	Refugee Protection Officer
RSD	Refugee Status Determination
RST	UNAIDS Caribbean Regional Support Team
SA	South Asian
SARS	Severe acute respiratory syndrome
SSA	Social Security Administration
SSM	Social Science and Medicine
STD	Sexually transmitted diseases
STI	Sexually transmitted infections
SU	Substance user
TB	Tuberculosis
UN	United Nations
UNAIDS	United Nations Programme on HIV and AIDS
UNDP	United Nations Development Programme
UNESCO	United Nations Educational, Scientific and Cultural Organization
UNFPA	United Nations Population Fund
UNGASS	United Nations General Assembly Special Session on HIV/AIDS
UNHCR	United Nations High Commissioner for Refugees
UNICEF	United Nations Children's Fund
US	United States
USA	United States of America
USAID	United States Agency for International Development
USDHHS	United States Department of Health and Human Services
UWI	University of the West Indies
UWP	United Workers Party
VCT	Voluntary Counseling and Testing
WB	World Bank
WCAR	World Conference against Racism
WHO	World Health Organization

List of Figures

List of Maps

List of Tables

Chapter 1
Refugees, Immigrants and HIV/AIDS

HIV/AIDS has emerged as one of the most damaging diseases humankind has experienced over centuries and is listed near the top among the causes of death globally. In the last three decades, AIDS has affected more than 60 million people and killed nearly 30 million (United Nations 2010). HIV/AIDS is both a medical and a social issue due to threat it poses to economic, social and human development. Medically, HIV/AIDS has reached pandemic proportions and poses a major challenge in searching for measures for cure and containment. Socially, it has resulted in enormous complexities in perception and response patterns that disrupt community life and cause uncertainty, fear and stigma.

Since the identification of HIV/AIDS virus, the pandemic has spread rapidly worldwide, particularly in the region of sub-Saharan Africa (SSA). According to the UNAIDS, 47.5 million[1] people across the world were infected with HIV/AIDS (people living with HIV/AIDs or PLWHA)[2] in 2011. Refugee populations are significantly affected by this pandemic; in fact, the number of HIV-positive individuals and the number of refugees across the globe are almost identical. This fascinating statistical similarity should not be interpreted to mean that all refugees are HIV positive. Rather, this is a numerical coincidence but helps to demonstrate the magnitude of the number of infected population. In general, however, refugees are more vulnerable to infection than the general population as they suffer from loss of proximity to family, property, food insecurity and lack of access to healthcare and education.

It is necessary to begin the discussion with an overview of global patterns, flows and magnitude of the refugee movements in relation to the HIV/AIDS pandemic. This chapter outlines the main argument(s), research problem and questions and brings together the analysis of global data on refugees, HIV/AIDS, its identification

[1] The numbers may vary across sources, but the significance is undeniable.

[2] We throughout the manuscript will be using terminologies suggested by UNAIDS terminology guidelines (2007). Words such as 'HIV positive' and 'People living with HIV' are gradually replacing other terms, such as 'AIDS sufferers' and 'victims of the disease' (UNAIDS 2007:10–11).

A.A. Ullah, A.S. Huque, *Asian Immigrants in North America with HIV/AIDS*,
DOI 10.1007/978-981-287-119-0_1

and spread worldwide and consequent impacts on refugees. These issues have a noticeable impact in shaping the political, economic and social landscape of the contemporary world.

The growing number of refugees has become a matter of global concern. Refugees are entitled to protection under the 1951 *Convention Relating to the Status of Refugees* (Refugee Convention) and 1967 *Protocol Relating to the Status of Refugees* (Refugee Protocol) in any of the 147 countries that are signatories to these conventions. Refugee status is important, as it bestows upon individuals specific rights under international law. A refugee is entitled to reside, at least temporarily, in the host country and is protected by the principle of *non-refoulement*. Host states are obliged to ensure civil and economic rights, and refugees enjoy access to social services and protection under national laws (Ullah 2014). On June 30, 2012, the federal government implemented cuts to its Interim Federal Health Program (IFHP), which covers basic healthcare for refugees, refugee claimants and certain other noncitizens.

AIDS itself is considered the fourth biggest cause of death globally (UNAIDS 2012), after heart disease, stroke and respiratory disease (UNAIDS 2011b). UNAIDS states that 'there are now 34 million adults and children in the world living with HIV/AIDS, nearly 70 % of them in sub-Saharan Africa, of those, 55 % are women' (UNAIDS 2012:6). UNAIDS has reported that there were five million or more newly infected patients with HIV-related illness globally in 2004, which was considered the highest number of cases since the onset of this epidemic during the 1980s. It is estimated that the total number of deaths since 1981 may be as high as 20 million (Dodds et al. 2001:2).

In 2008, the number of people suffering from HIV was 33.4 million worldwide, while it was estimated that over 5,400 individuals died from HIV/AIDS each day (CATIE 2010:5). The HIV infection may take two different forms: 'concentrated' or 'generalized'. Concentrated HIV infections are those that occur in specific vulnerable groups, such as men who have sex with men (MSM), drug users who use injection and commercial sex workers (CSW). Generalized infections are those that exist within the whole population, whether those at risk or in a general category (CATIE 2010:5).

A number of myths have developed surrounding this pandemic, and these have evolved over time. At the outset, HIV/AIDS was characterized by the global North as an African disease. On the other hand, it was viewed as a Western disease by the global South. Later, it became known as a disease of the poor. At present, it is recognized as a disease that knows no geographic boundaries and does not discriminate between culture, class, race and religion, making it a global concern. Nevertheless, the perception was based on an uneven geographic distribution of cases and continues to persist. Evidence suggest 95 % of HIV infection occurs in poor regions and in developing countries (UNAIDS 2011a; WHO 2010). One area of debate is related to the possibility of a direct correlation between poverty and HIV prevalence (see Chap. 3). This may or may not be the case, but it is clear that not all regions possess the same capacity to respond to the pandemic.

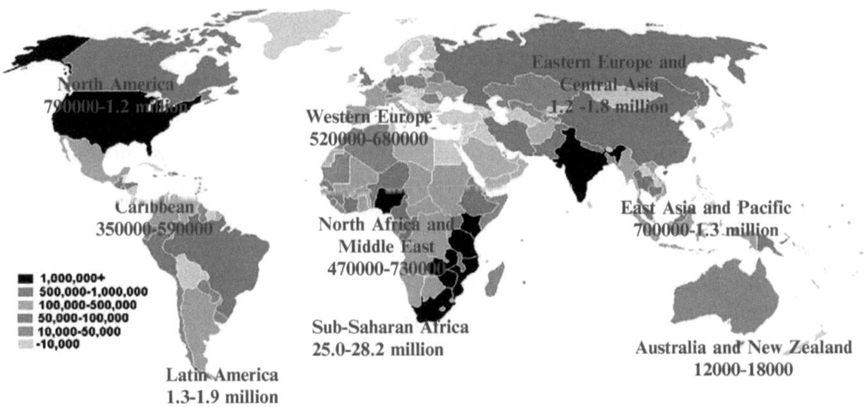

Map 1.1 Showing distribution of HIV/AIDS infection (Data Source: UNAIDS 2011a)

In SSA, approximately 30 % of the entire population lives with AIDS which threatens an entire generation. The virus is also present in the Caribbean, India, China, Southeast Asia, Eastern Europe and Central Asia. In these countries, injecting drug use (IDU) is a significant means by which the virus is transmitted (CPHA 2005:12).

The incidence of HIV/AIDS varies somewhat by region. The Map 1.1 presents regional statistics of HIV/patient with HIV-related illness. The darkest colour represents the highest rate of incidence. Though these statistics do not show data on South Asia as an entire region, India is included among countries with the highest prevalence rates in the world. SSA represents the highest HIV/AIDS prevalence in the world, with 67 % of the world's HIV/AIDS population (UNAIDS 2006, 2011a), more than half of whom are women (WHO 2010). Currently, it is estimated that around five million people living with HIV reside in India (Mayank 2012). HIV/AIDS is a critical global health problem and is not restricted to any specific territory; therefore, it needs to be addressed globally as well as regionally.

HIV prevalence in South Asia is relatively low, but absolute figures of PLWHA are higher when compared to other countries (Care India 2011). Of the global total, about 10 % of the AIDS sufferers live in South Asia (UNAIDS 2010). According to Care India (2011), the South Asian region is second only to SSA in terms of the absolute number of people infected with HIV. South Asia has experienced relatively rapid economic growth in recent years, yet South Asian countries are particularly vulnerable to the rapid spread of HIV. Factors such as stigma and cultural impediments to discussion about sexual issues, high rates of sexually transmitted infections (STIs), widespread incidence of unsafe sex, an expanding sex-work industry, low social status of women, porous country borders, poverty, inequality, illiteracy and high levels of mobility, including widespread rural–urban, interstate and cross-border migration (Care India 2011), contribute largely to the spread of HIV/AIDS in South Asia. India alone accounts for approximately 93 % of those infected in

South Asia. The estimated adult HIV prevalence in India was 0.31 % (0.25–0.39 %) in 2009—0.25 % among women and 0.36 % among men in 2009 (WHO 2010).

The notion of HIV/AIDS as a disease of the poor has been reinforced due to the fact that the majority of the infected people of concern to UNHCR are located in the global South in medium- to low-income countries. The access to antiretroviral (ARV) treatment is limited by citizen-focused public health systems in the Global South (WHO 2008). This is of particular concern to refugees residing in these regions. Refugees' access to public health programmes is further restricted by their isolation from host communities. Despite the widely held belief that refugees increase infection rate in the host community, research has shown that prevalence among the refugee population is lower than those within the host community in both refugee camp settings (UNHCR 2007) and urban areas. Yet HIV sufferer refugees often face hostility from the host community, in refugee camps and detention centres, in addition to losing the support of their social network within the refugee community due to HIV stigma. In many of their operations, the UNHCR aims to integrate refugee-focused programmes within national health programmes of the host country (UNHCR 2014).

AIDS is generally perceived as someone else's problem. Emanating from this notion, AIDS stigma and discrimination are alarmingly embedded in the mindset of healthcare providers as well as the general public in developing countries in particular and globally in general. The past decade has seen numerous physical attacks on HIV-positive individuals, including one who was set on fire and scorched in Bangladesh. In India, an HIV-positive teacher met the same fate (Ullah 2011). In a case of misinformation, an individual in Mexico was fired after he developed tuberculosis and fellow workers thought that he was HIV positive. A pregnant woman in Ukraine was coerced into sterilization during delivery upon discovery of her HIV status. In Cambodia, community members avoided the local temple after the monks began supporting AIDS orphans. Relatives confiscated a woman's property in Kenya after her husband died of an AIDS-related illness and was accused of being the bearer of HIV. In South Africa, a woman was stoned to death when she disclosed her HIV status (Brouard 2006).

Mann identifies three phases of the HIV/AIDS epidemic: the epidemic of HIV, the epidemic of AIDS and the epidemic of stigma, discrimination and denial (1987). This framework has been one of the surprising revelations in HIV research and helped put social science in context. Mann placed significant emphasis on the third phase, which remains among the least studied aspects of HIV/AIDS. In a similar vein, Parker and Aggleton suggest that 'early AIDS metaphors—as death, as horror, as punishment, as guilt, as shame, as otherness—have exacerbated these fears, reinforcing and legitimizing stigmatization and discrimination' (Parker and Aggleton 2002:1).

One of the most intriguing questions in this study remains, where do refugees and HIV/AIDS intersect? The risk of transmission is higher among refugees than the general population for a number of reasons. First, they lose the means to their livelihood and networks and face the risk of weakening social support and diminishing linkages with institutions. Second, health and education services are disrupted and this has an impact on access to preventive education, treatment and healthcare. Moreover, women and girls are at a greater risk of sexual violence and exploitation. Rape is used as a weapon of war, and refugees may be forced to use sex as a way of securing survival and basic necessities. Sexual interactions between civilians and combatants increase the risk of infection, as often there is no scope for them to negotiate safe sex. Potential of sexual transmission of HIV is even more likely in cases of rape during displacements and conflicts. The pervasive myth in Africa that raping a virgin or a child cures HIV also increases the potential spread of HIV/AIDS. While it is true that not all of these situations necessarily put refugees at direct risk of HIV infection, being subject to sexual abuse in any of these ways increases the likelihood of a refugee finding herself/himself in a situation where she/he is unable to negotiate sexual behaviour, thus increasing the risk of HIV infection (UNFPA 2006).

Globally, discrimination against PLWHA is embedded in social and state structures. 'An HIV positive person is suddenly faced with more tests that need to be conducted, lifestyle changes that need to be considered, people that need to be told, doctors that need to be consulted, stigma that needs to be lived with, and so the list could continue' (White 2004:47). This seems to suggest that an HIV-positive diagnosis could result in the shrinking of the territory of a person's identity and losing touch with a 'particular and valued sense of who they are—a 'sense of myself'' (White 2004:47).

Stigmatization, prejudice and xenophobia have similar impacts in terms of severity. The burden that they add to an individual's life is compounded by the gender, ethnic identity, origin and cultural background of the individual. Migrant populations in destination countries in general and refugees in particular face far more severe discrimination than native-born citizens. Discrimination may vary, depending on the country of origin, economic class and legal status. Infection with a deadly disease like HIV/AIDS adds enormously to the degree of discrimination.

In analyzing discrimination and stigmatization, the issue of human rights is important. 'Human rights are inextricably linked with the spread and impact of HIV on individuals and communities around the world' (United Nations 2010:1). AIDS and poverty are mutually reinforcing forces in many developing countries; poverty is considered by some to be a violation of human rights. Throughout this book, a key theme is that certain groups are more vulnerable to HIV. Social scientists argue that some groups are vulnerable because they often fail to realize their civil, political, economic, social and cultural rights (United Nations 2010; Ullah 2011). The unequal status of women in many communities means that their capacity to negotiate in the context of sexual activity is severely undermined, leaving women, particularly young women, more vulnerable to infection (United Nations 2010). Discrimination against individuals and groups who are particularly vulnerable to HIV/AIDS pushes many into hiding, depriving them of their rights to medical service.

Discrimination, Stigma and Xenophobia

The theoretical framework, discussed in details in the second chapter, provides further conceptualization of the terms discrimination, stigma and xenophobia and why and how these concepts are linked in the discourse surrounding HIV/AIDS. This section offers an overview of these concepts, putting HIV/AIDS into context.

Depending on the context, discrimination can be defined in various ways. A number of human rights instruments of the United Nations define the meaning and content of the principles of discrimination. 'The Charter of the United Nations prohibits discrimination on the basis of race, sex, language or religion. The Universal Declaration of Human Rights, adopted in 1948, enlarged the list to include colour, sex, political or other opinion, national or social origins and other status' (United Nations 2001:1).

Stigma is a social process, characterized by exclusion, rejection and blame, that results from experience, reasonable anticipation of an adverse social judgment about a person or group. It is generally contended that the study of stigma focuses too heavily on psychological approaches and seems to neglect to sufficiently incorporate understandings of stigma and stigmatized individuals as embedded in local moral contexts (Kleinman and Hall-Clifford 2013). The field of sociology broadened the understanding of stigma by identifying social processes that occur within the sociocultural environment whose effects can be observed within the individual. Anthropologists have focused on stigma as embedded in moral experience. Xenophobia is a sensation of fear or phobia towards a person or a given group of people deemed strange or foreign. The collective sensation may lead to rejection of the 'other'. Xenophobic violence 'is a pernicious form of discrimination in which individuals are targeted because of their race, national or ethnic origin, religion, sexual orientation, gender, gender identity, disability, or other similar status. Refugees, asylum seekers, stateless persons, displaced persons, and migrants are particularly vulnerable to such forms of violence as they are often distinguished by their appearance, language, religion and customs, particularly in largely homogenous societies' (Human Rights First 2011:1).

The Cambridge Dictionaries Online defines discrimination as 'treating a person or particular group of people differently, especially in a worse way from the way in which you treat other people, because of their skin colour, religion, sex, etc.'. This may be manifested in different ways, depending on the context and subject of discrimination. In case of HIV/AIDS sufferers, discrimination may be based on the socially constructed stigma associated with the disease, while others do so on the basis of the effects of the infection itself. Discrimination–stigmatization in some societies holds a horizontal relationship, while in some other communities, it is vertical (André 2004). This means that the role of health providers in responding to both stigmatization and discrimination is crucial. A report of UNAIDS on HIV/AIDS stigma in India and Uganda indicates that while discrimination against PLWHA was high in India, discrimination in Uganda was declining because many families had lost loved ones to AIDS, leading to increased awareness and empathy

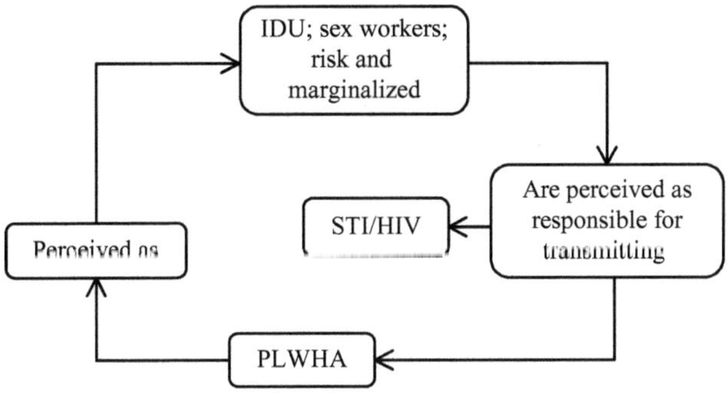

Fig. 1.1 The circle of stigmatization and marginalization (Source: Adapted from UNAIDS 2005)

with PLWHA and their families. Ugandan healthcare workers and counsellors were also credited with helping to fight stigma by assisting people to accept and understand their HIV status (Fig. 1.1).

According to the International Center for Research on Women (ICRW), 'stigma operates by producing and reproducing social structures of power, hierarchy, class, and exclusion and by transforming difference—such as class, race, ethnicity, health status, sexual orientation, and gender—into inequality' (2002:3).

> Discrimination [against AIDS sufferers] occurs on a daily basis. When we are diagnosed with HIV, experts predict our death. I have survived simply because I became involved with fighting against the discrimination and stigma. (Interview)

Discrimination and stigmatization of PLWHA thrive on intolerance and xenophobia. Xenophobia has become a serious concern for policymakers, PLWHA and migrant populations. This is primarily because throughout the course of the HIV/AIDS crisis, many countries sought to place the blame for HIV and AIDS on foreigners. For instance, the USA, Cuba and India have implemented policies that prescribe selective testing for people that come from countries considered to have a high risk for HIV infection. The USA and South Korea—important political players in the world—in 2010 lifted the travel ban on PLWHA from other countries. One of the major reasons for lifting travel bans on PLWHA was to facilitate holding significant HIV/AIDS-related conferences. It is believed that the ban had robbed these two countries of a small stream of income from conference visitors. PLWHA face the acute and home-grown problems of stigma and discrimination. Blaming does not result in solutions. Progress against the epidemic is only possible when communities own the problem of HIV/AIDS themselves (Cullinan 2001).

Ullah's (2011) study conducted in Bangladesh confirms that AIDS sufferers are discriminated against by health professionals as well as healthcare providers. This discrimination may be compounded in cases where these individuals are foreigners. In many cases, health practitioners are not willing to overcome cultural differences and language barriers due to assumptions that foreigners are refugees who take resources away from native-born patients. This may result from the belief that HIV-positive foreigners flee to destination countries to avail themselves of the healthcare facilities (Kollapan 1999). Of course, there are inequalities in healthcare between developing and developed countries. This inequality may contribute to decision-making to migrate for availing healthcare facilities.

Bronwyn Harris (2002) provides a theoretical perspective on xenophobia. According to Harris, the level of xenophobia depends on three elements based on scapegoating, isolation and the biological–cultural hypothesis. The biological–cultural hypothesis suggests that outward characteristics, such as hairstyles, accents, vaccination marks, dress and physical appearance, can be read as indexical markers or signifiers of difference and point out foreignness in a way that is immediately visible. As signifiers, these features have a common role in facilitating xenophobic behaviour. Exclusion, alienation and hostility operate in a complex, ongoing manner across the lines of nationality, such as between South Africans and foreigners, particularly African foreigners. Studies by Sinclair (1998, 1999) and Morris (1998) reveal that xenophobia impacts directly on foreign identity. Xenophobic behaviour among natives makes foreigners feel as unwanted outsiders. This leads to exclusion and alienates foreigners further from society. It also contributes to foreigner hostility, which is occasionally manifested as violence towards the host population. A general tendency to blame foreigners for bringing HIV infection in the countries of destinations prevails throughout the world. Deacon et al. (2004) find some rationale for such claims. For instance, foreigners represent competition in the labour market, fuelling xenophobic behaviour which has implications for stigma and discrimination (Deacon et al. 2004).

Stigma is frequently layered over other forms of social inequalities and characteristics, such as race, gender, class, sex work, homosexuality, religion, xenophobia, transgender, drug use, mental and/or physical disability, caste and disease. AIDS was generally considered a disease affecting mainly people of African descent until the year 2000. However, due to the growing incidence of HIV infection in India, the racialization of the disease partially shifted to Asia, and it is now suggested that AIDS is an Asian disease. The HIV/AIDS epidemic developed during a period of rapid globalization and growing polarization between rich and poor (Castells 1996, 1998). The perception that HIV/AIDS is an African or Asian disease, or that it is a disease of the poor, is an obvious example of class-based and racialized perceptions.

The HIV/AIDS-related stigma is particularly harsh upon women due to both gender-based and economic inequalities found in most cultures throughout the world. On average, South Asian women have lower social status than men and less access to safe housing and are largely dependent on their male partners or family members as breadwinners for support. Although the circumstances have begun to change, much more need to be done to address this problem. These factors render them vulnerable to sexual abuse because the dependency jeopardizes their social authority in negotiating safe sex or declining unsafe sex (Fig. 1.2).

Women living with HIV are often blamed by society for the spread of HIV, as they are seen as sexually promiscuous, as prostitutes and as dirty and immoral, while men living with HIV are culturally absolved of blame for the incidence of HIV infection—and even praised at times for exhibiting masculine characteristics in

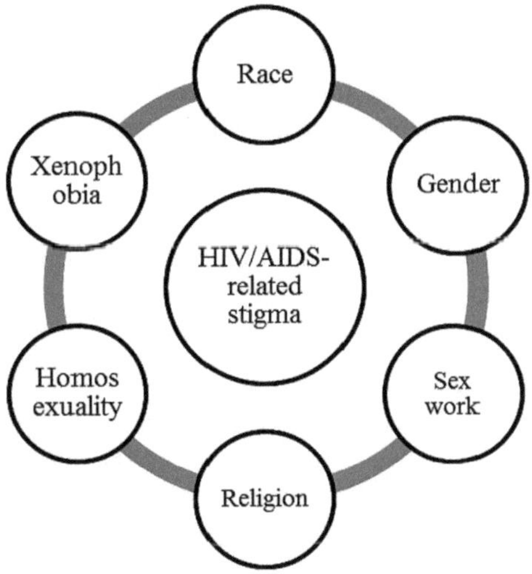

Fig. 1.2 Elements of HIV/AIDS-related stigma

their 'use' of women. Indeed, deaths due to AIDS have exacerbated scapegoating and the re-stigmatizing of women, who may be blamed for their husbands' HIV-related deaths.

Stigma and Sex Work In the mid-1990s, the state of Maharashtra in India was devastated by a disease called 'plague' that claimed hundreds of lives in a few short months. The 'plague' was later diagnosed to be HIV/AIDS related. In response to suggestions that sex workers were responsible for the spread of this 'plague', sex workers in Indian brothels took to the streets, saying they are not the only agents spreading the life-threatening disease.

Sex workers have often been exclusively blamed for the spread of HIV/AIDS. In many Asian states, such as India, Bangladesh, Nepal, the Maldives and Sri Lanka, sex workers are often synonymously described as 'AIDS carriers'. In some countries in Southeast Asia (SEA), especially Thailand in the late 1980s, when HIV reached epidemic proportions, sex workers faced severe discrimination and stigma due to the erroneous belief that they were the primary agents of transmission. AIDS stigma tends to silence open discussion, limiting understanding of its causes and appropriate responses. Open discussion is important in ensuring successful mobilization of government, communities and individuals to respond to the disease, and concealment delays urgent action (UNAIDS 2005).

Stigma can lead to violations of human rights, such as the right to non-discrimination, which affect the well-being of PLWHA. The principle of non-discrimination, based on recognition of the equality of all people, is enshrined in the Universal Declaration of Human Rights (UDHR) and other human rights instruments. Global consensus on the importance of tackling AIDS-related stigma and discrimination is highlighted by the Declaration of Commitment adopted by the United Nations General Assembly Special Session on HIV/AIDS in June 2001 (for details, please see Declaration of Commitment on HIV/AIDS, United Nations 2002).

Stigmatization of PLWHA contributes to feelings of shame among affected individuals, which 'can have a powerful psychological influence over how HIV sufferers see themselves and adjust to their status, making them vulnerable to blame, depression and self-imposed isolation' (UNAIDS 2005:5).

Stigma and Religion AIDS is no longer a disease confined to a particular race or region; nor is it associated with any particular religion. However, members of certain religious groups denigrate people who are HIV/AIDS-positive individuals due to stigma associated with the disease, and that stigmatization of certain religions in general can affect individuals who are HIV/AIDS positive in accessing treatment.

Homosexuality Homosexuality is severely stigmatized in many parts of the world and is considered by many to be antireligious, unsocial and deviant. In some countries, homosexual behaviour has been criminalized. Homosexuality was considered as a mental illness until 1973 according to the Diagnostic and Statistical Manual (DSM) of the American Psychiatric Association. It does not necessarily mean that homosexuality is not associated with psychopathology in the contemporary world. Whether or not homosexuality is criminalized, negative attitude towards homosexual behaviour, identity, relationships and community persists and can lead to homophobic behaviour among the larger communities. Homophobia is common, and the tendency to associate HIV/AIDS with homosexuality persists, leading many HIV-positive MSM to hide their status for fear of being ostracized as homosexual and being rejected and isolated from their communities.

Community Stigmatization

One of the principal observations advanced by researchers is that PLWHA are often stigmatized within their own community. Who constitutes this community? This question is particularly important when discussing double or multiple discriminations. The notion of double or multiple discriminations describes how it can have numerous directions and levels. Discrimination may be based on gender, race, sexual orientation, colour, country of origin or HIV status. Discrimination and stigmatization reinforce the pre-existing prejudices based on sexual orientation, gender, race and/or socioeconomic status (Parker and Aggleton 2002). Differences in race and ethnicity cause stigma and discrimination in most populations, no matter what sexual orientation an individual may hold. Raymond and McFarland conducted research on race and ethnicity among gay men to investigate determinants of selection of sexual partners, partner preferences and perceptions of HIV risk (zRaymond and McFarland 2009). Among all race/ethnicity groups (African, Asian, Caucasian and Latino), black gay men were perceived to be the highest risk group for contraction of HIV during sexual intercourse (Raymond and McFarland 2009; Smit et al. 2012).

The attitudes of the general population towards PLWHA have rarely been sympathetic in developing countries. This does not necessarily mean that they are embraced by their own social community—for example, gays, lesbians, bisexuals or transsexuals. The attitudes of these communities can in fact result in the isolation, exclusion and rejection of those affected (Courtenay-Quirk et al. 2006; Weatherburn et al. 2009; Maxwell 1998). There has been a clear and growing rift between HIV sufferers and HIV-negative people within their own community (Botnick 2000; Courtenay-Quirk et al. 2006).

In a study conducted by the Dutch HIV Association on 667 AIDS sufferers, the majority of participating gay men (79.5 %) reported experiencing one or more forms of stigma. In particular, 70.2 % of the gay respondents had experienced stigma within their own community. This means that even their community was a significant source of stigmatization (Stutterheim et al. 2008). It was expected that others within the community would understand and sympathize with the challenges experienced by its members. However, this study suggested that the reverse can be true. In some cases, individuals within the community are extremely intolerant. HIV-negative community members blame HIV-positive members for contributing to their stigmatization within the general population; as one HIV-negative individual stated,

> … because of the small number of stupid people who got infected, we the whole community is stigmatized. We are not responsible for other peoples' infection. We are not positive, still people look at us in a way that we are. Then who is responsible? How should we treat the positive then? We are already under a bad name. We are gay. Ok. We accept that we are often looked down upon. But we cannot accept being thought of as positive by others…. (Interview)

When this community interacts with the general population, they are often subjected to double discrimination. Refugees and immigrants, already facing xenophobic discrimination, face additional discrimination for both their sexuality and for their HIV status (Fig. 1.3).

How is it possible to recognize an infected person, if his or her status is not disclosed? In many cases, changes in body shape or physical appearance (generally lipoatrophy) take place due to HIV and its treatment. These are the distinct physical markers of a person's HIV-positive status. In such cases, PLWHA face greater stigmatization and discrimination (Fernandes et al. 2007; Persson 2005).

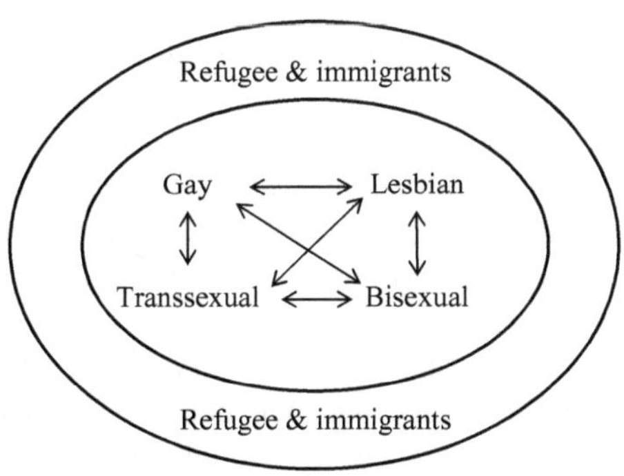

Fig. 1.3 Multiple layers of discrimination and stigmatization

The level of impact of internal stigma depends on the perceived avenue through which HIV is acquired. Rape victims and children born to HIV-positive parents are considered innocent. People infected with HIV as a result of extramarital sexual activities or through IDU are considered guilty. Therefore, it is likely that internal stigma will be exacerbated by the views of innocence or guilt held by the person living with HIV (Brouard 2006).

Contextual Factors

One important factor is the environment in which HIV sufferers operate. It may be supportive or hostile, depending on whether they are the only HIV sufferers in the community. The relative power between HIV sufferer and their partner or family influences the degree of internal stigma experienced by them. The position of the HIV sufferer in the familial power hierarchy determines how they will be treated by the community and how they treat themselves. Living conditions determine the sense of control, which can result in diminished self-efficacy. In such situations, a higher level of internal stigma may result.

Self-Factors

Internal stigma may be easier to deal with if one is relatively well at some point of time, although it could be argued that increasing sickness could force disclosure, which may prove beneficial in the long run. Accepting an HIV-positive status is important in internalizing the diagnosis and acting accordingly. Most HIV sufferers go through a process of moving from denial to acceptance. This may take time and differs from one person to another. Evidences suggest that if they are able to incorporate the experience of being positive into their meaning and belief systems, HIV sufferers are better able to cope. Undereducated individuals are disproportionately represented in HIV statistics worldwide. However, higher education does not, in itself, protect individuals from acquiring HIV. Where self-esteem and self-efficacy are linked to education level, it is likely that the more education and information an individual has, the easier it may be to overcome internal stigma. Some people cope with difficult life situations by withdrawing, while others reach out and become more proactive and assertive (Table 1.1).

An overview of challenges facing immigrants and refugees is important because the empirical basis of the study is grounded in these groups. A detailed account of their tribulations is presented in the second and third chapters. This section analyzes the fact that immigrants and refugees are already burdened under several sources of stress and that HIV status, along with its resultant trauma, makes their life more difficult. This further helps explain how prepared they are to endure multiple stressors. It is fair to ask why considerations of stigma and discrimination are important in the study of HIV/AIDS among refugees and immigrants.

Table 1.1 Commonly used stigma instrument items grouped according to ICF[a] domains

Domain[a]	Item
Interpersonal interactions and relationships	Problems in/quality of an ongoing marriage/problems with spouse or partner
	Affected people are concealing the condition/keep it a secret
	People avoid someone with this condition/distance themselves socially
	Problems for the affected person to get married
	Is the person with the condition treated with respect by family, community members and health workers
	Allowed to or problems to play with/be around/look after children
	Do friends avoid you/is your relationship with your friends affected negatively?
	Problems for the children or relative of the affected person to get married
	Negative attitude of relative/abandoned by family
	Does the opinion of the affected person count in (family) discussions
	It is easier to avoid new friendship than worry about felling someone that I have this condition
Major life areas	Do you have an equal opportunity as your peers to find work?
	Loosing work or diminished employment prospects
	Working with/employing an affected person
	Are you able to work as hard as your peers do/has your ability to work been affected by your condition?
Stereotyping	It is possible/easy to tell if a person has this condition
Domain[a]	Item
Major life areas	Has your condition affected your educational plans or opportunities?
Community, social and civic life	Visiting or being invited by friends, family and/or others
	Being socially active
	Attending social/community function and/or meetings
	Anyone with (a history of) this condition should be excluded from taking public office/difficult to function as a leader
Domestic life	Does the affected person do household work (the way they want)
Dom	Having equal opportunity to buy or rent accommodation
Self-esteem/self-efficacy	I'm not as good a person as others because of my condition/think less of yourself

(continued)

Table 1.1 (continued)

Domain[a]	Item
	Others would think less of the person because of his/her condition
	Having this condition has spoiled my life
	I'm a person of worth; I can have a good, fulfilled life, despite my condition
	I feel comfortable being seen in public with a person who has/is known to have this condition
Fear of contagion or of being affected	Being afraid of (persons with) this condition
	Being afraid you or other may catch the condition from an affected person
	An affected person should be isolated/live separately
Shame/embarrassment	Is the condition associated with shame or embarrassment
Blame/guilt	I feel guilty because I have this condition
Pity	People feel sorry for a person with condition/others pity you
Perceived stigma	Others would think less of the family

Source: Adopted from Van Brakel (2005)
[a]Domains of the (International classification of functioning) ICF or stigma components

Buehler (2013) has introduced a framework for stress emanating from relocation. Any kind of relocation involves psychological stress, and they are stronger in cases of forced relocation. We attempt to reframe Buehler's concepts of stresses during and after relocations (Fig. 1.7).

Social integration and adaptation are primary defining issues in determining how newcomers are able to settle in their new environment. Adaptation encompasses a number of variables such as language, education, skills, personal traits and origins. Networks play a significant role in facilitating settlement process and meeting immediate social needs and offering information on children's school, available health services and entitlements and other facilities. However, not all newcomers or refugees have networks or personal contacts to draw upon (Ullah 2010a, 2013). Even if they have, an HIV sufferer may not be supported by the fellow countryman. This places them into a particularly vulnerable situation. Language barriers, marginalization and social exclusion, and legal obstacles are the most pronounced factors that make life difficult for them. Cultural attitudes, religious beliefs, taboos, limited social capital, fear of discrimination and limited knowledge of HIV within these communities were highlighted as factors that increase vulnerability, as were negative social attitudes towards migrants, racism, poverty and services that are not culturally sensitive.

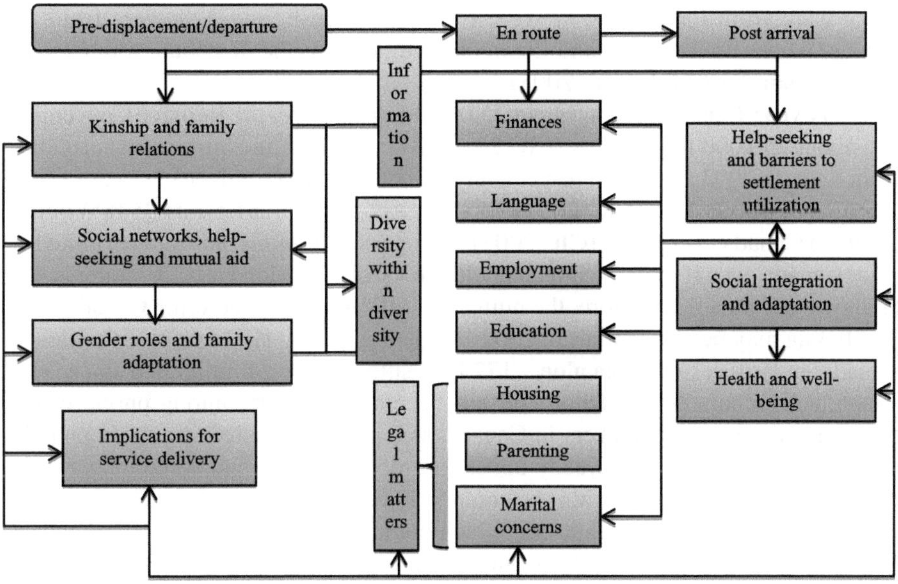

Fig. 1.7 Stressors in the migration trajectory

The Research Problem

How do HIV-infected South Asian residents in North America, in general, and Canada, in particular, negotiate their everyday lives within their community and the broader societal environment? By negotiation, we mean how human agency and structural factors interplay in the daily lives of South Asian PLWHA (Sztompka 2008:30). Discussing 'everyday lives' opens up a host of micro and macro issues. It allows us to assess whether people are experiencing discrimination. This can generate rich data as to where this discrimination comes from and how it is experienced.

There is limited published literature on health issues of South Asians, and there is no known systematic study so far on HIV prevalence and treatment among South Asians in North America. Anecdotal evidence shows that many South Asian women in Canada discover their HIV status only when they begin prenatal care and are tested for HIV as part of routine procedures in early pregnancy (Sheth 2001; Yoshioka and Schustack 2001). Disclosing HIV status is an emotionally difficult task for any individual because it raises issues of privacy, vulnerability, identification with a stigmatized role and feelings of imposition on others. A small study conducted by Yoshioka and Amy on nine Asian HIV+ women found that fear of stigma concerns over disappointing and/or burdening others and fear of discrimination strongly influenced the women's decisions to disclose their status to others (Yoshioka and Schustack 2001). Another study conducted in the USA showed that of all known South Asian HIV/AIDS cases, 73 % were from India,

19 % were from Pakistan, 6 % were from Bangladesh, and 2 % were from Sri Lanka (World Bank 1998), and it can be assumed that the distribution in Canada would be similar (Zaidi et al. 2005).[3]

Every year, Canada accepts about 25,000 refugees under the Refugee Convention and about 250,000 immigrants (CIC 2013). About half of the immigrants originate from Asia. In 2003 and 2006, respectively, 6,989 and 2,000 refugee claimants originated from South Asia (CIC 2007). On average, India alone sends 35,000 immigrants to Canada every year (CIC 2007). Refugees and immigrants are permitted to enter Canada even if they are infected with HIV/AIDS (as long as CD4 count is 400 or above/cell/mm^3). Therefore, the number of HIV+ migrants entering Canada from South Asia may be substantial. In 2002–2003, around 700 HIV+ refugees settled in Canada; in British Columbia alone, 172 HIV sufferers have immigrated since 2000 (Haag and Gilbert 2007). This trend has become a concern among public health professionals and policymakers in Canada, as it places an increasing strain on public health systems that are already under enormous pressure and could increase the risk of HIV transmission within the country. For those immigrants to Canada, their HIV status causes additional stress, which compounds their level of vulnerability. HIV/AIDS-related stigma and discrimination remain the main barrier for them in accessing support and services.

South Asians immigrants and refugees, particularly women, are often faced with multiple barriers which include socioeconomic inequality, systemic marginalization, gender inequality and cultural and language barriers. These barriers increase their vulnerability to HIV infection and reduce the likelihood of testing, while their isolation heightens the impact of HIV/AIDS on their lives. These individuals are potentially facing multiple discriminations that can risk their own health and that of others. At present, however, little is known, empirically or anecdotally, about the extent of this risk and its impact on health.

Despite remarkable progress made in treating HIV, many people continue to face problems accessing care and treatment. These problems are exacerbated by a shortage of physicians and other healthcare providers and the increasingly complex care needs of people with HIV (PHAC 2005a). A significant proportion of people with HIV also have coinfections that threaten their health and complicate care. For example, as of December 1999, about 11,194 people living with HIV in Canada—more than 20 % of the total—were coinfected with hepatitis C (Blumberg 2000); this number has since grown to close to 14,000. Many people living with HIV are coping with complex issues, including the effects of stigmatization. Between 40 and 60 % of people with HIV suffer from depression, which can lead to a weakening of the immune system, faster disease progression, lack of adherence to treatment regimens (which, in turn, can lead to treatment failure and the development of

[3] Based on the 29 states with confidential name-based HIV surveillance systems, between 1999 and 2002, 17.4 % of APIs diagnosed with HIV were born in India compared to 1.1 % Pakistani- and 31.9 % US-born APIs. Between 1985 and 2002, 4.9 % of AIDS cases were among people born in India, compared to 1.0 % Pakistani and 39.6 % US born (Zaidi et al. 2005).

drug-resistant strains of HIV), greater risk of suicide and less rigorous adherence to safe sex and drug use practices (Carlisle 2000).

The financial impact of HIV is often exacerbated by the lack of flexible employment opportunities or disability plans that can accommodate the needs of people who go through extended periods of ill health during which they cannot work. As a result, a growing number of people with HIV are trapped in poverty and are unable to secure adequate housing. Many people living with HIV/AIDS also struggle to manage sexual relationships in the context of a life-threatening sexually transmitted infection (PHAC 2005a).

Research Objectives

This book seeks to identify the ways in which HIV+ immigrants, refugees and asylum seekers from Asia are coping with the challenge of living with HIV/AIDS. The objective is to determine the extent to which healthcare and treatment regimen for HIV/AIDS are known to, and accessed by, immigrants and refugee claimants in Canada and their perceptions about discrimination relating to HIV/AIDS issues. The specific goals of the research are to explore:

(a) The extent to which refugees and immigrants living with HIV/AIDS face discrimination from within their own ethnic communities, gender groups and the general Canadian population
(b) The impact of this discrimination on health outcomes (morbidity and mortality, social isolation, mental health, overall well-being)

We make a further distinction between what we see as the two major types of characteristics addressed in the literature on stigma—disease and deviant identity. Identity is the way people think of themselves. When people conceive that they are deviant, they are more likely to engage in further deviant behaviour. The essence of deviant identities includes the ways that they develop, factors that foster their development and consequences of having them (Kitsuse 1962). Based on these distinctions, researchers have developed a typology of the functions of stigma and prejudice. They propose that there are three functions of stigma and prejudice: (a) exploitation or domination, (b) enforcement of social norms and (c) avoidance of disease (Phelan et al. 2008).

Significance and Rationale

Generally, socioeconomic status, race, ethnicity, gender and sexual orientation are among the characteristics that may determine which social groups have a higher prevalence of morbidity or mortality (US Department of Health and Human Services 2000). Two components of stress—general stress and stress that is generally attributable to prejudice—are potential causes of disease. In addition, coping resources, such as personal resources and social support, are resources that can moderate the impact of stress on disease, acting as stress buffers (Wheaton 1985).

The debate about stigma by human rights proponents and bioethicists has routinely raised the question of who will bear the burden of stigma and whether such burdens are unfairly distributed. Stigma is almost always imposed by those with power or authority on those who have less power. Socially vulnerable groups face greater stigmatization, and this adds to the burden they already bear. Generally, it is believed that women are exposed to more stress than men; however, some researchers argue that women, as a group, are not exposed to more stress than men (Turner and Lloyd 1999). Rather, women and men are exposed to different types of stressors. Kessler et al. (1999) however, found no gender difference in exposure to discrimination. We are not in complete agreement with this particular assertion.

Disclosure is one of the most challenging issues facing HIV+ individuals—'to disclose or not to disclose, who to disclose to, how to disclose and when to disclose'. The tension between the need to maintain control over personal information and the moral and ethical obligation to warn others of the potential risk is at the core of the debate about disclosure. Many individuals find it desirable to share information about their status with their partners. While some are able to tell their partners immediately, others may hold back due to concerns over potential negative consequences. Some people may be reluctant to disclose while trust is yet to develop, while some do while it is still developing. Given the costs and benefits of revealing one's diagnosis, why do people choose to conceal or disclose their status? When do people determine that disclosure is risky or safe? When do they risk rejection to obtain needed support? We attempt to answer these questions by investigating motivations for disclosure.

Discrimination based on race has received moderate attention in research and is of continuing academic and political interest in terms of understanding the persistence of racial discrimination for racially stigmatized groups (Blank et al. 2004). Social and health researchers are examining the extent to which perceptions of discrimination, racial and non-racial, are stressful life experiences that adversely affect health (Clark et al. 1999; Dion 2001). For example, the institutionalized inequality of apartheid in South Africa and its legacy has been decisive for a broad range of outcomes in South African society (Moller 1998; Seidman 1999). Several researchers have noted that the oppressive nature of apartheid in South Africa had pervasive negative consequences for mental health (Turton and Chalmers 1990). It has long been recognized that this kind of unfair treatment can lead to negative emotional reactions and psychosomatic symptoms[4] (Adams 1965; Dion 2001).

[4]This involves both mind and body. There is a mental aspect to every physical disease. How we react to and cope with disease varies greatly from person to person. With some mental illnesses, one may not eat or take care of oneself very well which can cause physical problems. The term psychosomatic disorder, however, is mainly used to mean … 'a physical disease that is thought to be caused, or made worse, by mental factors'.

Both the recently popular and long-standing scholarly literature on Canadian immigration have emphasized the post-arrival experiences of immigrants in Canada and the effect of immigrants on the Canadian economy and social institutions (DeVoretz et al. 2003). The number of people living with HIV in Canada and the USA continues to grow rapidly. At the end of 2002, an estimated 56,000 Canadians were living with HIV, representing an increase of about 12 % from 1999. In terms of exposure category, in 2002 this included 32,500 MSM, or 58 % of the total; 11,000 IDU, or 20 % of the total; 10,000 heterosexuals, or 18 % of total; 2,200 MSM who also use injection drugs, or 4 % of the total; and 300 attributed to other exposures, or <1 % of the total (PHAC 2005).

Of the estimated 56,000 infections in 2002, about 17,000, or 30 %, were unaware of their HIV-positive status (PHAC 2010). Of these, there were an estimated 2,800–5,200 new HIV infections in 2002; between 600 and 1,200 were women, representing 23 % of all new infections (PHAC 2005a). Taking into consideration the status of these individuals is particularly important because, until they are diagnosed, they are not able to access support, treatment and prevention services that could help them manage the illness and extend their life span, as well as reduce the risk of transmission to others. A significant number of people in this group are not diagnosed until quite late in the course of infection disease, when medications are of little help.

The mechanisms through which stigma functions in relation to HIV/AIDS need to be explored. Castro and Farmer (2005:56) argue, 'stigma and discrimination are part of complex systems of beliefs about illness and disease that are often grounded in social inequalities'. They suggest that 'stigma is often just the tip of the iceberg; because it is visible and generally accepted in public health discourse without further qualification, the term has frequently served as a means of giving short shrift to powerful social inequalities that are much harder to identify and conceptualize' (Castro and Farmer 2005:53).

Outline of the Book

The first chapter offers an overview of the global pattern, flow, magnitude of the refugees and HIV/AIDS pandemic and outlines the main arguments, research problem and questions. It reviews global data on refugees, the identification and transmission of the HIV/AIDS virus and consequent impacts. This chapter also sets out the objectives of this book and outlines the content of all the chapters to highlight the common theme.

The second chapter is divided into two sections. The first section outlines the main theories of discrimination and stigma. It presents the theoretical framework that constitutes the basis for achieving the objectives and establishing the main argument of this book. The second section includes the methodology of the research. Both qualitative and quantitative techniques were used in collecting and analyzing the data. Research on refugees is a complex undertaking, and there is no tested method for studying both refugees and HIV/AIDS. This chapter also explains the process for handling confidential research material, developing intersectional analyses and answering specific questions related to multi-strategy research design that are crucial in researching refugees.

The third chapter examines the intersection of refugees and AIDS in Canada. It presents a critical analysis of the impact on Canada from the influx of refugees and HIV/AIDS and challenges the notion that HIV/AIDS is a disease of the poor. It poses a question to assess the place of Canada in the global scenario of refugees and HIV/AIDS and proceeds to answer the question.

The fourth chapter conceptualizes multilevel discrimination and stigmatization and differential health outcomes. Discrimination and stigmatization breed mounting trauma, complexities in relationships, dwindling confidence levels and conflict in treatment regimens. Living conditions are impacted by the experience of dehumanizing top-down structures of discriminations. This chapter also presents the research findings. Using a theoretical framework which outlines the hierarchies of discrimination and stigmatization, the empirics are triangulated with theories to better explain where, and in what ways, these populations are being discriminated against and stigmatized and the implications of xenophobic treatment. This chapter further discusses the consequences and implications of treatments provided on health outcomes.

The fifth chapter emphasizes the impact on mental health when discrimination, stigmatization and xenophobia combine to humiliate the PLWHA. It analyzes their resilience and coping mechanisms in such situations. The main arguments of this book are supported by a number of case studies in this chapter.

In countries where the HIV/AIDS epidemic is widespread, populations considered to be at risk of contracting HIV/AIDS are the generally neglected groups from social, economic and epidemiological points of view. Consequently, very little effort is made to provide HIV interventions for these groups who, in turn, are often excluded from mainstream HIV prevention services. However, transmission rates and HIV prevalence among high-risk groups can be up to around 10 times higher than other groups in the society.

The sixth and last chapter analyzes the performance of countries that are party to international conventions and their ability to comply with them. This chapter discusses the role of the existing policies in protecting the rights of the refugees and immigrants with HIV/AIDS. The objective is to formulate a set of policy recommendations based on the findings for policymakers, researchers, medical professionals and service providers.

Chapter 2
Understanding and Exploring HIV/AIDS and Discrimination

The previous chapter presented the nature of the problem under investigation, outline of this book, objectives and research questions. Research projects are expected to be methodologically sound, ethically transparent, theoretically underpinned and empirically grounded. This chapter analyzes the methodological and theoretical issues. This research is primarily based on qualitative data obtained from both primary and secondary sources. Interviews with participants were conducted using both open- and closed-ended questionnaires and checklists. The study placed emphasis on in-depth interviews, using ethnographic techniques to obtain information on life histories of immigrants and refugees, both before and after migration. The process was facilitated through partnerships with community organizations that work with immigrants, refugees and asylum seekers on issues of HIV/AIDS. An extensive review of relevant existing literature and databases to consider mortality and morbidity rates preceded the field research.

This chapter is divided broadly into two sections. The first section reviews and critiques the main theories relevant to discrimination and stigma. The second section sheds light on the methodology followed in the research. The objective is to present a theoretical framework that constitutes the basis for achieving the objectives and establishing the main arguments of this book.

Conceptual Issues

Theoretical models have greatly advanced the understanding of how stigma affects people through a broad array of psychological processes and social mechanisms. HsinYang and Kleinman (2008) argue that while these theories have generated much knowledge by highlighting different routes by which stigma acts upon the individual, the majority of theories limit the negative effects of stigma to individuals.

Social psychological models of stigma primarily deal with the aspects of 'social identity' applied to an individual, through examining the situational stimulus that

A.A. Ullah, A.S. Huque, *Asian Immigrants in North America with HIV/AIDS*,
DOI 10.1007/978-981-287-119-0_2

individuals respond to (Crocker et al. 1998). Sociological models describe the social domains of stigma as occurring when objects in the social world obtain meaning through symbolic interaction (Goffman 1963), while other authors describe these social dimensions as occurring through institutional, structural and hegemonic forms (Parker and Aggleton 2003).

Link and Phelan (2001) indicate that stigma is present when elements of labelling, stereotyping, separation, status loss and discrimination occur together. We employ two stigma-related theories—the concept of 'secondary deviance' (Lemert 1967) and 'modified labelling theory' (Link et al. 1989)—to highlight the possible linkages. The concept of secondary deviance considers whether and to what extent responses to behaviours that are initially viewed as problematic generate additional, secondary differentness that further sets the person apart from the mainstream (Lemert 1967). Thus, to the extent that institutional policies and practices aimed at controlling one set of behaviours disadvantage people with respect to the capacity to work productively, obtain housing, socialize with others and generally function effectively, new elements of differentness are created.

Link and colleagues (1989) built upon and modified the labelling approach of Scheff (1984), although the difference between the two approaches was mainly a matter of emphasis. Figure 2.1 represents the model of Scheff, looking at stigma in relation to mental illness (1984) (adopted from Link et al. 1989). Notable components in the modified approach are the negative consequences of stigma for self-esteem and earning power, as well as vulnerability to new disorders or repeat episodes of existing disorders. When an individual internalizes that he or she is 'a mentally ill person' and incorporates it as a central identity, the labelling of oneself is complete and the consequence is chronic mental illness (Scheff 1966 in Link and colleagues 1989:402).

Thus, a measure of self-perceived discrimination was to ask respondents if any of the following things ever happened to them because of their HIV status by exploring the following issues: (a) You had difficulty renting an apartment or finding housing, (b) you were turned down for a job for which you were qualified or (c) you were refused or charged more for health insurance because of your status. A framework was created to guide the research of stigma themes, experiences and management strategies along the lines described in the literature. The three central columns of the framework (Fig. 2.1) represent enacted stigma, perceived

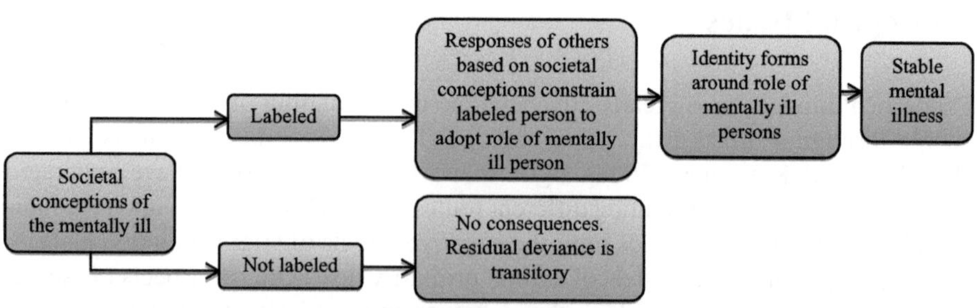

Fig. 2.1 Scheff's labelling approach

stigma and internalized stigma. The headings represent the major themes that emerged in support of each construct, women's experiences of stigma and management strategies they described.[1]

A conceptual framework of stigma would be incomplete without acknowledging both the dynamic nature of stigma and the role of organizations designed to deal with societal problems. These issues represent the newest foci of research, and while that presents a challenge to identifying the forces at work, they cannot be ignored (Basnett 2001; Cresswell 2005; Reidy 1993). While 'institutionalized stigma' (Corrigan and Kleinlein 2007) is not limited to the healthcare system, organizational norms in the healthcare system can, even inadvertently, enact prejudice and discrimination while paradoxically aiming to care for those suffering illness.

Some societies place great value on appearance, and ugliness and disfigurement are sometimes attributed to sin. It was noted in a study (Ullah 2011), where one participant stated 'that some people say I did something bad that made me ugly'. This is of relevance to PLWHA as the illness, particularly in its later stages, can result in noticeable physical changes and disfigurement. Person et al. (2009) in their study reveal that enacted stigma based on physical appearance can also be a contributor to loss of work and income. They described a case of a young Ghanaian woman with severe disfigurement, who experienced social and economic discrimination and income loss when people refused to shop at her stall following her disfigurement (Fig. 2.2).

These experiences of enacted stigma and feelings of perceived stigma contribute to internalized stigma. In addition, the woman's identification with a sick role, along with the loss of social interactions, contributes to devaluation of the self. Internalized stigma is experienced as a process of self-labelling with feelings of fear, guilt, shame, sadness, depression and diminished self-worth. Internalized stigma of this nature may be further heightened in the case of HIV/AIDS due to the moral judgments often normatively associated with the condition. The moral weight associated with HIV/AIDS stigma in China, for example, is greatly compounded by views common across cultures that immoral behaviours give rise to HIV cases. Mak et al. (2006) in their Hong Kong study revealed much greater stigma among the general population towards HIV/AIDS when compared with tuberculosis and SARS (Mak et al. 2006). Such moral judgments commonly focus on behaviours perceived to be associated with HIV, such as drug use, commercial sex or homosexuality (Fig. 2.3).

Despite the existence of strong legislation in China that protects confidentiality and guarantees access and equality of treatment, stigma continues to take place during healthcare practice (Yang et al. 2005). The continuation of stigma at an interpersonal level, despite legislative protection, illustrates how one's loss of moral standing remains a key. Some physicians in southern China contested treatment of HIV/AIDS patients as 'a waste of medicine on a morally contaminated individual' (Jing 2006:167). Another study in Yunnan Province shows that 30 % of healthcare workers were 'unwilling' and 81 % 'preferred not' to treat HIV sufferers (Hesketh et al. 2005; Yang et al. 2005). Ullah (2011) found similar results in a study in Bangladesh.

[1] For more on types of stigma, please see Chap. 3.

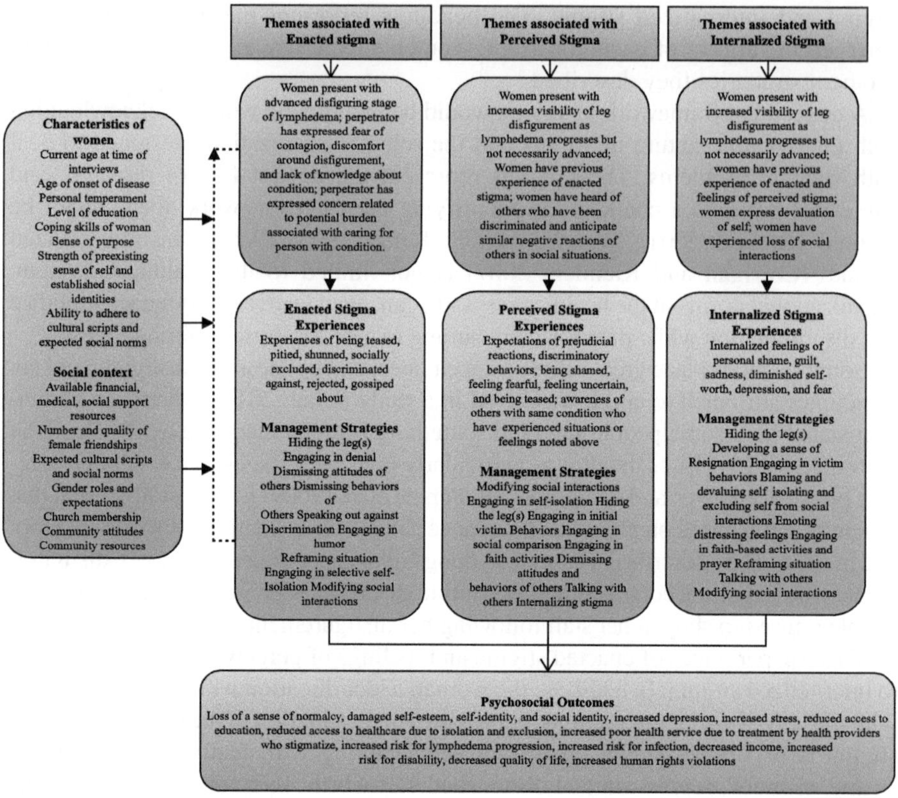

Fig. 2.2 Conceptual framework of health-related stigma as described by women with HIV/AIDS (Sources: Adopted from Person et al. 2009)

The theoretical framework for the understanding of AIDS-related stigma has developed over a decade of ethnographic research (Castro and Farmer 2005). The psychosocial field has clarified the cognitive processes that lead to labelling and stereotyping. However, as Castro and Farmer have noted in their review of the literature, most psychological research focuses more on:

> individualistic perceptions and attitudes than on the broader social context in which such perceptions are grounded. Most of these studies discuss the implications of these beliefs—in terms of misunderstandings, misinformation, and negative attitudes—as far as efforts to change the perceptions of the stigmatizers are concerned. (Castro and Farmer 2005:54)

More recently, some anthropologists (Smith 2011; Adam 2011) have challenged approaches that emphasize cognitivist explanations of stigma rather than the structural violence that generates the social inequalities in which stigma is invariably rooted (Castro and Farmer 2005). According to Stuber et al. (2008), stigma is generally conceptualized as negative labels and pejorative assessments, social distancing and discrimination that can occur when individuals lack power. Much research on

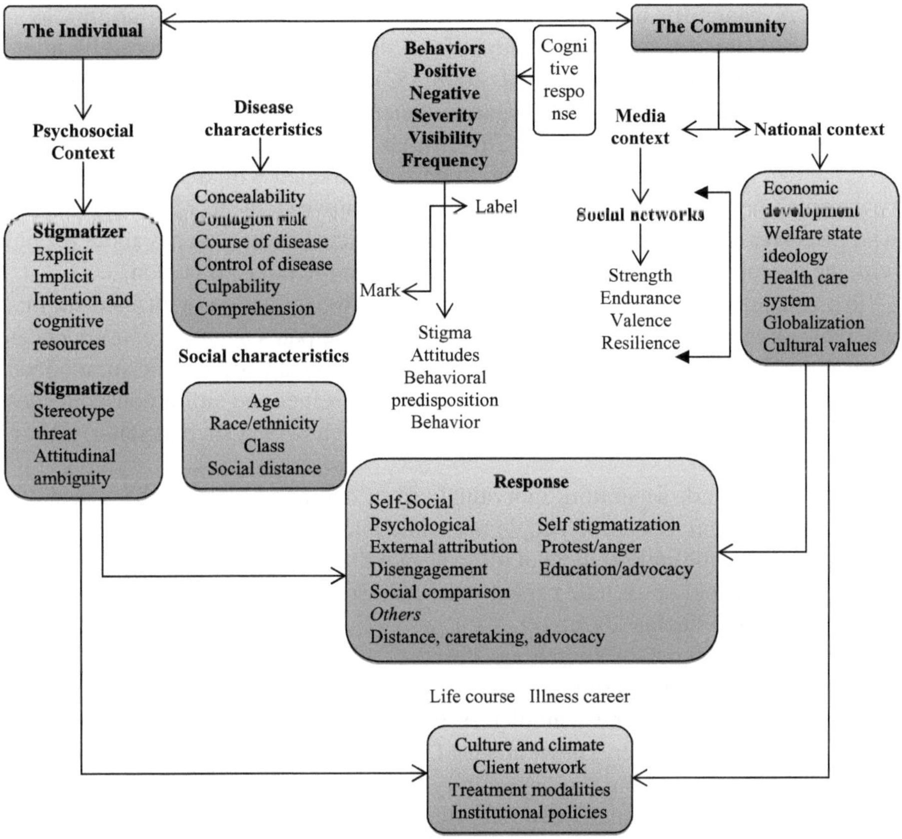

Fig. 2.3 Framework Integrating Normative Influences on Stigma (FINIS) (Source: Pescosolido et al. 2008)

stigma has drawn upon a framework developed by Goffman, which risks viewing stigma as a static individual attitude, rather than a dynamic and contested social process. Castro and Farmer argue that this has 'seriously limited the ways in which stigmatization and discrimination have been approached in relation to HIV and AIDS' (Castro and Farmer 2005:54).

Stigma, Discrimination, Prejudice and Xenophobia: Do They Overlap?

Stigma refers to the situation of an individual who is 'disqualified from full social acceptance' (Goffman 1963). The stigmatized individual is 'reduced in our minds from a whole and usual person to a tainted, discounted one' (Goffman 1963:3). The term stigma is used by those who experience it, and those who study it. 'Stigma researchers generally have two different ways of conceptualizing stigma as a psychosocial stressor, which are distinct from the types of stress induced by interpersonal discrimination' (Stuber et al. 2008:352). The stress induced by stigma has been described as the direction of negative societal attitudes towards the self, or the so-called internalization of stigma. The critique is that stigma researchers tend to describe the adverse effects of stigma on persons labelled with a stigmatized attribute, explaining stigma by examining the social cognitive elements of the stigmatizer, who perceives a stigmatizing feature, endorses the negative stereotypes about people with the perceived feature and discriminates against the targeted person.

Perceived or felt stigma is the fear of potential discrimination or enacted stigma, whereby someone with a stigmatizing condition anticipates negative consequences from social interactions (Van Brakel 2006). In internalized stigma, the stigmatized persons impose stigmatization processes upon themselves and suffer consequences of distressing feelings, such as shame or guilt, and behaviours such as self-isolation (Person et al. 2009).

Stigma is a mark separating individuals from one another based on a socially conferred judgment that some people are tainted, and this leads to negative beliefs (i.e. stereotypes), the endorsement of those negative stereotypes as real (i.e. prejudice) and a desire to avoid or exclude persons who hold stigmatized statuses (i.e. discrimination) (Link and Phelan 2001).

Generally two types of stigma are observed: enacted and felt. Enacted stigma refers to actual discrimination or unacceptability, whereas felt stigma refers to the fear of such discrimination (Scambler 1998). Causes, actions and consequences of these types of stigma differ. Tuberculosis (TB) patients who are HIV sufferers experience enacted stigma from the community throughout their life. In contrast, most HIV–TB patients experience only felt stigma during a short period. For the HIV sufferers, the enacted stigma greatly affected the patient and the family, psychosocially as well as economically. This study found that the common expressions of stigma towards HIV sufferers include keeping a distance from the patient, refusing foods cooked or sold by the patient and prohibiting the patient from participating in social gatherings (for details, see Chap. 4). The type and strength of stigma were closely linked with the type and strength of the categories 'defining oneself' and 'human bond' (Fig. 2.4).

> In Canada, we want to highlight that the human rights of the HIV/AIDS-infected groups are extremely marginalized by laws and policies. (Sandra Chu, a senior policy analyst at the Canadian HIV/AIDS Legal Network 2012)

Increased attention by researchers to the targets of prejudice in the 1990s (Crocker and Garcia 2006) resulted in combining theories of prejudice with theories of stigma. The concepts of stigma, prejudice and discrimination increasingly are used by the same authors in the same texts (Levin and Van Laar 2006). The undesired 'differentness' of a stigmatized category such as race can lead others to both turn away from and actively discriminate against the stigmatized (Goffman 1963). Thus, discrimination becomes an important component of stigma (Link and Phelan 2001). Where social inequalities exist, it is a key feature of intergroup relationships and

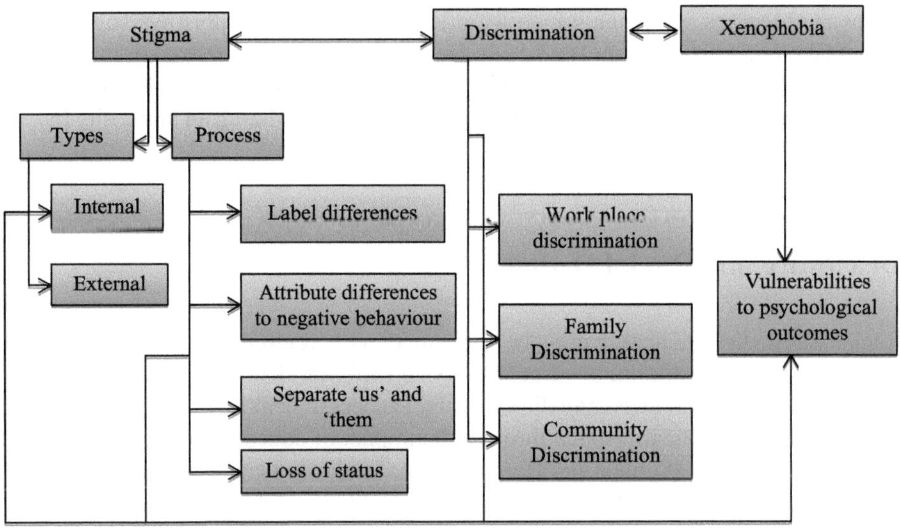

Fig. 2.4 Xenophobia and human rights dynamics (Source: Authors)

serves to reinforce the symbolic boundaries that separate social groups from one another (Jackman 1994).

Prejudice and discrimination are believed to be important contributors to the production of health disparities (IOM 2002; DHHS 2003; USAID 2000). Goffman's stigmas, blemishes of individual character and abominations of the body appear to cover every imaginable form of stigma or prejudice. Similarly, several of the prejudice models are not tied to particular in- and out-groups, and social identity theory is based on research showing that arbitrarily identified characteristics can serve as the basis of discrimination (Tajfel 1970). Clark et al.'s (1999) analysis of the stressful consequences of discrimination should apply to any characteristic that is the target of stigma or prejudice. However, in other cases, this substitution does not make sense. 'Prejudice reflects a general negative evaluation or orientation to a group or a member of a group, whereas stereotyping involves the association or attribution of specific characteristics to a group and its members. Both prejudice and stereotyping can produce discrimination, an unfair or unjustified group-based difference in behavior that systematically disadvantages members of another group' (Dovidio et al. 2008:478–9).

The studies on prejudice versus stigma give rise to another question. Phelan et al. (2008:361–2) ask 'why do particular characteristics become the object of stigma and prejudice, and are there different reasons for different characteristics?' Many of the models examined emphasize that the objects of stigma and prejudice are socially constructed and vary dramatically across time and place (*Ibid.*:362). Phelan, Link and Dovidio believe the reasons that particular characteristics are selected as targets of stigma and prejudice may represent an important variation that was revealed by the comparison of stigma and prejudice models. Goffman adds that there are many forms and degrees of stigma which were left unexplored and portrays stigma as a universal human experience (1963:127). He explains the incidence of stigmatization by stating that '[W]e construct a stigma-theory, an ideology to explain his inferiority and account for the danger he represents, sometimes rationalizing an animosity based on other differences, such as those of social class' (1963:5).

Disclosure and Racial Disparity

Racial disparities in health may be explained with reference to the differences between genetic populations' susceptibility to different diseases (Pettaway 1999). Socioeconomic differences may directly affect access to healthcare (IOM 2003) and indirectly influence health status through the impact of education on health literacy and health practices (Sentell and Halpin 2006). Studies on Canada suggest that the experience of unfair treatment, unrelated to race, induces stress and adversely affects psychological well-being for multiple social groups (Dion 2001). Empirical studies on the association between perceived discrimination and some indicator of health (Paradies 2006) found a positive association between discrimination and indicators of morbidity (Ren et al. 1999).

A study conducted by the National Center for Health Statistics (NCHS) on racial and ethnic disparities has attracted the attention of scholars in a range of professions and academic areas. Research shows that people who self-identify as 'White' are healthier than members of all other racial/ethnic groups, with the exception of people who self-identify as Asian or Pacific Islander (NCHS 2004). However, in the USA, obvious expressions of prejudice towards minority groups, and towards African Americans in particular, have declined substantially over the past 50 years. Bobo argues that 'the single clearest trend in studies of racial attitudes has involved a steady and sweeping movement toward general endorsement of the principles of racial equality and integration' (2001:269). Furthermore, there is some evidence to suggest that people rarely report experience of racial prejudice (Schuman et al. 1997). At the same time, however, racial disparities remain in economic (Blank 2001), physical (IOM 2003) and psychological health services (Surgeon General of the United States 2001).

The processes of conceptualization of stigma suggest that stigmatization occurs in the context of social forces that are mobilized to maintain specific dynamics of power (Parker and Aggleton 2003). The symptoms of illness 'kept many women out of the job market, locking them into poverty. The inability to work and earn money adds to the pain of living with a mental illness' (Collins et al. 2008). Within this study, there are stories about fathers who punish or rebuke their daughters for marrying darker men. Tensions between darker, poorer branches of a family and fairer, more affluent relatives; friends who marvel at the beauty of a child born with light skin, blue eyes and blonde hair; and perceived rejection of their own dark skin by in-laws with 'good hair' are common. Some of the participants in this study rejected these ideas, but admit that their relatives' ideas about race have influenced their actions in relationships. While women incorporate these experiences into their stories of relationships, few explicitly acknowledge experiencing race-/ethnicity-based discrimination (ibid). This study indicates the ways in which race, gender and ethnicity further impact the experience of illness, stigma and discrimination. Mentally ill women face a range of negative experiences, such as sexual health risks, that cannot be reduced to their mental illness, but to the intersection of these multiple stigmatized identities (Collins et al. 2008). Efforts to combat stigma and prejudice are ineffective if they do not account for multiple and interlocking identities (Crenshaw 1996). Similarly, the past 25 years of the AIDS epidemic have demonstrated that people who are vulnerable to gender inequality, racism and stigma carry the greatest burden of disease (Farmer 1997).

Given the degree of discrimination and prejudice experienced by PLWHA, social stigma often functions as a barrier to disclosure of one's HIV status. Crocker offered two interesting motivational factors in relation to disclosing one's HIV status: egosystem and ecosystem. Egosystem is made up of self-serving benefits, which boosts one's image. In constructing desired self-images, people present themselves in a certain way to get other people to see them as having particular qualities, so they can obtain resources such as relationship partners, jobs or admissions to college (Baumeister et al. 1996). The ecosystem goals focus on supporting others by avoiding being selfish, self-centred and harmful to others. We agree that fear of rejection leads people to conceal a stigma if they have egosystem goals, but not if they have ecosystem goals. When people have egosystem goals, they tend to enhance self-images and obtain desired social outcomes such as acceptance. Consequently, when stigmatized people expect rejection if they reveal their stigma, they attempt to conceal it from others. Ecosystem goals for disclosing stigmatized identities include consideration of the needs and well-being of others, in addition to the self. Instead of focusing on protecting the self, ecosystem goals focus on supporting others. People with egosystem motivations might be willing to risk disapproval for the sake of creating authentic relationships with supporting others (Crocker 2011). Disclosure and consequent depression have gender implications. Women who have been historically deprived of their due rights and disempowered are more exposed to varied kinds of stressors than men.

The most common barriers to disclosure that were mentioned by participants include fear of abandonment, fear of rejection/discrimination, fear of violence, fear of upsetting family members and fear of accusations of infidelity.

We consider the gendered effect of lying and how HIV status intersects with the power imbalance at the root of sexual assault. We discuss the tension between the need for women to protect both their medical information and their sexual integrity.

The subversion of self-esteem, shame and the desperate need to hide are the central elements of stigma and discrimination that emerge from disclosure of status (Bayer 2008a). Jennifer Crocker has made clear that the extent to which at least some of those who are objects of discrediting could resist the burden of prejudice and discrimination (Crocker, cited in Bayer 2008a, b:464). Healthcare providers are, therefore, faced with the challenge of how to address stigma in its own right if they want to maximize the quality of life for those they treat and maintain the benefits of treatment (Link et al. 1997) (Fig. 2.5).

Fig. 2.5 Impact of stigma

Stigma causes psychiatric morbidity by the fact that it restricts social participation. These variables are hard to measure quantitatively. Measurement of self-esteem, depression and social participation is therefore highly relevant to monitor the impact of stigma reduction interventions (Cardol et al. 1999). The emotional damage, for instance, caused by stigma can have deep ramifications in a person's life. The quality of life can be severely affected in terms of having problems in finding a life partner, building relationships and gaining employment. As an obvious effect of stigma, isolation deprives an individual of education, economic opportunities, socialization, sharing pain and grief with others and access to finance. These facts have a multiplier effect on the lives of those facing stigma. They may contribute to increased disability and reluctance to continue medication and obtain treatment.

Refugee Status Determination as a Burden

For those PLWHA who are refugees or asylum seekers, the refugee status determination (RSD) process itself can be the cause of additional stress and perceived discrimination. Therefore, the refugee status determination process merits attention. This analysis illustrates the extent of the burden the asylum seekers continue to carry until they are successfully granted refugee status. It is pertinent to outline the steps in this process for a better understanding of the potential refugees' experience of tribulations to go through the process. While it is true that claiming asylum in Canada is an easier process than in many other countries for resettlement, it is still a lengthy, complex and cumbersome process. Some reports suggest that some may be using Canada's asylum system to 'jump' the immigration queue (Brennan 2010). Nonetheless, claimants from designated countries of origin are still entitled to receive a fair hearing at the Immigration and Refugee Board (IRB). Hearings on these claims are expected to be held within 60 days, as opposed to the 90-day time frame for claimants from those countries that are not so designated.

In the event of a negative decision, claimants from designated countries of origin will have an expedited appeal process before the Refugee Appeal Division (RAD). These appeal decisions are expected within 30 days, unless a hearing is held, as opposed to the regular processing time, which is 120 days for all other claimants. A country can be considered for designation only if: the number of claims for refugee protection is equal to or greater than the number of claims specified in the regulations that will be developed later and the rate of acceptance by the RPD is equal to or lower than the rate set out in regulations. In addition, the following criteria will also be taken into account: the human rights record of the country and the availability in the country of mechanisms for seeking protection and redress (Government of Canada 2011).

The IRB considers a number of factors, including the protection available in the country of the claimant and the nature of the claim itself. The IRB then selects one of three possible ways to decide the claim: a fast-track expedited process, a fast-track hearing or a full hearing (Brennan 2010).

The fast-track expedited process applies to claimants from certain countries or for certain types of claims. The refugee protection officer interviews the claimant and makes a recommendation about the claim. A favourable recommendation is forwarded to a member who will decide if it should be accepted without a hearing. A hearing is held if the claimant is not granted refugee protection through the expedited process. Fast-track hearings are held for claims that appear to be simple because they may be decided on the basis of one or two issues. A refugee protection officer does not attend these hearings but may assist the member to ensure that all relevant evidence is presented. Representatives of the UNHCR may observe the hearing. The IRB will assign the claimant to one of these processes—the fast-track expedited process, a fast-track hearing or a full hearing.

Interdiction: These measures block refugees fleeing persecution, many of whom are forced to turn to human smugglers to help them reach a safe destination. In 2003, the Canadian Border Security Agency reported 6,439 airline interdictions.

Judicial Review and Stay of Removal: There are widespread claims that refugees are vulnerable to exploitation by incompetent and unscrupulous lawyers and immigration consultants. The British Columbia government withdrew legal aid for refugee claimants in 2003. Even in places where legal aid is available, it rarely covers a review of decision. If a person is accepted after the process, it only means he/she can temporarily reside in Canada. This does not provide a refugee status or permanent residency. The success rate for a judicial review is between 5 and 10 % (Noii-Van 2007).

Safe Third Country Agreement: The adoption of Canada's 'None Is Too Many' policy on December 29, 2004, effectively closed its land border to refugees, preventing at least 33 % of all refugee claims from ever being heard.

Deportation: Failed refugee claimants are called for an interview with an enforcement officer who sets a deportation date. Often the deadline is within a couple of days, and this can be followed by confiscation of the claimant's health and social insurance card. They may be detained without notice if they are visibly upset or display a high degree of stress. There are arguable claims that Canada regularly deports people to unsafe countries (Noii-Van 2007). Procedure to deport refugees to an unsafe condition is in clear violation of Canada's obligations under international law.

Without Legal Status: There are up to 200,000 people living without legal status in Canada which may mean that their application for status has been made but no decision has been reached or was turned down. Living without status may also mean that no application has been made at all, either due to fear, misinformation or lack of assistance and resources. It may also mean that someone's arrangement for sponsorship or work permit relationship has broken down. Canada has refused to resolve the situation faced by people without status in Canada including long-term residents who have been living in Canada for years because of a moratorium on removals. Entire families live in a state of constant stress and fear. Workers are exploited. Children of non-status immigrants, whether Canadian-born or not, are denied the right to education. Children and entire families lack adequate and affordable medical coverage. Some refugees have been forced to seek sanctuary in churches across Canada. In March 2004, Canada violated this sanctuary by arresting Mohamed Cherfi in a church (Canadian Council for Refugee—CCR 2005). In 2004, the immigration minister, Judy Sgro, criticized churches offering sanctuary and incorrectly stated that refugee claimants have 'between 6 and 20 avenues of appeal' (Canadian Council For Refugee—CCR 2005:2).

Resettlement: Through the UNHCR, Canada chooses a limited number of refugees who meet certain criteria to resettle in Canada. The country accepts less than 0.1 % of the world's refugees. In 2004, Canada reduced the funding for these refugees and reduced the number to 7,300. Thus, refugee applicants must have enough money to support themselves through government or private sponsorship. Many applications for refugee status are denied because they have small children or have survived torture and therefore do not meet the successful establishment criteria (Noii-Van 2007).

CD4 Count Dynamics

The level of discrimination and stigma often is determined by whether or not the condition of the HIV sufferer has degenerated into AIDS. It is therefore important to understand the transformation stages and the clinical progression towards AIDS. Generally, the clinical indication of this progression relies upon the CD4 count as a measure. CD4 counts and HIV viral load are the best indicators known so far for monitoring the degree of damage to the immune system from HIV and the risk of clinical progression to AIDS. CD4 are the main cells in the body affected by HIV. A normal CD4 count in a person who is HIV− can range from 400 to 1,600 (Srinivasula et al. 2011).

There is another way to check the status. HIV reproduces in the bloodstream. The viral load is a measure of the amount of HIV virus in blood, expressed either as a number ranging from 48 to 10,000,000 copies/ml or as the log of the viral load. The higher the number, the more quickly HIV will damage the immune system and the more likely one is to feel sick from the HIV infection. When the viral load rises to over 100,000 copies/ml (log 5.0), the medical provider may prescribe medications to combat HIV. These medications bring down the viral load, aiming for less than 48 copies/ml or 'undetectable' (Vajpayee and Mohan 2011:801). The viral load is expected to decrease by 1.0 log after one month on the medication.

White blood cells are produced by the body to fight off infection as a part of the immune system. CD4 cells are a type of white blood cell called lymphocytes, which have a marker on the outside of the cell called a CD4 marker. These are also called 'T cells' and occasionally 'T helper cells'. These are the cells that HIV infects and destroys (Vajpayee and Mohan 2011). Usual CD4 counts for a newborn baby are around 3,000–5,000 and for an adolescent or adult about 700–1,200 cells/ml. If the count falls below 200 cells/ml, the patient is diagnosed with AIDS. This is not a different disease from HIV infection; instead, it means patients are vulnerable to unusual infections that other people do not get, called 'opportunistic infections'.

Usually a medical provider may start medication to treat HIV if the CD4 count falls below 350 cells/ml. However, one can start medication before the CD4 cells drop below 200 because the body responds better to medication when they are commenced at above 200 cells/ml. HIV medicines attack the HIV virus in the body, allowing the body to produce more CD4 cells. The amount of CD4 cells varies and may rise and fall. To determine if a change in CD4 cells is significant, the medical provider may refer to the 'CD4 percentage', that is, the percentage of lymphocytes with CD4 markers on the surface. For example, if the CD4 count was 400 (18 %) and then was 325 (19 %) at the next check, the HIV infection is not getting worse and hurting the immune system more because the CD4 percentage is stable or improving. When the CD4 percentage is less than 15 %, one is still vulnerable to opportunistic infections and should take medication to prevent sickness (Rodriguez et al. 2005; Zhou et al. 2010).

Methodological Issues

Research on refugees is a difficult undertaking, and there is no established method for examining both refugees and HIV/AIDS with a single framework. The challenging nature of research with refugees is made more complicated by the precarious conditions under which refugees reside. Moreover, there are additional issues of sensitivity involved in undertaking research on HIV/AIDS. This study aimed to address a gap in the literature and prepare the ground for designing research based on geographical and political context, and propose alternative strategies for addressing methodological challenges. This is expected to be an important contribution to the methodological underpinnings of refugee research. Ethical issues pose a significant challenge as this research involves human subjects and deals with delicate and sensitive issues. This section also explains the process for handling confidential research material, developing intersectional analyses and answering specific questions related to multi-strategy research design that are very important for researching refugees.

Methodology

A constructivist grounded theory (GT) approach has been selected as a theoretical and methodological framework to guide this research. Grounded theory is a widely used qualitative research technique that explores social processes and reveals how people anticipate and respond to various life experiences. This approach is crucial for this study as it intends to examine the life experience of the research subjects. GT seeks to inductively distil issues of importance for specific groups of people and creates meaning about those issues through analysis of theory (Mills et al. 2006). Unlike the original grounded theory, first developed by Glaser and Strauss (1967), constructivist grounded theory is not 'objectivist' (Charmaz 2003), which recognizes that the 'viewer creates the data and ensuing analysis through interaction with the viewed' (Charmaz 2003:273), and therefore the data does not provide a window on an objective reality. Thus, the background of researchers influences their interpretations of the data. They cannot avoid being influenced by 'disciplinary emphases' and 'perceptual proclivities' (Charmaz 2003:259).

Grounded theory seeks to foster 'the development of qualitative traditions through the study of experience from the standpoint of those who live it' (Charmaz 2000:522). Rather than beginning with a pre-established theory, a constructivist grounded theory approach aims to develop theory grounded in data that were systematically gathered and analyzed (Strauss and Corbin 1998:25). Therefore, the approach is appropriate for this study, particularly because there is scant information about the life experience of Asians living with HIV in North America. The study has, therefore, designed with the objective of understanding the lifestyle and psychosocial experience of Asians living with HIV. In order to identify a culturally appropriate HIV prevention and treatment strategy for this population, it is important to understand the way in which Asians living with HIV in North America operate within their social and systemic community.

The Interpretative Phenomenological Analysis (IPA) yields good results in analyzing qualitative data. One of the methods this research uses to interpret and analyze field data is embedded within interpretive phenomenology. The primary advantage of this technique is that it facilitates, by exploration, delving into the personal experiences and perceptions of research subjects (Creswell 2003). This technique is useful because of its ontological and epistemological significance and helps to ensure that the participants' subjective experiences are valued and their experiences can be understood by interacting with and listening to them (Fouché 2005). The objective of the discussions with the participants was to understand their daily ordeals in carrying the burden of the disease and related tribulations of stigma and discrimination. Qualitative research designs are best suited to this task of understanding the complexities of lived 'experiences from the perspective of those who live it and in order to understand this world of meaning, one must interpret it' (Willig 2001:150). Interpretive researchers are interested in what is meaningful or relevant to the participants and how these participants experience daily life. Neuman (2000) argues that social life is a socially constructed meaning system that is based on social interactions and people's definitions of reality (Neuman 2000).

Since the primary objective of this research is to understand the perceptions and perspectives of the PLWHA in relation to enduring stigma, a phenomenological approach is appropriate. This approach helps researchers identify people's perceptions, perspectives and understandings of a particular phenomenon (Creswell 2003; Fouché 2005). The most interesting aspect of this method is the three distinct phases of contemplation: epoche, phenomenological reduction and imaginative variation (Leedy and Ormrod 2005). Epoche is the suspension of presuppositions, assumptions, judgments and interpretations with the intention of being fully aware of what is being presented (Willig 2001). Phenomenological reduction is the description of the phenomenon itself, which includes describing the physical features and the experiential features (Willig 2001). Imaginative variation involves accessing the structural components (such as time, space and social relationships) of the phenomenon (Leedy and Ormrod 2005).

Sample Frame and Sampling

Determining the sample frame is crucial to generating the sample and thus the quality of the analysis. It is a major determinant of the extent to which the samples are representative of the population (Bilsborrow 1998:89). There are currently no reliable statistics on Asians living with HIV in North America in general and South Asians in Canada in particular due to the fact that the disclosure and testing rates for the community are low. In the absence of a list of actual estimates of South Asian living with HIV in Canada, there remains a challenge as to how the sample frame could be defined. The geographical region identified as South Asia includes eight countries—Afghanistan, Bangladesh, Bhutan, India, the Maldives, Nepal, Pakistan and Sri Lanka. For convenience of sampling, this study covers immigrants from Bangladesh, India, Pakistan and Sri Lanka.

A number of factors are considered to determine the appropriate sample size for a study. In quantitative approaches, they include the level of precision, the level of confidence or risk, and the degree of variability in the attributes being measured (Miaoulis and Michener 1976). The level of precision—sometimes labelled as the 'sampling error'—is the range in which the true value of the population is estimated (Israel 1992; Smith 1983). However, there is always a chance that the sample obtained does not represent the true population value. Degree of variability refers to the distribution of attributes within the population. The more heterogeneous a population, the larger is the sample size required to obtain a given level of precision. The less variable (i.e. more homogeneous) a population, the smaller the sample size would need to be (Cochran 1963; Mian 1999; Sudman 1976). Given the challenges of knowing the sample frame, we had to choose snowball technique in order to select the sample.

Recruitment of Participants and Interview Process[2]

Most interviews were conducted face to face in person. A few organizations that claimed to have been working with the PLWHA promised to lend assistance in conducting this research. After two years of consistent attachment and constant communication with those organizations, they were unable to present any of their clients to the authors. This is obviously a part of challenge inherent in such kind of research. Participants were recruited through a snowball and purposive sampling method. Some interviews were conducted online through various chat rooms used exclusively by PLWHA. In order to recruit a diverse group of participants, the recruitment process utilized a sample fraction for ensuring the inclusion of a proportional number of South Asian nationalities. Interviews were conducted at different times of the day to ensure accessibility and convenience for the participants. Participants were provided with information on the study, research goals and methodology, and efforts were made to develop trust and rapport with potential participants. Familiarity with South Asian culture and language and personal associations and knowledge made it easier for us to connect with participants and facilitate the interviews (for more information, see Appendix).

Based on the literature and knowledge of South Asian cultures, some specific issues were identified for approaching the research in a culturally appropriate manner. These included issues related to family, social support, dating, relationships, sexuality and awareness about STIs and safer sex practices (Eysenbach and Till 2001). Gender issues are also important here, as this is highly relevant in terms of women's ability to negotiate safer sex and men's feelings of conforming to certain standards of masculinity in regard to sexuality. We used these thematic topics as a general guideline during the interviews to explore participants' lived and psychosocial experiences. However, no specific set of questions were developed for the interviews; rather, unstructured, open-ended questions were used to explore these issues. In doing so, it was possible to solicit not only the factual information required for the study but also allowed participants to attribute meanings and interpretations to events and relationships in their own terms and discuss issues that are most relevant and important to them (Mann and Stewart 2000). This method of unstructured in-depth interviewing was useful in generating insights about participants' experiences of themselves in their own worlds. It also provided an opportunity for us to hear participants' stories in their own terms (Anderson and Jack 1991).

In many Asian cultures, sex and sexuality are sensitive topics that are often excluded from open discussion. As in most cultures, there are many South Asian

[2] For further details on the interview process, please see Appendix.

men who are attracted to other men physically, psychologically and/or emotionally, and yet did not identify themselves as gay, bisexual or even as MSM. One of the most vulnerable exposure categories in terms of HIV globally is MSM. The sexual practices of MSM include anal sex, which—when practised without protection—carries a higher risk of transmission than unprotected vaginal sex. Unlike communities of openly gay men who are routinely targeted under HIV/AIDS prevention programmes and campaigning, MSM are often excluded or neglected in such interventions, and therefore high rates of transmission and infection remain among this group. Since the onset of the HIV/AIDS pandemic, consistently high levels of HIV infection have been found among this group.

Given the sensitivity of these issues, particularly pertaining to sexuality and sexual practices, rapport building with the interviewees was critical for allowing participants to discuss these kinds of issues without feeling embarrassed or being subjected to judgment. Moreover, it was important that participants were interviewed in locations they found comfortable, to 'allow communication to flow with a minimum of self-consciousness and self-restraint'. Moreover, by feeling more comfortable and less restrained, participant–interviewer interactions were expected to be more direct and may led participants to 'greater self-disclosure even about sensitive issues' (Mann and Stewart 2000:200).

Each interview lasted approximately one and half hours. Before the interview began, the interviewer carefully explained the research goals and methodology to every participant and informed them that they could withdraw at any time during the interview. A letter of consent was reviewed with each of the participants before starting the discussions. To ensure that they met the criteria for participation, each participant was asked to ethnically identify him or herself before the interview began. People who work during the day prefer to be interviewed at night, while students and young people who live with their parents tend to interview more often during the day than at night while their parents were not home. These aspects were given careful consideration.

It is important to nail down the process followed in interviewing using semi-structured questions. Marvasti (2004) and Smith and Osborn (2003) mentioned five phases of this process, only three key phases were followed in this research. Primarily, preparation for the interview involved the construction of an interview guide for field research (Marvasti 2004; Smith and Osborn 2003). The second stage involved serious consideration of the relationship between the interviewer and interviewees, that is, establishing relationships, conducting interviews and dealing with contingencies if the interview did not proceed according to plan. Finally, termination took place when the conditions of the research agreement were met, the proposed objectives were achieved and the saturation point was reached. In some cases, interviews were terminated and participants were offered the opportunity to have a debriefing and feedback session.

The basic principles that were incorporated in all the interviews included respect and courtesy, acceptance and understanding, confidentiality, integrity and individualization. The strategies included observation (both participatory and non-participatory), and care was taken to maintain ethical norms, timeliness and clear communication with participants. The objective was to address any conflict or misunderstanding promptly. Simple observations throughout the fieldwork process were recorded and included in the reflexive notes. These included describing the research context and the participants, noting participants' nonverbal behaviour during the interviews, interpreting the situation and including a reflexive analysis. These simple observations were not subjected to the stages of Interpretative Phenomenological Analysis (IPA), but were used for their value in describing the research sample, setting and for reflexive insights. Unlike participant observation, this simple observation is not time consuming or labour intensive and does not create an enormous amount of data (Strydom 2005).

Snowballing

The snowballing method was not intended at the outset in order to keep the sample as random as possible. Snowballing carries a risk of adding bias to the data. This technique of sample selection has gained popularity among researchers. However, this technique is useful in difficult research conditions and for obtaining information from population that is hard to reach. As research progressed, the difficulty of accessing the target population group was increasingly realized. It was not easy to collaborate with organizations working among HIV/AIDS patients. Incidentally, an enthusiastic, helpful and cooperative person who became infected around 8 years ago agreed to be interviewed. This person had already been interviewed by a number of researchers. This led us to a number of his friends who were willing to share their experiences. Thus, there was an inadvertent effect of a snowballing technique, and we consider it to be a by-product of the constraints imposed by the nature of this particular research context.

Online Research Participants

The constraints in accessing our target population compelled us to consider alternative methods, and we resorted to exploring online communities and support groups for PLWHA. This was not a planned or anticipated method for accessing the target sample, yet it proved to be very effective in reaching the population that helped us gain insight into another aspect of their life experience. This channel was useful in providing a safe place to find respite from stigma, seek support and build community. In many of these sites, users can upload their profiles onto the system, and they can only be seen by other members and they are able to conceal them at any time. It cannot be claimed that complete interviews were obtained from the people on these sites. Rather, it was possible to complete a few in-depth interviews, while many others were left partially completed. It should be stated that the half-done interviews were not considered as part of the sample. Some participants did not feel well and had to leave the chat room, and it was not possible to reconnect with them. These chat rooms have separate rooms for HIV sufferers, and that helped to identify the target population. It took a few days to get to know some of the participants. Once a certain level of rapport was achieved, participants agreed to be interviewed. The same procedure and standards (such as confidentiality and ethical issues) were maintained for the online interviews as for those conducted face to face.

The chat rooms could be accessed by any person from anywhere in the world. Therefore, the identification of the participant depended on his and her own desire to disclose honestly. We confirmed that they were living in Canada, that they were of Asian origins (especially from South Asia) and that they were willing to participate in the study. Interviews were conducted after obtaining their consent. Online chat was not considered as interview, but it in fact helped us to get to know each other and at some point we exchanged our telephone numbers and Skype IDs. Some of them agreed to meet and to be interviewed face to face. Some of them were interviewed via Skype. The sites we explored ranged from those broadly targeting gay men wanting to meet one another to those dedicated to PLWHA.[3]

Interviews

Neither unstructured nor semi-structured interview restricts the participants to specific questions spelled out on the questionnaire; rather it offers flexibility and easy integration into the research context (Greeff 2005; Silverman 2006; Smith and Osborn 2003; Ullah 2012). This technique was used to gather information about the social lives of PLWHA (Silverman 2006), to understand the participants' lives and to generate in-depth information (Greeff 2005; Willig 2001). Participants have the opportunity to further expand, modify and add to their answers throughout the semi-structured interview process. The freedom is also there if they need to clarify anything (Marvasti 2004). During the process of narrative interaction, the researcher and participant give and take from each other, and this underlines the complexity of

---

[3] www.Gay.com chat room

http://www.hivandsingle.com/

http://www.experienceproject.com/groups/Am-HIV-Positive/19015/forum

http://www.13km.com/—this is an amazing site which is absolutely designed for HIV-positive persons.

www.HIVDating.info—HIV dating site reviews, free to join the best HIV dating service for HIV-positive singles dating and dating with HIV-HIV POZ personals for HIV POZ dating

www.HIVMingle.com—online community for HIV-positive dating, where one can meet other HIV-positive singles for friendship, relationships, love and chat.

www.HIVPositiveMagazine.com—this site welcomes all HIV positive. The mission of this site is exactly the same as the mission of the print version of HIV Positive magazine. The mandate of this site is to help one live a long, productive, fantastic life with HIV.

MenLivingWithAIDS.ning.com—this site is for guys who are infected and their friends.

SOFLpozgroup.com—this is a social group for HIV gay men ages 21–40 in South Florida who would like to meet others like themselves.

the area of interest being explored and, in turn, gains density as the conversation about meaning ensues. Therefore, the interview becomes the 'site for the construction of knowledge, and clearly the researcher and informant produce this knowledge together'. In the construction of such knowledge, the information generated needs to reveal depth, feeling and reflexive thought (Mills et al. 2006).

The semi-structured interview allows for flexibility, unlike the structured interview where questions are adhered to in a consistent and highly structured manner. In structured interviews, the insight gained into the interviewees' world is limited to responses given to the questions that are being asked (Greeff 2005; Marvasti 2004). While semi-structured interviews provide for the relatively systematic collection of data within a reasonable time frame and, at the same time, ensure that important data is not omitted, the in-depth interview is a time-consuming method that generates vast amounts of data that are difficult to manage and organize (Silverman 2006; Smith and Osborn 2003).

Semi-structured interviews are extremely helpful in exploratory studies in furthering and developing the ongoing research questions and framework. In exploratory research, there is ample room to clarify concepts and problems, and it allows for the establishment of a list of possible answers and solutions, which in turn facilitates the construction of more structured interviews. Semi-structured interviews also facilitate the reformulation of ambiguous questions and the elimination of superfluous ones and allow for the discovery of new aspects of the problem by exploring in detail the explanations supplied by participants (Bless et al. 2006).

It should be mentioned that there are some problematic sides of this technique as well. While it offers flexibility and freedom, the personalities of participants may be overly deterministic in the answers being given (Bless et al. 2006). This was obvious during the interviews. At the same time, there is a risk that the interviewer plays an overly deterministic role in influencing the data by recording the information inaccurately—either by translating the ideas of the participant into the interviewer's own words or interpreting the answers according to his/her 'own views or by recording only a summarized version of the answer' (Bless et al. 2006:12). This research required extra care to ensure objectivity. The semi-structured approach to in-depth interviews required more time than it could have been in using a structured questionnaire. However, this was offset by the quality of data gathered.

Data Processing and Analysis

Participants were purposively selected to generate data that fills conceptual gaps in the development of a formal theory. Data collection and analysis proceeded simultaneously and in an interactive manner. Analysis relies upon an inductive approach 'to develop open coding categories and then, through axial coding, to interrelate these categories' that represent phenomena (Creswell 1998:209). The transcripts of the interviews were carefully read, and coding conducted line-by-line to highlight key phrases that represent themes. Similar coded phrases were then grouped together to develop a list of emerging themes and categories. This helped to further reduce themes and create clusters.

Measuring Stigma

In analyzing the data generated, a key lens of analysis was the experience and perception of stigma by research participants. In order to theoretically organize the experience and perception of stigma, the study focused upon five theoretical domains of stigma: attribution theory and stigma, fear or peril and stigma, policy and stigma, power and stigma, and social norms and stigma. This framework is aligned with Van Brakel's (2006) five categories of health-related stigma: the experience of actual discrimination (enacted stigma), attitudes towards affected people, perceived or felt stigma, self or internalized stigma and discriminatory practices in (health) services.

Stigma and health conditions have become inseparable phenomenon (Van Brakel 2005). HIV is inextricably associated with stigma primarily because of the prevailing discriminatory idea that HIV is a disease that is contracted through immoral activities. Theories of stigma suggest that people who have contracted a stigmatized illness through methods beyond their control (e.g. a person who has contracted HIV through a blood transfusion) are associated with less blame and anger than towards someone who contracted the illness through high-risk behaviours, which in turn guides the inclination to either punish or assist the person (Corrigan 2000). The psychosocial consequences of stigma generate indescribable torment to the stigmatized (Frist 1996; Nyblade et al. 2003).

The effects of stigma include psychological stress, depression and other psychiatric morbidity, fear, marital and relationship problems, other social participation restrictions such as loss of employment or reduced employment opportunities and reduced education opportunities, increased (risk of) disability and advanced disease and risk of being victims of violence. Some examples of the effects are delay in diagnosis and treatment resulting in continuing risk of disease transmission in case of infectious diseases and in more severe morbidity and poorer treatment prognosis in most conditions (Van Brakel 2005; Jaramillo 1998; Nicholls et al. 2003; Piot and Coll Seck 2001). Concealment may result in continued risk behaviour and failure to embrace preventive behaviour among sufferers of conditions such as HIV/AIDS (Adetunji and Meekers 2001; Rahlenbeck 2004) and in poor treatment adherence or default from treatment, as has been reported in leprosy, TB, HIV/AIDS, mental illness and epilepsy (Conrad 1985; Heijnders 2004; Sumartojo 1993; Weiser et al. 2003). It is noticeable that in spite of wide cultural diversity, there is remarkable similarity in the way life is affected by stigma in different countries and health conditions. They include marriage, interpersonal relationships, mobility, employment, access to treatment and care, education, leisure activities and attendance at social and religious functions (Van Brakel 2005).

Despite the knowledge that we have about the interplay between stigma and HIV, little progress has been made in systematically addressing stigma. It is recognized that many stigma reduction interventions have struggled to effectively measure and evaluate its impact. Obviously, it is not easy to reliably measure such a complex psychosocial phenomenon. Brakel's (2005) review of more than 60 stigma-related papers found that the indicators developed so far apply only in a single particular field of health. Development of appropriate instruments of stigma assessment for a range of health areas would help develop stigma reduction strategies. Since this research is based on a mixed method technique, it is important to have instruments in place in order to undertake quantitative measures, as and where required.

Generic Instruments

Based on his extensive review of the literature, Van Brakel (2005) found only one generic measurement instrument—a stigma scale. The scale contains 12 items and is only one part of a catalogue of instruments used to study different cultural and epidemiological aspects of a health condition. Responses are coded on a 0–3 ordinal scale (0 = no, 1 = uncertain, 2 = possibly of conditionally and 3 = yes). The scale covers only certain areas of life that may be affected by stigma, such as concealment, avoidance, pity, shame, being made fun of, respect and marriage prospects.

HIV/AIDS-Specific Scales

The 'AIDS Attitude Scale' (AAS), developed in the USA, has been used in a number of studies since 1992 (Froman et al. 1992; Froman and Owen 2001). Another scale for measuring public attitude is the 'Attitudes towards AIDS' scale developed in Brazil (Moriya et al. 1994). It consists of 25 items and the psychometric properties have been found to be good. Yet another type of instrument is the 'protocol for identification of discrimination against PLWHA' developed by UNAIDS; this is an indicator based on a checklist of 37 possible ways discrimination may occur (2000).

The 40-item 'HIV Stigma Scale' developed by Berger et al. measures stigma perceived and experienced by PLWHA (Berger et al. 2001). The items are formulated as statements and responses are requested on a 4-point agreement scale. It is possible to test the psychometric properties of the scale in a large sample of population with diverse backgrounds. The indicators in the set measure stigma and discrimination both from the perspective of PLWHA and of the community. Each indicator asks for the number of PLWHA who have experienced a particular type of discrimination or the number of people who have a particular opinion about or feeling towards PLWHA.

Ethical Issues[4]

Ethical issues are not new in social sciences research; however, stricter application of the ethics approval process has become increasingly important in recent times. Research in the past, including those that are often cited nowadays, rarely went through the protocol of ethical approval required today when research involves human subjects. This study involves extensive interaction with human subjects, that is, people living with HIV/AIDS, and required approval of research ethics obtained through rigorous procedures.

Adherence to ethical research processes is highly relevant to this study for a number of reasons. First and foremost, this research involves a vulnerable group of people, and their informed consent and participation is critical to avoid objectifying or exploiting their experiences. Ethical lapses in research can significantly harm human subjects (Shamoo and Resnik 2009), particularly those who are already marginalized or at risk, and research cannot claim to be academically sound if it does not demonstrate ethical treatment of its subjects and data.

Discussions of the importance of ethics in research have identified a number of reasons why ethical considerations are critical in research. Shamoo and Resnik (2009) discuss some of these points. First, adherence to ethical standards helps promote the aims of the research, for instance, prohibitions against fabricating or misrepresenting research data ultimately promote higher standards of accuracy. Ethical standards also promote the values that are essential to collaborative work, such as trust, accountability, mutual respect and fairness. The guidelines for authorship, copyright and patenting policies, data sharing policies and confidentiality rules in peer review are designed to protect intellectual property interests while encouraging collaboration. Ethical norms help to ensure that researchers can be held accountable to the public. Funders feel comfortable to provide research funds when projects can ensure the quality and integrity of research. In sum, ethics processes promote moral and social values such as: social responsibility, human rights, animal welfare, compliance with the law, and health and safety (Social Research Association 2003; Shamoo and Resnik 2009).

The Web Center for Social Research Methods stated that during the 1990s questions surrounding the ethics of medical research took a new turn (http://www.socialresearchmethods.net/kb/ethics.php). In many cases, it has been the lack of attention paid to ethics over the previous three decades that has resulted in the high degree of rigour in today's ethical approval processes. The last few years have witnessed major changes in the ethics of research, but a new consensus is evolving to involve the stakeholder groups most affected by a problem so they can participate more actively in the formulation of guidelines for research (Shamoo and Resnik 2009). This study required similar vetting after a lengthy process of review of the proposal.

[4] For further information on the ethical processes adhered to in this study, please see Appendix.

Protection of Human Participants

In order to ensure the participation and protection of the research subjects, respondents were provided with background information, aims, objectives and methods of the study. They were informed that participation was voluntary and that they could withdraw from the project at any time. Respondents were also assured of the confidentiality of information obtained from the interviews. Following this explanation, the willing respondents signed a written consent form to participate.

There are a number of key phrases that describe the system of ethical protection created by contemporary social and medical research establishment for trying to better protect the rights of research participants (http://www.socialresearchmethods.net/kb/ethics.php). The principle of voluntary participation requires that people not be coerced into participating in research. Closely related to the notion of voluntary participation is the requirement of informed consent. Essentially, this means that potential research participants must be fully informed about the procedures and risks involved in research and must give their informed consent to participate. Ethical standards also require that researchers do not place participants in a situation where they might be at risk of harm. A broad definition of harm is used in this case to include both physical and psychological harms.

Participants in this study were offered one of two levels of privacy in order to ensure protection of their identities. Confidentiality of all participants is guaranteed, and they are assured that this information will not be available to anyone who is not directly involved in the study. The stricter option available is the principle of anonymity, which essentially means that the participants remain anonymous throughout the study—even to the researchers themselves. Clearly, the anonymity standard is a stronger guarantee of privacy, but it is sometimes difficult to maintain, especially in situations where participants have to be measured at multiple points of time. This type of research must adhere to the principles of honesty, objectivity, integrity, carefulness, respect for intellectual property, openness, responsible publication, confidentiality, social responsibility, respect for colleagues, non-discrimination, competence, legality and human subjects protection (Shamoo and Resnik 2009).

Reliability and Validity

Unlike quantitative research, the validity and reliability of a qualitative study is commonly judged by four criteria: credibility, transferability, dependability and conformability (Lincoln and Guba 1985; Trochim 2000). Quality research must have a degree of reliability in its data and analytical appropriateness. To ensure the quality and reliability of the research, a number of measures were adopted for this study. A field-test of the questionnaire was conducted before administering them to the respondents, and the data was crosschecked. 'The quality of a grounded theory study can be judged through the 'validity, reliability and credibility' of the data within the standard canons of scientific research' (Creswell 1998:209). In this study, credibility was established through triangulation of qualitative interviews and community consultations. Validation was enhanced through the consultation process with participants to verify and expand the understanding of participants' experiences developed through the data analysis. Dependability was enhanced through the process of data analysis: that is, the data was coded and then, in collaboration with an expert, core categories were developed through mutual consensus (Lincoln and Guba 1985; Creswell 1998).

Anonymity and confidentiality were ensured by not publishing information on the identity of the participant. Code numbers were assigned to the notes for identifying their views and using them correctly. Participants were reassured that information generated from the interviews would remain confidential and would not be used for any other purpose outside of the research study. Access to the audiotapes was limited to the researchers only. Since data collection involved working with HIV/AIDS patients, it was important to outline the extent of time required, the potential impact, limitations and outcomes of the research (Creswell 2003).

Challenges

The topic of this research is extremely sensitive because it deals with human subjects, and a great deal of attention was dedicated to ensuring non-discriminatory and appropriate language and attitudes. The language in the text of the questionnaire and other relevant documents, as well as in the practices and question formation of the researchers, had to be carefully screened. Since this study deals with the South Asian community, sensitive issues needed to be managed with reference to a cultural perspective. Accessibility to the respondents has been a major challenge throughout the course of this research. Community organizations dealing with counselling of PLWHA were considered as important partners in undertaking this research. However, organizations have their specific objectives and interests, and sometimes they are accorded more importance instead of providing full cooperation with external researchers. Building collaborative research partnerships with these organizations was a major challenge and, on some occasions, posed a barrier to accessing research participants. Nevertheless, the cooperation of these agencies was invaluable for the study and contributed to more convincing findings. Finally, the question of representativeness and reliability remains a challenge in undertaking this type of research where the sample frame is unknown, and personal perspectives of both participants and researchers present a risk of influencing the outcome of research.

Chapter 3
Poverty, Migrants and HIV/AIDS in Canada

The AIDS pandemic has gained momentum during the past quarter century, expanding to all regions of the world. AIDS affects both the rich and the poor, but the hardest-hit countries are among the poorest in the world. Unless more vigorous actions are undertaken to combat the disease and its effects, the HIV/AIDS epidemic portends a grim future for many countries, especially the poorest countries. (United Nations United Nations 2005:V)

The previous chapter presented the methodology of the research and outlined theoretical issues relating to stigma, discrimination and xenophobia. This chapter reviews the literature on the interplay between poverty and the HIV/AIDS epidemic. This is particularly important in order to dispel myths surrounding ownership of the disease. Studies suggest a significant correlation between poverty and HIV/AIDS, which perpetuates the poverty trap for millions of people worldwide (Pottie et al. 2011). Researching the relationship between HIV/AIDS and poverty is a complex task because of their evolving characteristics and divergent scholarly approaches. Therefore, it is hard to isolate the cause–effect relationship. Despite these difficulties, substantial research has been devoted to exploring their correlation. The United Nations has broadly categorized the determinants of HIV/AIDS as biological and social. Poverty is the primary social determinant of HIV (United Nations 2005:12).

Most researches seem to conclude that there is a strong correlation between the condition of poverty and HIV/AIDS. While a cure has not yet been discovered, an antiretroviral treatment (ARV) has been developed; however, although ARV treatment has proved to be successful, the drugs are too expensive for many people, particularly those from the poorer regions of the world. This causes ongoing problems in treatment as well as prevention, which helps account for the fact that while developing countries hold '80 per cent of the world's population, the area contains 95 per cent of the world's HIV/AIDS cases' (Fenton 2007:17). One potential cause for this discrepancy may be that people who are impoverished are more likely to turn to prostitution as a way to support themselves. This profession is considered a breeding

A.A. Ullah, A.S. Huque, *Asian Immigrants in North America with HIV/AIDS*,
DOI 10.1007/978-981-287-119-0_3

ground for the HIV/AIDS virus, allowing the disease to quickly and anonymously pass from one person to another.

Not only does poverty contribute to HIV/AIDS, it seems to perpetuate poverty. The virus causes physical deterioration in infected people, so much that it becomes very difficult to improve their socioeconomic conditions. In the African continent, the pandemic has had a significant impact on primary education. HIV/AIDS was found to lower primary school enrolment by as much as forty per cent, with many orphans dropping out following the death of their parents. A low level of educational attainment has severe implications for a country's long-term development (Cheru 1999).

In addition, HIV/AIDS causes reduced earnings and lower agricultural productivity, which can cause household income to fall by up to 30 % (Friis 1998). With dwindling food security, it is becoming increasingly difficult for families that are already surviving on the margin. The correlation between food intake, level of nutrition and immune system is strong. Because of malnutrition that is caused by a lack of food, people infected with the virus become even more vulnerable to the disease's physical impacts as their immunity decreases.

The fact that AIDS has been perceived as an African disease since the onset of this pandemic, we argue, emanates from the notion that AIDS is a disease of the poor. This chapter presents a critical analysis of the impact of migrant populations and refugees and HIV/AIDS in Canada and challenges the notion that HIV/AIDS is a disease of the poor. It assesses the position of Canada in the global scenario of refugees and HIV/AIDS and its response. Canada is one of the most generous countries for refugee resettlement and accepts a large number of convention refugees in order to provide them with protection. The central point is that protection is not restricted to physical, political or economic conditions but should extend to the protection of refugees' mental stability. HIV/AIDS-related discrimination and stigmatization can cause severe psychological instability and damage.

Poverty

Poverty is not the only factor contributing to the spread of HIV/AIDS; however, the link between HIV/AIDS and poverty is incontrovertible. Conventional wisdom suggests that people from lower income groups are most at risk of contracting HIV; this is borne out by existing research that shows HIV/AIDS has struck the lowest income countries in the world mercilessly and that these countries have the highest HIV prevalence rates. 'HIV/AIDS appears to interact strongly with poverty and this interaction has increased the depth of vulnerability of those already vulnerable to shocks' (ILO 2005:7; Ganyaza-Twalo and Seager 2005). Figure 3.1 explains the bi-causal relationship between HIV/AIDS and poverty.

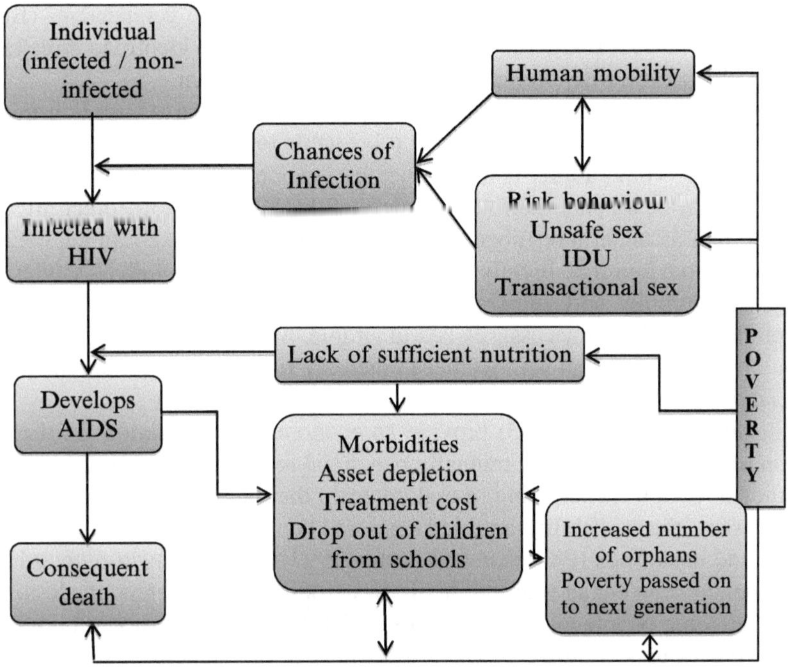

Fig. 3.1 HIV/AIDS and poverty-bi-causal relationship (Adapted from Seager et al. 2005)

HIV/AIDS and poverty are related to each other in a number of ways. HIV/AIDS both causes and is caused by poverty. Poverty increases the risk of HIV/AIDS when it propels the unemployed into unskilled migratory labour pools in search of temporary and seasonal work (ILO 2005; WHO 2010; Ullah 2010a, 2011). However, it is not always necessarily the case that the poorest countries have the highest prevalence rates. Some countries with very high HIV prevalence rates are also among the rich. However, due to the lack of good governance, weaknesses in strategy, policy and programme implementation, poorer countries are at greater risk (ILO 2005). Poverty and HIV/AIDS, independent of one another, are powerful enough to reverse development processes. The negative impacts of these two phenomena together can pose even greater challenges. Poverty is not simply having an income below the poverty line; it is a multidimensional state encompassing deprivation from a number of basic necessities (Fig. 3.1).

Economic Theory of the Pandemic

The onset of the HIV epidemic was followed by an economic approach to HIV/AIDS. This section reviews relevant literature dealing with the economic approach to poverty and the HIV/AIDS pandemic and offers a framework for understanding it. This approach is considered from both macro and micro perspectives (Barnett and Whiteside 1999, 2002). Topouzis and du Guerny (1999) identified three factors at this level: susceptibility, vulnerability and risk environment.

Susceptibility is viewed as an increase in social predisposition to virus transmission. A society is vulnerable to the extent that it is unable to resist or mitigate the impact of an epidemic. Vulnerability is determined by the coping mechanisms available to society, such as healthcare facilities (Cameron 2007). Unlike some other infectious diseases, such as malaria or tuberculosis, individuals may make rational decisions about risky behaviour that directly affects their risk of infection with HIV (Gersovitz 2000). Susceptibility and vulnerability are independent concepts—if a society is susceptible, it might not necessarily be vulnerable. A risk environment is formed by any number of factors that act together to increase risk, such as gender inequalities or social disruption.

Philipson and Posner (1993) provide an economic interpretation for the transmission of HIV by means of a mutually beneficial sexual transaction. According to their model, people anticipating sexual contacts that have potential of HIV transmission assess the probability-adjusted costs and benefits of other practices, such as safe sex and unsafe sex (Philipson and Posner 1993). This means in economic term that the person who engages in safe sex is aware of the cost which is 'the less enjoyment'. But some people go for unsafe sex which bears the risk of getting infected. Rational individuals compare the cost of unsafe sex and benefit of safe sex. Some people who are not optimistic of the future, thus, could engage in unsafe sexual activities. This is not because of frustration with poverty; this behaviour is prompted by the thought that they have nothing to lose.

Gaffeo (2003) noted that the model developed by Philipson and Posner has particular application to the spread of HIV in sub-Saharan Africa and South and Southeast Asia, where the primary method of transmission has been heterosexual intercourse. Kremer (1996) and Kremer and Morcom (1998) suggest that information about HIV infection risk is critical for individuals to makc rational decisions about high-risk behaviour. In the absence of information about HIV infection risk (such as in the early years of the epidemic in sub-Saharan Africa), individuals have little incentive to adjust their behaviour. Market failures—for instance, in the markets for sex or drug injection equipment sharing—may result where not all market participants have complete information or where only one partner has complete information about the risks (Lloyd 1991). Individuals tend to change their behaviour if the information that they receive is credible and sufficiently increases the probability-adjusted costs of unsafe sex. However, it is also possible that the accumulation of information in itself is insufficient to encourage a substitution of unsafe for safe sex (Ford and Kittisuksathit 1996; van Landingham et al. 1997). Steinfatt (2002) suggests that low-risk individuals are unlikely to change their behaviour even with substantial knowledge, as the probability-adjusted cost of HIV infection is very low. For these individuals, the cost of future death or disability from AIDS has a very low present value, such that they are unlikely to avoid risky behaviour (Becker and Kilburn 1994; Philipson and Posner 1993).

It is relevant to consider the ideas of Gary Becker (1976) about the nature of human behaviour. He argues that human beings tend to maximize utility. The general law of economics is that everything has a cost. Rationality implies that individuals attempt to make good choices, estimating the nature and probability of the consequences of the choices from among which they can choose in an effort to maximize their utility (Ojteg 2009). Rational choice theorists suggest that economic theory can help analyze human sexual behaviour (Ojteg 2009). The market for sexual trades is seen as one where people engage for mutual benefit (Philipson and Posner 1993), and in economic sense, most prices of nonmarket goods and services are 'shadow prices' in that they are not necessarily pecuniary costs. Ojteg (2009) presents his argument with the example of an individual choosing between safe and unsafe sex and rationalizes that the shadow price of engaging in an unsafe sexual activity can be the expected cost of becoming infected with STD.

There is of course utility in sex activity. Levy (2001) argues that if safe and unsafe sex yields the same amount of utility, the only rational choice would be to engage in safe sex given that protection is inexpensive. Nonetheless, people tend to engage in unsafe sex, meaning that they do not want to compromise the pleasure with the cost of protection, namely, condoms. In many countries, condoms are not easily available or buying them is a matter of shame or the supply is restrained due to religious traditions. In an economic sense, therefore, safe sex is not a perfect substitute for unsafe sex. If the costs of safe sex are considered higher than unsafe sex, the latter may be preferred despite the risk of infection (Levy 2002).

Further, evidence suggests that individuals may be compensated for engaging in high-risk behaviour. In commercial sex market, sex workers may be compensated for higher risk in the form of an additional payment for unsafe over safe sex when the customer prefers unsafe sex (Gertler et al. 2005). Similar models could be developed for transmission of the HIV through injection drug use. Here, individuals who are contemplating injecting drugs compare the probability-adjusted costs and benefits of, for example, needle sharing, with the alternative of new needles and effective disinfecting practices. Increasing risk of infection should lead rational individuals to shy away from needle sharing, thus reducing the rate of transmission. Again, information is important as it provides incentives to adjust behaviour.

In many circumstances, there are constraints which directly reduce the individual's ability to select the safe alternative. The individual might not have access to a 'safe' method. More importantly, there may be cultural or gender issues which prevent the individual from being able to completely exercise authority in the decision-making process with regard to safe behaviour. For example, in some developing countries, shame mechanisms restrain people from buying condoms, storing them at home or using them during sex.

There are many explanations for the association between HIV and poverty grounded in the theory of economics of HIV/AIDS and sexual behaviour (Cameron 2007; Holmqvist 2009; Zulu et al. 2002). In the developing world, power relations between genders are significant. Females generally hold less power than males, contributing to their inability to negotiate safe sex conditions (Gordon and Crehan 1995; Gray et al. 1999; van der Straten et al. 1995). A similar situation applies to commercial sex workers, particularly trafficked women and children, who are unlikely to be in a position to negotiate with employers or clients (Ahlburg and Jensen 1998; Archavanitkul and Guest 1994). Power relations are correlated with economic conditions. Nonbiological factors, such as poverty, are also responsible for increased vulnerability to HIV/AIDS. Poverty has affected women more severely than men (Ullah 2003; Dunkle et al. 2004; Hunter 2007).

A growing body of literature suggests that there may be a negative linkage between poverty and the HIV/AIDS pandemic (Fenton 2004; Masanjala 2007). For example, people living in wealthier households in developing countries may tend to face a higher prevalence of HIV (Lachaud 2007; Mishra et al. 2007; Fox 2010). Individuals from higher echelons of society may lead reckless lifestyles and engage in risky sexual relationships, such as having multiple partners (Hargreaves et al. 2002). This class of population does not interact with the general population on a regular basis, and thus disclosure is not a significant issue for them. If infected and diagnosed, they have the means to travel out of the country for treatment. 'The fact that the positive association between wealth and HIV infection tends to be stronger for women may be attributed partly to wealth increasing partnership networks by increasing mobility and social interaction, and partly to women improving their economic situation by having more than one concurrent partner' (Shelton et al. 2005:2).

There is no doubt that HIV/AIDS leads to financial, resource and income impoverishment. 'Although the problem of AIDS related impoverishment might usefully be thought of as a livelihood problem, this framework may ultimately turn out to be limited. A livelihood approach only provides an entry point to a problem. This perspective has applications beyond HIV/AIDS and is relevant to consideration of the effects of other communicable Diseases' (Barnett and Whiteside 2002:4–5). Illness and death leads to an erosion of social capital and socially reproductive labour. Many researchers suggest that national economies would grow more slowly in HIV endemic countries than in non-endemic countries. Again, we notice renewed interest in further study of macro impact of HIV on development as the consequences of the disease are becoming apparent (Barnett and Whiteside 2002). For example, AIDS reduced Africa's economic growth by less than one per cent in the 1990s, and more than one per cent decrease in per capita growth between 1990 and 1995 resulted from HIV/AIDS and malaria combined (Bonnel 2000).

Poverty, HIV and Stigma in Canada

Is HIV/AIDS a disease of the poor? This question has been prevalent since the onset of the pandemic. How does HIV/AIDS figure in developed countries like Canada? Many people from Asia think there is no poverty in the Western world. Defined contextually, poverty is prevalent in all parts of the world. People who experience poverty struggle for their basic needs: food, medicine, education and shelter. What exacerbates the problem of poverty is its heightened prevalence and severity of HIV/AIDS within vulnerable groups, such as refugees and immigrants in Canada (Rollason 2009). Poverty occurs when 'someone lacks any item required to maintain long term physical well-being' (deGroot-Maggetti 2002:10). This is, in fact, the deprivation of basic necessities of life. People facing poverty cannot obtain the amount of food required for survival. They lack warm, dry and safe housing, clothing appropriate to climate, sufficient personal hygiene items and healthcare. The absence of one or more of these necessities compromises long-term physical well-being (Hulme 2000; Hashemi 2001; deGroot-Maggetti 2002:10; Ullah and Routray 2003, 2007).

The UN definition of poverty is more encompassing than many others found in the literature. Poverty is not just about low income; rather, it reflects poor health and education, deprivation in knowledge and communication, inability to exercise human and political rights and the absence of dignity, confidence and self-respect (Donald and Mottershaw 2009, UN 2007a; Galabuzi 2005:18). Poverty is the denial of opportunities and choices most basic to human development—to lead a long, healthy, creative life and to enjoy a decent living, freedom, dignity and self-esteem (Neal 2004:25).

While poverty is contextual, it prevails in all societies, and Canada is no exception. The task of measuring poverty is, therefore, both relative and contextual. The level of poverty in Canada is best measured by indicators such as usage of food banks and emergency shelters and the lack of adequate housing (Canada Without Poverty 2012). The problem of homelessness is obvious from the fact that a large number of people live on streets and in emergency shelters. Another obvious example is the growing number of youth and young families who are homeless, many of whom remain so throughout adulthood (deGroot-Maggetti 2002:4). Poverty lines are either restrictive or inclusive. Restrictive measures conceptualize poverty as 'that point at which people's physical/medical survival is at risk' (Gordon 1972). Inclusive measures conceptualize poverty as 'the cost of meeting the physical, emotional, social and spiritual needs of individuals and families' (deGroot-Maggetti 2002:4). There are specific groups who are at risk of poverty in Canada, such as families headed by single parents, new immigrants, disabled persons and Aboriginal families (Ullah 2008a). In addition, young families that are headed by individuals under 30 are particularly vulnerable to poverty. In 1997, the high-risk groups represented 53.9 % out of all families living in poverty (deGroot-Maggetti 2002:15).

Poverty and unemployment are interrelated phenomena. Though the figures below represent the state of poverty among Canadians in general, the extent of poverty among refugees and migrants is much worse (Fig. 3.2).

For the purpose of making international comparisons, the LIM is the most commonly used low-income measure. It explicitly defines low income as being much below average, and it is calculated at one-half the median income of an equivalent household (Statistics Canada 2012).

The unemployment rate can be defined as the number of people actively looking for jobs as a percentage of the total labour force. From 1976 to 2012, the unemployment rate in Canada averaged 8.5 %. In 2010, almost 12 % of immigrants who had been in Canada for 5 years or less were unemployed. This number is about double the unemployment rate of native-born Canadians (Fig. 3.3).

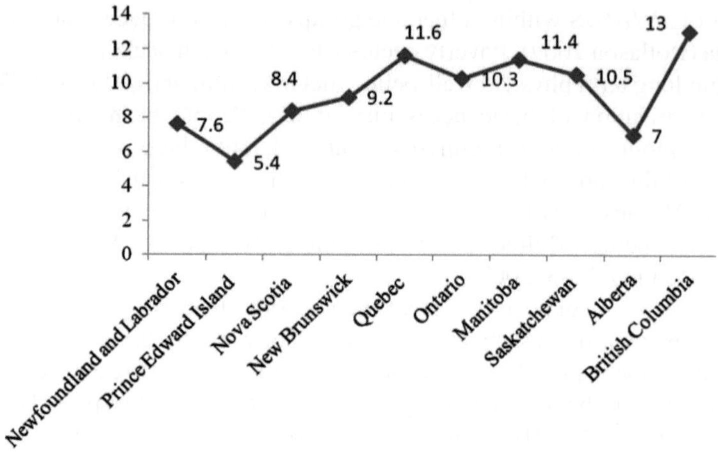

Fig. 3.2 Prevalence of low-income (after-tax) Canada and the provinces, 2006 (Source: Statistics Canada 2012)

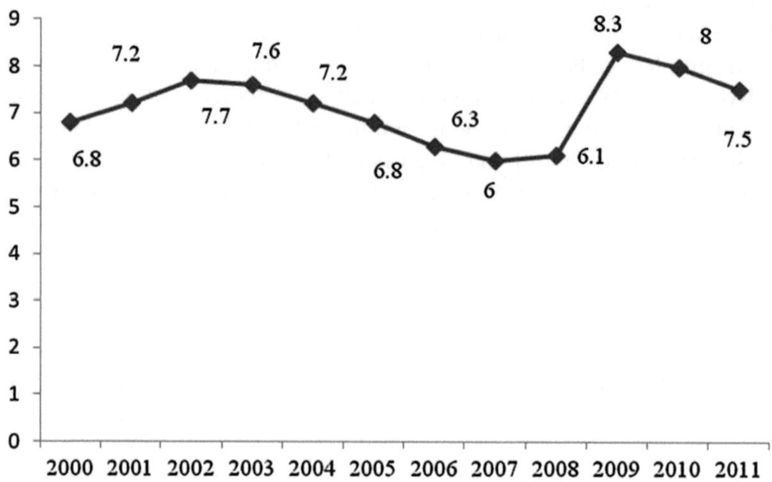

Fig. 3.3 Unemployment rate in Canada (Source: Human Resources and Skills Development Canada 2012)

Poverty in Refugee and Immigrant Community

In simple terms, refugees are persons who seek refuge or asylum outside their homeland to escape persecution (Ullah 2014; UNHCR 2011; Ministry of Education 2009:4). Canada accepts refugees irrespective of their countries of origin. The first chapter discussed the names of countries that send the largest number of refugees and immigrants to Canada. Most refugee population comes from poverty- and disease-prone areas. Canada has designated a number of countries where sufficient conditions exist to produce refugees. Most designated countries are from the African region. Since immigrants constitute approximately 20 % of the Canadian population, the impact of their vulnerability on the overall poverty statistics is significant (Galabuzi 2005:5).

People migrate to Canada with the belief and hope that they would be able to secure a better life in comparison to that in their country of origin. In most cases, disillusionment sets in quickly. Evidence suggests that Africans, Caribbeans, Arabs, South Asians and Latin Americans are among the groups with high incidence of poverty in Canada (Galabuzi 2005:19). Gender elements are also significant to the analysis of refugees, racial groups and poverty. In most cases, females constitute the dependent category in applications for immigration.

A lack of resources and opportunities pushes individuals and families into poverty. Immigrants, refugees and racial groups are overrepresented among the poor in Canada. Low income and unemployment are the principal factors that contribute to poverty. Racism—a critical issue in Canada and deeply connected to poverty—is widely spread across society, such as workplace, schools, social institutions and media (Galabuzi 2005:10).

It is obvious that there are pockets of poverty in Canada. Refugee and immigrant populations are often trapped in these pockets. Though social assistance is available from the government, most individuals pass a window period (a period for adjustment, job search and overall settlement) after they arrive during which they are unaware of, or unable to, access such programmes and facilities. This period is critical to successfully overcoming their poverty situation and settling down. Social assistance meets a bare minimum of their needs. Although these populations can play significant roles in the economy, sufficient efforts are not made to employ newcomers in appropriate positions. Some immigrants tend to complain that they are brought to Canada to provide services to the elderly, and no other opportunities are available to them. Besides, access to employment is largely affected by market conditions and problems of refugees' integration (DeVoretz et al. 2004:29). Therefore, this group is not represented in high-paying positions. On the contrary, they generally work in low-skilled and low-paying positions (Galabuzi 2005:12), leaving them unable to cross the poverty line. Social assistance has a dark side, in that it can affect people's motivation to look for employment. This may be a contributing factor to the high rate of unemployment among the migrant community. However, we found some of them happy at least because of the fact that their children will have better opportunities in the future to succeed in life.

In Canada, poverty among refugees and immigrants is exacerbated by unemployment and low income. The challenge of getting a job in Canada for refugees and newcomers is partly attributable to 'downward occupational mobility among immigrants and refugees' (Sherrell 2011:18). Unemployment rates among these groups are higher than that of the general population. Particularly, immigrants are overrepresented in unemployment and low-income groups, which gets them trapped in poor living conditions (OCASI 2005:2). In 2001, while the rate of unemployment was 6.7 % overall, it was 12.6 % among racial groups. Specifically, women and youth face a higher rate of unemployment within racialized groups (Galabuzi 2005:13; Sherrell 2011:19).

Generally, refugees and immigrants are subject to discrimination based on their racial status regardless of their qualifications (Galabuzi 2005:14). However, there are claims that refugees and immigrants who came from European countries can become successful in Canada. On the other hand, refugees and immigrants who come from Africa or Asia constitute the poorest groups in Canada (DeVoretz et al. 2004:8). This contributes to a perception that refugees from Europe are more skilled and better educated than those from other regions (DeVoretz et al. 2004:10). This may not be the case. It is also claimed that names are often an important determinant for selection by employers, and non-European names act as yet another obstacle to gaining employment for immigrants from other regions of the world.

The racialization of poverty is often considered a disaster because poverty is not distributed equally among all Canadians, and a similar pattern prevails among refugees and immigrants. Racialization of poverty is 'a process by which poverty becomes more concentrated and reproduced among racialized group members' (Galabuzi 2005:16). The racialization of poverty is caused by structural socioeconomic features that predetermine the disproportionate incidence of poverty among racialized group members. This directly and severely impacts the social, economic and health status of people who face racism.

Poverty has an adverse impact on health and education of refugees, immigrants and racial groups in Canada. The income of these groups is severely affected by discriminatory attitudes among employers towards specific vulnerable groups. This contributes to poor housing, inadequate nutrition, challenges in accessing services and mental and physical health risks (Khawaja 2003; Galabuzi 2005:15). Poverty has pushed many women to engage in transactional sex in order to earn a living (Neal 2004:27). This tendency puts women at risk of being infected with HIV/AIDS due to inability to negotiate safe sex and avoid unsafe sexual behaviour, contributing to additional vulnerability.

The lack of appropriate and sufficient funding for specialized healthcare programmes serving refugees, such as the Interim Federal Health Program (IFHP), places refugees in a vulnerable situation (OCASI 2005:3). The recent changes to the IFHP suggest a new approach to debates about the problems the refugees face in accessing healthcare services. The IFHP covers temporary, basic healthcare coverage to resettled refugees and asylum claimants in Canada. Activists, healthcare providers and civil society members are seriously concerned that this may adversely affect patient care. Erica et al. (2012) fear that these changes will create two tiers of refugees: those from designated countries of origin (DCO) and those from non-DCOs. Refugees and refugee claimants from non-DCOs will be adversely affected by the proposed changes in the IFHP because the suggested cuts may lead to worse health outcomes, higher costs and increased risk to public safety as many refugees will be left without adequate healthcare.

The changes to the IFHP are justified by projected cost savings. However, it is well established that primary and preventative care is cost-effective and saves taxpayer dollars. The per capita cost for refugee claimants under the current IFHP is approximately 10 % of the average per capita cost for Canadians (Dewar 2012). The Minister of Health argued that refugees 'abuse the healthcare system' and seek asylum to avail themselves of healthcare benefits (Ball 2012). Research shows that refugees experience higher rates of poverty than nonimmigrants when they first arrive in Canada. Poverty is arguably the most important social determinant of health. Erica et al. (2012) point out that the burden of additional debt and the complications of untreated disease can, in no way, help them to improve their conditions.

Many refugees experience torture or trauma before coming to Canada, which means that they could need psychological care. In Canada, no one without a status can access social and health services (OCASI 2005:3–4). Inequity in the healthcare system may push people without status into the risk of contracting HIV/AIDS. Likewise, they tend to avoid healthcare because of the racist approaches often manifested in healthcare in Canada. Because of the poor conditions they live in, refugees do not prioritize health issues, as they are primarily concerned with meeting their basic needs (Galabuzi 2005:24). Homelessness is an associated problem for refugees living in Canada (Neal 2004:16). Two aspects of poverty—unemployment and low income—are the principal reasons for the continuation of homelessness.

> Over the past two decades homeless people are increasingly evident on the streets in Canada. Only a handful of attempts to count the homeless have been made at both local and national levels in Canada. These attempts have failed for a lack of a consistent definition of who the homeless are, as well as the elusiveness of the population. (Hargrave 1999)

It is the harsh reality that social exclusion targets people from specific backgrounds (Galabuzi 2005:23). Access to healthcare services for HIV/AIDS patients is beset with several obstacles such as language, cultural, religious and racial barriers. When faced with discrimination and stigmatization based on both HIV/AIDS status and ethnocultural characteristics, patients become increasingly unwilling to undergo treatment and neglect their healthcare needs in order to avoid such problems. This is reflected in their deteriorating health and well-being and higher risk of infection.

Unemployment and housing are intimately connected (Hargrave 1999); the higher the income, the greater the choice households have in the size and quality of housing. People with higher incomes can afford better quality housing, while those who do not have an adequate income lack the means to be selective in their choice of housing (Sherrell 2011:162). Many individuals do not have the option to reject houses that are available to them within their price range (Galabuzi 2005:24). The ability to obtain adequate nutrition is similarly affected by low income; for example, individuals may be forced to choose between adequate housing and nutrition or to compromise on both or one of the two (Sherrell 2011:167).

Education, too, is adversely impacted by poverty. Where people share limited living space, a place for study is difficult to find (Sherrell 2011:174). Furthermore, people with low income living in poverty also lack access to technology. Many lack computer access and Internet; therefore, students need to go to libraries, public facilities and settlement agencies in order to do their homework—facilities which are not necessarily easily accessible on a regular basis, especially for the refugee population. The incidence of poverty is impacted by gender as well, with more women living in poverty than men. There are an estimated 2.2 million adult women living in poverty in Canada, and poor women represent 19 % of all women in Canada (Sherrell 2011:172–6). While poverty among men is related to low wages, poverty among women is related to low wages, their marital status and the problems they face. Single mothers, separated wives and divorced women are overrepresented among those in poverty (Whitzman 2010).

The healthcare system in Canada is not immigrant friendly. New immigrants must wait for a period of 3 months in order to obtain access to provincial healthcare. During this period, new immigrants must either seek private healthcare or wait for becoming eligible (OCASI 2005:1). In practice, this means that these groups are not able to obtain basic assistance or services for healthcare.

Regardless of the non-discriminatory principles that Canada is committed to, inequality is apparent in dealing with minorities and racial groups (see Chaps. 4 and 5). In fact, Canada 'puts vulnerable groups under a second tier or third tier of the health care system', and while the policy of equity needs to be implemented for all Canadians in general, it should be applicable for refugees and immigrants in particular due to their vulnerable circumstances (OCASI 2005:1). On practical grounds, the health status of newcomers usually deteriorates after they arrive in Canada and they arise from homesickness, trauma and travel-related experiences. Settlement and integration into the new society—which is stressful in most cases—remain as major reasons for poor health status. Additionally, lack of employment and inability to pay for private healthcare services have adverse impacts on their mental health.

Canada has legal obligations towards people living within its borders and is required to preserve 'the right to adequate food, clothing and housing, the right to the highest attainable standard of health, the right to education, the right to social security, the right to freely chosen work, the right to decent working conditions' (Galabuzi 2005:34). The country is legally committed to protecting refugees and asylum seekers. Moreover, Canada is obliged to offer them permanent rather than temporary resettlement (DeVoretz et al. 2004:1). It is a signatory to several human rights treaties such as International Covenant on Economic, Social and Cultural Rights (ICESCR) and International Convention on the Elimination of Racial Discrimination (ICEARD). Therefore, the country has legal obligations under international human rights law to protect the rights of the most marginalized groups among its population.

Poverty hinders normal lifestyle of people. Certain groups who are at risk due to racism, immigration and refugee status are severely threatened by poverty, as they do not have the same rights as native-born Canadians. Although Canada is perceived to be a country where rights are well protected, in practice this may not be the case. A research report by UNICEF Canada questioned if Canada was fulfilling the rights of 7 million children and 14 % of Canadian children who are living in poverty and found the child poverty rate to be worse than two-thirds of other industrialized nations (UNICEF Canada 2012). Living up to its commitments will help to utilize Canada's diverse population as a source of human capital and benefit the country.

Although Canadian legislation does not explicitly debar HIV-positive individuals from seeking refugee status, precautionary measures can have a discriminatory impact against people who could pose challenges to public health in the country. This could be an issue as there can be evidence that the HIV sufferers engage in high-risk behaviour, such as sharing needles or engaging in unsafe sex, and refuse to cooperate with public health authorities. However, protected people, convention refugees or a person in similar circumstances are exempt from medical inadmissibility. Human rights activists and researchers argue that allowing HIV-positive refugees and migrants to enter Canada creates no direct risk to the health of Canadians. Claiming that immigrants with HIV are a threat to public health simply because they are HIV sufferers stigmatizes all people with HIV as dangerous to public health. It is discriminatory and unjust to automatically preclude persons with HIV from migrating to Canada.

Allowing an HIV Sufferer: A Floodgate Argument

How do, then, Canadians feel about allowing people with HIV to migrate to Canada, given the fact that HIV/AIDS is a deadly disease? Does this justify the prevailing discrimination and stigmatization? Canada is home to a significant number of immigrants and refugee claimants,[1] who represent about 20 % of the population of the country (Statistics Canada 2011; Census 2006), and the country receives about 265,000 immigrants every year. Many ethnic and religious groups live and work in Canada, and the largest groups are the English, French, Scottish, Irish, German, Italian, Chinese, Aboriginal, Ukrainian, Dutch, South Asian and Scandinavian. Since the 1970s, most immigrants have come from Asian countries (Statistics Canada 2011). People migrate to Canada in various categories, such as skilled worker programmes, family sponsorship, refugee claims, business persons and other nominee programmes.

South Asians originate from the Indian subcontinent, which includes India, Bangladesh, Pakistan, Sri Lanka, Maldives, Bhutan and Nepal (Map 3.1). The combined population of these countries is about 1.5 billion (World Bank 2011), representing more than 20 % of the global population (Statistics Canada 2012). The South Asian region accounts for about 40 % of the total poor in Asia, and in 2000, according to the headcount ratio, about one-third of the population lived below the poverty line (World Bank 2011; Salthouse 2010; Thapa 2004) which correlates with high rates of death and disease (APIAHF 2006). Along with widespread poverty, South Asia occupies a prominent place in the landscape of ethnic and

[1] Claimants are a larger pool of refugees who first must clear certain security checks before being accepted as convention refugees (for details, please refer to Chap. 2).

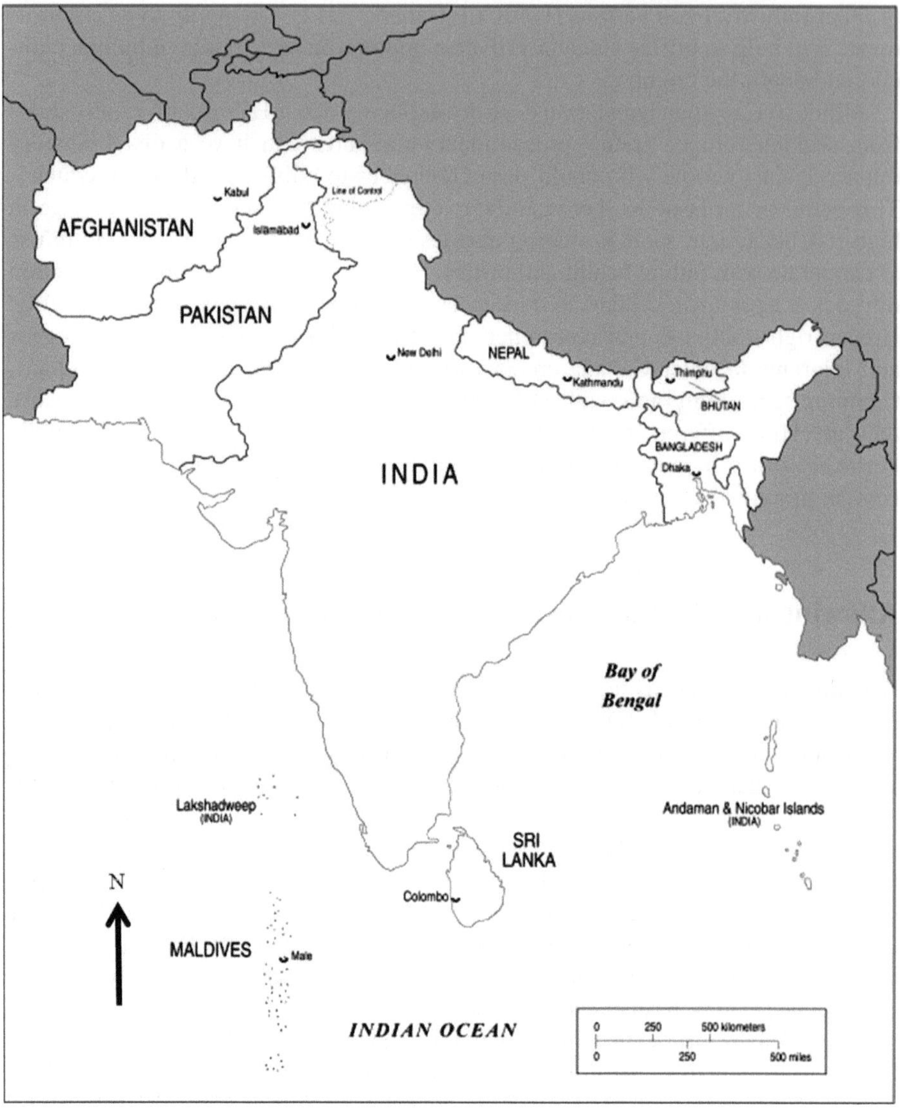

Map 3.1 Map of South Asia

religious conflict[2] (Sahadevan 1999) that has generated many refugees and economic migrants over centuries. For example, Maoist conflict in Nepal, Tamil-Sinhalese conflict in Sri Lanka, internal tribal conflict in Pakistan, ethnic tensions and

[2] Such as Maoist conflict in Nepal, LTTE issues in Sri Lanka, Kashmir and Nagaland issues in India, refugee issues in Bhutan and Nepal.

Naxalite insurgencies in India[3] and Muslim insurgencies in Afghanistan have each triggered significant refugee movements. South Asians represent 3.1 % of the Canadian population and are the fastest-growing immigrant population and the second-largest visible minority in Canada. They are expected to be the most prominent visible minority group in Canada by 2017, at an estimated 1.7 million (Statistics Canada 2012).

Within the past 10 years, about 74 % of immigrants who have arrived in Canada were of non-European origin. Of these, approximately 53 % were from Asia, 15 % from Latin America, 6 % from Africa and 26 % from other areas of the world (Statistics Canada 2011). In 2001, South Asians were the second largest and the most diverse visible minority group in Canada numbering 917,000,[4] belonging to a range of ethnic, religious and linguistic groups whose ancestries, immigration histories and personal experiences are quite varied (Tran et al. 2005). South Asians have settled in different parts of this country, though the majority (70 %) resides in Toronto and Vancouver. In 2001, they accounted for 10 % of the population of Toronto and 8 % of Vancouver (Tran et al. 2005).

The significant increase in the South Asian population in Canada has become a challenge for the healthcare system. Many (such as, Long 2010) argue that South Asian refugees and immigrants typically arrive with poor health. Premigration circumstances, including conditions in refugee camps, inadequate healthcare and insufficient nutrition at home, contribute to poor health on arrival. These obviously present wide-ranging health problems. In addition, ethnic, religious, socioeconomic and cultural differences between and within groups of refugees may result in community fragmentation (Long 2010). Therefore, additional attention and resources will be required to appropriately provide this population with medical care.

This population group can be considered as 'vulnerable population'—a group that is at higher risk for poor physical, psychological and social health outcomes. These vulnerabilities are shaped by political and social marginalization and a lack of socioeconomic and social resources (Pitkin et al. 2007).[5] While mental and emotional health problems affect many refugees and immigrants,[6] HIV infection

[3] The Naxalites first emerged in 1967 in the village of Naxalbari in West Bengal and spread throughout the central states of Bihar, Orissa and Andhra Pradesh until it was violently suppressed by state and paramilitary forces by 1972. This militant left-wing movement fractured into more than 40 distinct groups, which began to remobilize, consolidate and become more active in the 1980s and 1990s, particularly in the state of Andhra Pradesh (Ramana 2011).

[4] They trace their origins to South Asia, which encompasses India (from where 44 % of immigrants have come), Pakistan (8 %), Bangladesh (1 %) and Sri Lanka (formerly Ceylon, 9 %). Most South Asian Canadians are immigrants or descendants of immigrants from these countries (Statistics Canada 2011; CIC 2007).

[5] Pitkin and colleagues (2007) identified factors that influence immigrants' vulnerabilities including socioeconomic background, immigration status, language proficiency, welfare reforms, residential locations, stigma and marginalization.

[6] Migration 'stress', loss of personal and cultural identity, depression and post-traumatic stress disorder are commonly identified.

compounds other challenges that this population faces[7] (PHAC 2005). In addition, South Asia faces an HIV endemic, with an estimated six million people infected.[8] At least 60 % of HIV sufferers in Asia live in India alone (UNAIDS 2007; World Bank 2006:xi). However, both UNAIDS and the World Bank report that significant reductions in HIV prevalence rates occurred in South Asia overall from 2001 to 2009, and even in India where actual numbers are high, prevalence rates remain low on a global scale. Previously, it was thought that around five million people were living with HIV in India—more than in any other country. New data, including the results of a national household survey conducted in 2005–2006, led to a major revision of the existing estimate in July 2007. It is now thought that around 2.39 million people in India are living with HIV. Of these, an estimated 39 % are female and 3.5 % are children. Data discrepancy is a common phenomenon; however, despite these revisions, there is no reason for complacency.

Is HIV imported in Canada by the immigrants or refugees? How does the endemic in the country of origin impact the country of destination? These are important questions that arise in this context. Although it has not been established, it may be conjectured that as the Asian migrant and refugee population forms a significant portion of the Canadian residents, there may be links to the increased incidence of HIV in the country. In Canada until 2006, 62,562 HIV+ and AIDS cases were diagnosed (CIC 2007) and in 2009 it rose to 69,844 (Public Health Agency, Canada 2010). Estimates based on the 1996 census suggest that approximately 439 South Asian adults may be infected with HIV in the Greater Toronto Area alone (ASAAP 2007). This number today after 15 years could be much higher, and the number for the entire country could be substantially higher. However, HIV/AIDS remains largely invisible for the majority of South Asians living in Canada (see disclosure section below).

Discussions about HIV/AIDS within the South Asian community are limited, as HIV/AIDS is often perceived to be a Western phenomenon linked with homosexuality, drug use and promiscuity.[9] HIV is commonly linked to the issues of sex, sexuality, religion and culture. These are still considered as taboo or issues that are off-limits to many South Asians. This may explain why the South Asian community remains one of the lowest tested communities in Canada (Sidhu et al. 2003).

The sensitivity of HIV and the peculiarities of the specific community have largely muted opportunities for a constructive response to HIV/AIDS infections and prevention. Chances are high that the necessary care, support and services for the South Asian communities are less than those available to the general population (Sidhu et al. 2003). Since Canada is a country that respects the diversity and the

---

[7] Those burdens often include being uprooted living in unfamiliar surroundings with minimal, if any, resources, support or livelihood and, sometimes, enduring illness and the seemingly inescapable consequences of violence, rape, abuse and loss many refugees have experienced, in particular the loss of family and friends (PHAC 2005).

[8] The epidemic was driven mainly by the region's flourishing sex industry and injecting drug users.

[9] There is a popular South Asian myth saying HIV/AIDS happens only to non-monogamous, white, heroin-injecting sex workers and homosexual men.

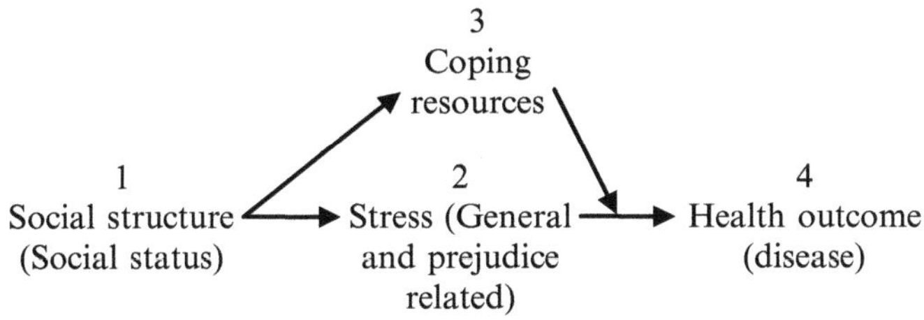

Fig. 3.4 Causal model of social structure and health (Source: Adopted from Meyer 2008)

cultural specificities of its population, there may be a lack of awareness as to how to penetrate cultural and social mores to raise awareness of HIV/AIDS among immigrant and refugee communities. However, regardless of the challenges of gathering and disseminating information, the lack of information clearly suggests that there is an absence of systematic knowledge about how HIV/AIDS issues are dealt with by specific ethnic communities of Canada, how discrimination functions within and outside their community, the magnitude of the problem and how health-sensitive issues can be approached with respect to both cultural particularities and universal health principles (Fig. 3.4).

Ethnic Composition and HIV/AIDS Incidence

The literature suggests that perceived discrimination is a neglected stressor that adversely affects the health of immigrants irrespective of colour and race (Paradies 2006; Williams et al. 2003). Stigma and prejudice may be experienced from exposure to negative attitudes, structural and interpersonal experiences of discrimination and violence against persons who belong to disadvantaged social groups. The social processes of stigma and prejudice are quite similar; but the historical reasons underlying why societies stigmatize or are prejudicial tend to vary.

Goffman (1963) presents stigma as a damaging social label affecting individuals, influencing social interactions and jeopardizing opportunities for social inclusion. Labelling occurs through stereotyping and assigning differential statuses (Link and Phelan 2001). Weiss et al. (2006) characterize it as health-related stigma, exclusion, rejection and assigning blame. People fearful of being stigmatized by others may act in ways that undermine their ability to cope with illness or that exacerbate the disease by not practising healthy behaviours, not adhering to treatment regimens and in some cases terminating treatment (Dasgupta 2001; Eastwood and Hill 2004) (Table 3.1).

The 2001 Census confirms that 18.4 % of the population was born outside Canada. About 13 million which is almost half of the total population of Canada came as immigrants during the past century (Statistics Canada 2003). Of the total, about one-half (46 %) reported only British, French and/or Canadian ethnic origins.

Table 3.1 Ethnic composition in Canada

Ethnic origin	Total
British Isles origins	11,098,610
Other North American origins	10,408,735
Canadian	10,066,290
European origins	9,919,790
English	6,570,015
French origins	5,000,350
French	4,941,210
Scottish	4,719,850
Western European origins	4,372,750
Irish	4,354,155
German	3,179,425
Eastern European origins	2,998,220
Southern European origins	2,723,675
East and Southeast Asian origins	2,212,340
Aboriginal origins	1,678,235
Italian	1,445,330
Chinese	1,346,510
South Asian origins	1,316,770
North American Indian	1,253,620
Ukrainian	1,209,090
Northern European origins	1,120,805
Dutch (Netherlands)	1,035,965
Scandinavian origins	1,009,735
Polish	984,565
East Indian	962,670
Caribbean origins	578,695
Russian	500,600
Arab origins	470,580
Welsh	440,960
Total	**31,241,030**

Source: Statistics Canada (2006) Census of Population. Last modified: 2009-07-28

Non-Europeans have origins in Asia, Africa, Central and South America, the Caribbean, Australia and Oceania (Statistics Canada 2003). Vibrant ethnicity and multiculturalism are prime character of many cities in Canada. A walk down the street reveals the multi-ethnic composition of the population in Canada. In Toronto, for instance, Indians, Pakistanis and Bangladeshis are concentrated in particular pockets of the city (Table 3.2).

Figure 3.5 demonstrates a near linear growth in economic immigrants, while flow of refugees declined slightly from 2001 to 2010 (Statistics Canada 2011).

People living with HIV/AIDS (PLWHA) who are part of minority ethnic or cultural communities such as Lesbian, Gay, Bisexual, Transgender, Intersex, Questioning (LGBTIQ) people, Aboriginal people and people from HIV endemic countries often experience stigma and discrimination from within their own communities, as well as from the general population (Fig. 3.6). This has implications for both HIV sufferers

Table 3.2 Top 10 source countries

2008	REF	A	A (%)	R	AB	W	P
USA	969	6	2	205	16	97	324
Czech Republic	859	84	43	5	11	95	195
Nigeria	766	210	55	128	11	35	384
El Salvador	587	95	52	71	4	14	184
India	561	102	25	179	97	35	413
Total	22,598	4,217	37	4,816	586	1,866	11,485
Mexico	9,322	515	8	3,397	422	1,769	6,103
Hungary	2,426	3	1	5	55	208	271
Colombia	2,310	2,443	76	662	29	94	3,228
Czech Republic	2,210	93	10	76	32	728	929
China	1,597	992	58	543	92	90	1,717
2009							
Haiti	1,583	1,051	42	1,260	37	127	2,475
Sri Lanka	827	986	91	60	12	29	1,087
Nigeria	763	440	66	147	29	48	664
Saint Vincent	651	129	40	145	26	23	323
Al Salvador	532	63	29	114	13	26	216
Total	22,221	6,715	39	6,409	747	3,142	17,013

	REF	A	A (%)	R	AB	W	P	F
2010								
Hungary	2,300	22	2	72	117	967	3,534	1,178
China	1,644	881	53	579	95	96	2,959	1,651
Colombia	1,384	1,266	52	1,019	32	95	2,692	2,412
Mexico	1,299	563	11	3,437	331	1,406	9,322	5,827
Sri Lanka	1,200	513	76	138	10	11	1,284	672
Haiti	1,062	2,490	55	1,778	151	144	3,937	4,563
Nigeria	846	593	64	251	47	40	1,552	931
Saint Vincent	710	136	32	409	41	49	1,047	735
India	532	124	30	206	33	55	1,144	418
Pakistan	526	255	58	119	32	36	821	442
Total	11,503	7,033	37	8,008	889	2,899	28,292	18,829
2011								
Hungary	4,423	165	8	738	249	838	5,975	1,990
China	1,913	957	53	666	80	96	3,080	1,799
Colombia	904	639	37	972	18	103	1,882	1,732
Pakistan	882	433	67	138	27	46	1,069	644
Namibia	859	65	47	48	12	14	1,055	139
Mexico	763	1,042	17	4,184	284	600	3,997	6,110
Nigeria	696	840	63	422	41	33	913	1,336
Saint Vincent	682	288	35	457	45	34	905	824
Sri Lanka	635	281	57	183	14	14	1,432	492
India	632	111	18	381	37	76	1,173	605
Total	12,389	4,821	31	8,189	807	1,854	21,481	15,671

Source: IRB Refugee Status Determinations (1989–2011 Calendar Years)

Source: Immigration and Refugee Board Canada – Refugee Protection Division

YR year, *REF* referred to IRB, *A* accepted, *R* rejected, *AB* abandoned, *W* withdrawn/other, *P* pending, *F* finalized

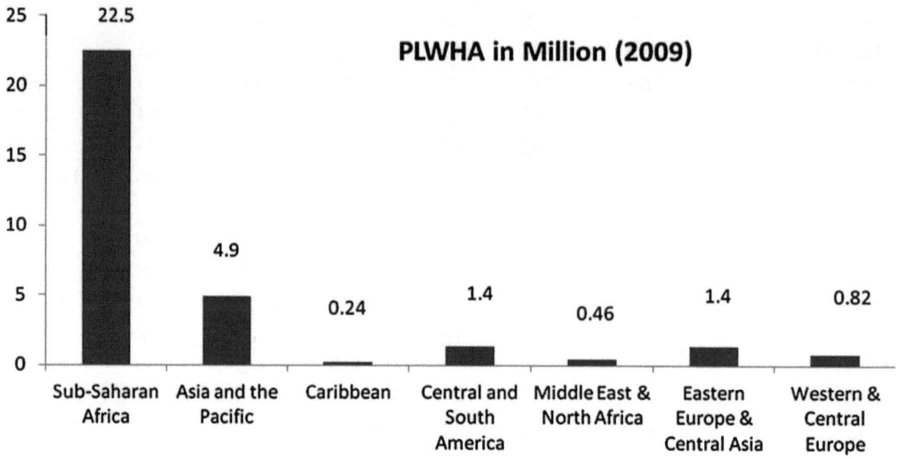

Fig. 3.5 People with HIV/AIDS in 2009 (UNAIDS 2010)

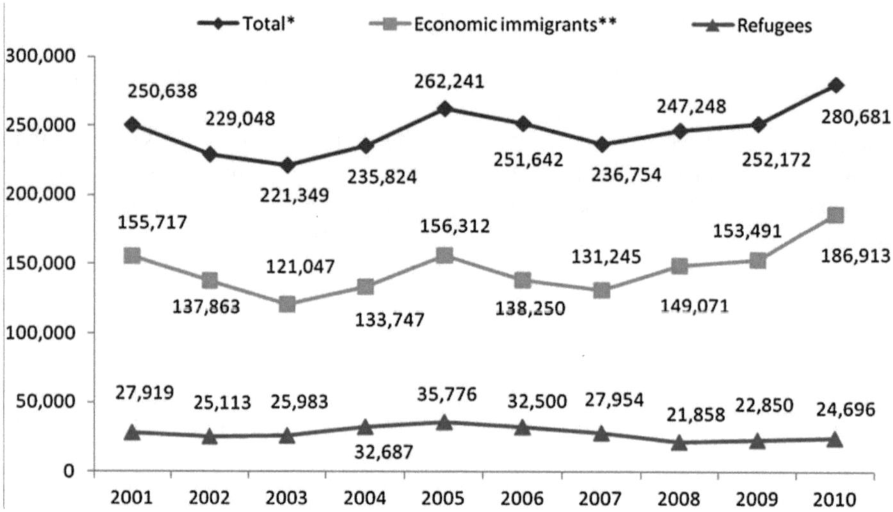

***Includes all categories; **Excludes Refugee, Family class and other immigrant categories**

Fig. 3.6 Flow of immigrants and refugees in Canada, 2001–2010 (Source: Canada Immigration and Citizenship 2011)

and for the community. Individuals become highly isolated, and the community is unable to hold open discussions to reduce the risk of transmission or provide support for those who are ill. The stigma associated with HIV isolates PLWHA and affects their quality of life, as well as those who care for them. It can make people who are at risk of HIV/AIDS less willing to be tested or to seek treatment (Klovdahl et al. 2001). For people who belong to marginalized groups, the stigma associated with HIV is

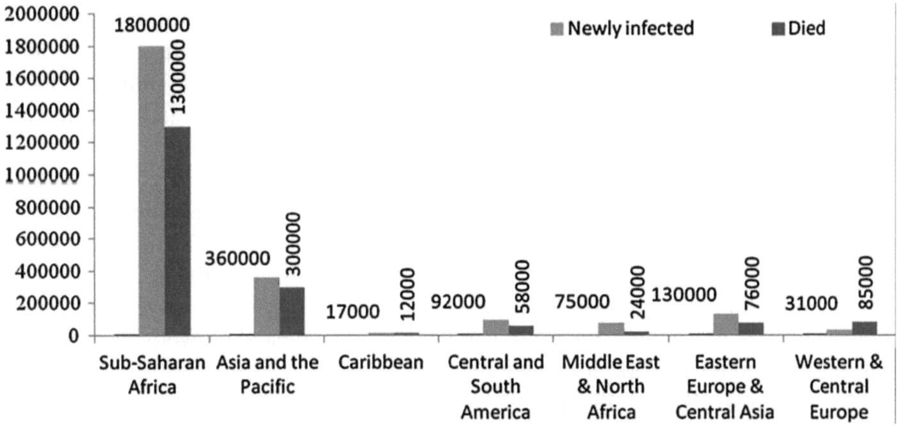

Fig. 3.7 Newly infected and died of HIV/AIDS in 2009 (region wise) (UNAIDS 2010)

compounded by other forms of discrimination, including homophobia, racism, gender inequality and negative attitudes towards drug use and sex workers (PHAC 2005).

Newly Infected and Died of HIV/AIDS in 2009

An individual who experiences employment discrimination due to HIV status may make two types of claims. The first type of claim may be made in cases where an employer has treated an applicant or employee differently than other applicants or employees due to that person's HIV status. Cases in which an employee might make such a claim include situations in which an employer has terminated or refused to hire, rehire or promote an employee based on that person's HIV/AIDS status. The second type of claim may be made by an employee who experienced job discrimination due to HIV status where an employer had failed to provide reasonable accommodation, such as an adjustment in job requirements or policies which enables HIV-positive individuals to continue to perform the essential functions on their job (Fig. 3.7).

Immigration Process and Stressors

Immigrants and the capacity of refugees to adjust to their new environment remain a critical factor for both migrants and host communities. There are a range of complex issues a refugee must deal with when moving to the country of resettlement. This is particularly important to broadly understand the burdens faced by them.

The unhealthy environment in which migrants live contributes to increased exposure to infection and inaccessibility of medical services. Immigrants remain under constant stress to survive financially in the host state and send money to their families back home (Lawson et al. 2006:35). Unemployment and insufficient sources of earnings add further stress to their lives. When immigrants come to a new country and are unable to find suitable means of livelihood, they may resort to sex work to meet their financial needs. Additional pressures regarding settlement issues such as lack of housing and accessing the education system may further exacerbate their vulnerability (Lawson et al. 2006:19). In an attempt to validate the conventional claims that immigrants are more exposed to poverty than native Canadians, conversations with a small sample of sex workers who posted on websites revealed that most of them were born outside of Canada.

Migrants with HIV/AIDS struggle to cope in isolation, as being separated from their families and support networks places further strain on their ability to psychologically cope with the stress of their HIV/AIDS status. Most immigrants often lack sufficient financial sources to return home to their families in their countries of origins or to bring them to Canada, which may imply that they do not disclose their status to their families (Lawson et al. 2006:34). Lack of precise information about this disease may lead migrants to fail to understand its significance. Lack of translation services, transportation, culturally appropriate materials and information about existing services and professionals who can address HIV/AIDS issues can increase the risk of infection or eliminate opportunities to access treatment and medical services (Interagency Coalition on AIDS and Development 2008:5).

Migration stressors add tremendous psychological burden on top of the infection. Many epidemiological studies suggest that PTSD and depression are the two of the most prevalent mental disorders among forced migrants and refugees (Steel et al. 2002). Refugees and migrants go through the acculturation process, which is a complex construct that can be measured across several dimensions, including language, cultural identity, values and norms (Miller et al. 2006) and social contact with people native to the country of immigration (Knipscheer and Kleber 2007). This process has a significant impact on the quality of life of immigrants. The World Health Organization (WHO) identified immigrants living in highly stressful situations as one of the five priority groups in an international quality of life (QoL) assessment (Orley and Kuyken 1994).

Evidence shows that the traumatic experiences which accompany forced migration are associated with high rates of stress and poor mental health outcomes. Trauma, PTSD symptoms, depression and poor QoL are associated with problems in social integration among war-wounded refugees (Hermansson et al. 1996). The primary stressors related to migration have been identified as unemployment, social isolation, cramped housing, fear and stigma, difficulties in the migration process, poor language acquisition, traumatic stress, xenophobia, poverty and discrimination. Status incongruity and/or the perception of discrimination is associated with psychological distress among refugees and immigrants (Fuller 1993; Furnham and Shiekh 1993; Matsuoka 1993) (Fig. 3.8).

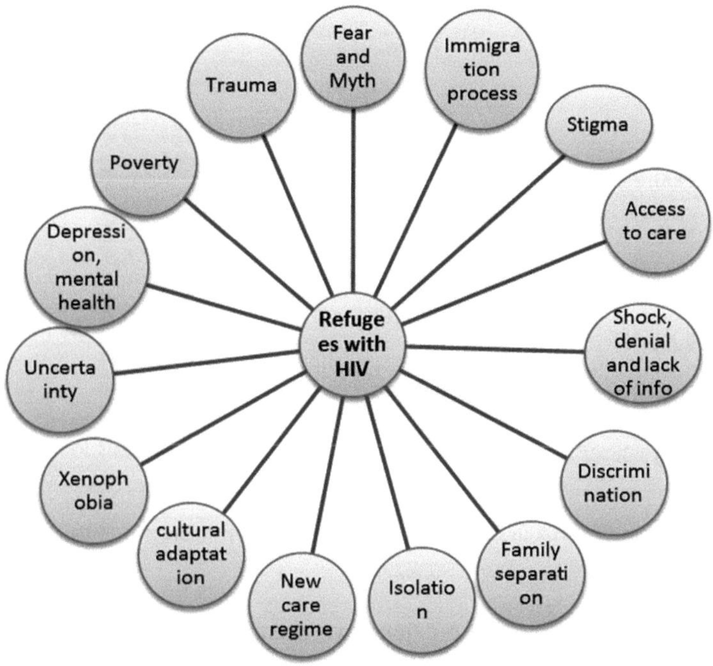

Fig. 3.8 Migration-related stressors

The type of HIV/AIDS epidemic that prevails in North America is largely the 'concentrated' type (CPHA 2005:12). The number of people infected in Canada continues to grow and increased by almost 12 % from 1999 to 2002. Of the infected, MSM comprises 58 %, 20 % are IDU and 18 % contracted HIV/AIDS through heterosexual transmission (CPHA 2005:7). In 2002, among infected individuals, 30 % were unaware of their infection, which resulted in delayed access to support and treatment services which could have been helpful in managing the disease. Approximately 47,000 HIV cases were recorded as of 2000, which rose to 69,844 by 2011. In 2011, 17,165 HIV cases developed into AIDS, which is 20 % higher than it was in 1995. Seventy per cent of individuals who developed AIDS eventually died of the disease (Dodds et al. 2001:2). These figures represent only the known cases; however, there are many others who have not been tested or diagnosed and therefore are not aware of their infection (Fig. 3.9).

Responding to the Challenge

Although there is a declining trend in the newly infected cases over the last decade, the overall number is, however, alarming. Two significant steps in tackling HIV/AIDS by the government can be seen in Public Health Agency of Canada (PHAC)

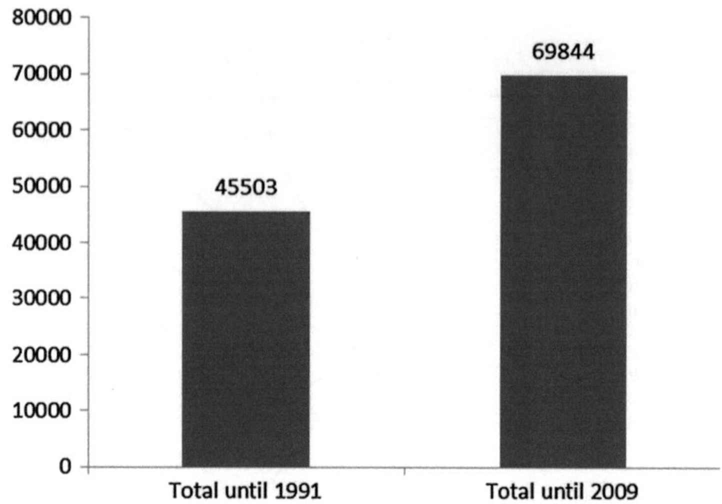

Fig. 3.9 Number of PLWHA in Canada (Source: Public Health Agency of Canada 2010)

and the vaccine plan. Over the previous two decades, Canada has achieved some degree of success in managing HIV. Research has opened up access to more knowledge about the disease and its transmission, as well as the available service delivery and treatment. Parent to child, that is, vertical transmission of HIV, has been effectively eliminated. New infections among Canadians have been minimized and blood supplies have been made as safe from contamination as possible (PHAC 2004:3). The first national official step towards tackling HIV/AIDS began in 1990 through the National AIDS Strategy, a 3-year initiative which was renewed in 1993 for another 5 years. Nevertheless, these efforts were not enough to entirely halt the spread of the disease, and it became clear that the epidemic was and is a serious health and social problem. Therefore, the Canadian Strategy on HIV/AIDS (CSHA) was established in 1998, as a collaborative effort among legal, ethical and human rights sectors, along with representative members from the affected communities.

The Federal Initiative—an initiative to address HIV/AIDS in Canada—is a key element of the Government of Canada's comprehensive approach to HIV/AIDS. It includes efforts to strengthen the role of nongovernmental organizations, enrich practice through research work, engage human rights standards to address HIV/AIDS and ensure participation of PLWHA (PHAC 2004:6). Through these initiatives, the federal government was able to 'develop discrete approaches to addressing the epidemic for people living with HIV/AIDS' in order to increase cooperation among governmental sectors and to raise awareness among the public (PHAC 2004:7). The first policy objective outlined by the Federal Initiative is to increase partnership among people and organizations. This engagement would be enriched through voluntary, professional and private sectors, international partners and vulnerable communities. The second objective is to develop an integrated approach to primary healthcare for HIV/AIDS and similar infections, which requires medical cooperation among HIV/AIDS-related health programmes and service providers at all levels (PHAC 2004:8).

Through this collaborative programme among researchers, government and the community, a vaccine plan has been established to better manage HIV and related problems. This plan includes the development, production and distribution of an HIV vaccine, trials and testing of cases and engagement of community members (PHAC 2010; CPHA 2006:7). There are two types of vaccines—preventative vaccines aimed at protecting individuals from infection and therapeutic vaccines to manage manifestations of HIV/AIDS (CPHA 2006:8).

CANVAC (Canadian Network for Vaccines and Immunotherapeutic) contributed internationally through its collaborations in Africa between 2000 and 2006. This initiative brought together '75 of the most highly recognized Canadian researchers specialized in the field of immunology' (CPHA 2006:9). Canada made its commitment to the HIV vaccine plan in 2002 at the International AIDS Conference in Barcelona (International AIDS Society 2002). This commitment was reinforced in 2004 when Canada joins other countries in leading the global HIV vaccine plan by financially contributing to global research. The Action on HIV/AIDS 2005–2010 is a further instance of the active involvement of Canada in vaccine development and delivery. It supported the UNGASS Declaration of Commitment on HIV/AIDS, which encouraged governments to put HIV vaccine research on national research agendas (CPHA 2006:11).

Engagement among a range of Canadian sectors should be recognized for contributing to the success of the vaccine plan. This includes engagement with the general public to gain support for expenditures, engagement with vulnerable populations that would most likely be targets for testing and receiving the vaccines and engagement with organizations working with those populations (PHAC 2009; CPHA 2006:33). Since 2001, Canada has contributed $62 million to IAVI and $5 million to the African AIDS Vaccine plan (CPHA 2006:40). However, currently there is no fund for HIV vaccine research in Canada itself.

Despite the participation of Canada in many initiatives around the world, 'none has been specifically targeted to HIV vaccines research in Canada' (CPHA 2006:12). 'While Canada has an effective regulatory system for approving vaccines for testing, it has not fully addressed the issue of liability for any harm that results from participating in a trial' (CPHA 2006:22). The Canadian HIV/AIDS Legal Network has created a guide for lawyers and activists in order to help people who may have suffered harm as a result of participating in a vaccine trial. In Ontario, a number of academics and community members have been working on developing specific guidelines to be used in such cases (CATIE 2010:24). However, Canada has taken many steps to deal with HIV/AIDS efficiently; however, further and more concentrated efforts are still needed.

In one case, the Supreme Court of Canada decided 'people living with HIV must disclose their HIV status before engaging in sexual behavior that poses a "significant risk of transmitting the virus"' (CATIE 2010:23).

Exposure Category and HIV

HIV is more prevalent among certain groups, such as youth, migrant communities and Aboriginal populations. The prevalence of HIV among youths aged 15–19 years old is 1.5 % of all HIV cases, while cases between the ages of 20 and 29 constituted 25 % in 2008 (CATIE 2010). Also, youths represent the highest percentage of new HIV-positive cases among MSM. The estimates of new infections in the same year are fairly ambiguous, which ranged between 2,300 and 4,300. In terms of exposure categories, MSM continued to comprise the greatest proportion (44 %) of new infections in 2008, which was only slightly lower than the estimated 45 % in 2005. The portion of new infections in the same year among IDUs was slightly higher than in 2005 (17 % compared to 16 %) (Statistics Canada 2011; PHAC 2008).

Aboriginal people in Canada are also particularly vulnerable to HIV/AIDS. In 2008, an estimated 4,300–6,100 Aboriginal persons were living with HIV or AIDS. This represents an increase of 24 % from 2005 (PHAC 2008, 2010). An estimated 300–520 new HIV infections occurred in Aboriginal persons in 2008 (12.5 % of all new infections), higher than the corresponding figure of 240–430 in 2005 (10.5 % of all new infections in 2005) (PHAC 2010). The overall new infection rate among Aboriginal persons was about 3.6 times higher than among non-Aboriginal persons in 2008.

The picture of newly infected persons among exposure category is more horrific: 66 % IDU, 23 % heterosexual, 9 % MSM and 2 % MSM-IDU (PHAC 2010). By gender, in 2008, from 12,200 to 16,400 women were living with HIV or AIDS in Canada, which is 22 % of the national total. According to Health Canada, there were an estimated 600–1,120 new HIV infections among women in 2008, while the corresponding figure for 2005 was 590–1,100. The proportion of all new infections among women remained the same from 2005 to 2008 (26 %).

The CCDIC of the Public Health Agency of Canada received 67,442 positive HIV tests from November 1985 to December 2008. It can be assumed that since there was an estimated total of 65,000 persons living with HIV in Canada in 2008, the remaining 16,900 (range of 12,800–21,000) persons, or 26 %, were unaware of their HIV infection. A remarkable number of PLWHA are unaware of the infection. By exposure category, it is almost the same as among the general population: 19 % of infected persons in the MSM and 25 % of infected persons in the IDU (PHAC 2009).

According to Interagency Coalition on AIDS and Development (ICAD) (2008), Afro-Canadians constitute a significant number of HIV/AIDS cases in Canada. According to the 2001 Census, there were 662,215 individuals of African descent in Canada. Around 45 % of the Afro-Canadian population was Canadian born (Interagency Coalition on AIDS and Development (ICAD) 2008:3). The rate of HIV infection among this population in 2005 was 12.6 % times higher than the rate among Canadians generally. *Springboarding*, a national HIV/AIDS strategy for Afro-Canadian, African and Caribbean Communities, was tasked to develop to a national HIV/AIDS strategy for these communities (Interagency Coalition on AIDS and Development (ICAD) 2008:1). Burdens and obstacles faced by Afro-Caribbean individuals, and particularly Black immigrants, are higher and varied than those faced by other HIV sufferer groups, making them more vulnerable than any other group (Lawson et al. 2006:34).

Immigrant communities are particularly vulnerable to HIV/AIDS. Refugee and immigrant populations are subject to stigma related to HIV/AIDS. The stigma of racism deepens this stigma and makes it worse. It is often believed that HIV/AIDS is brought to Canada by (im)migrants from HIV/AIDS epidemic countries, particularly those from Africa (Lawson et al. 2006:9).

The belief that HIV is a disease affecting MSM within African and Caribbean communities results in further discrimination against, and isolation among, Afro-Caribbean MSM. 'Gossip and ostracism have a particularly damaging impact on those who are already separated from their families through immigration or who are dealing with settlement issues' (Lawson et al. 2006:31). Under these circumstances, immigrants are subject to discrimination and face double stigma within the Canadian community because of their HIV status; therefore, they can be considered one of the most vulnerable groups that face HIV/AIDS problem.

HIV/AIDS is much more than a health problem. It is a global challenge that encompasses a wide range of social, economic and political issues. According to Lawson and colleagues (2006), dealing with a problem of this scale requires two parallel approaches: social elements and governmental policies. Socially, HIV/AIDS touches on complicated factors such as stigma, gender, and psychological health. These social elements affect both sources of infection and channels of treatment.

In addition, discrimination and marginalization against specific groups affect the ability of the state and service providers to address HIV/AIDS. HIV testing during immigration is considered a challenge especially with the 'poor counseling and moreover, new immigrants face the challenge of transition from federal to provincial support, which exacerbates the challenges faced by HIV persons' (Interagency Coalition on AIDS and Development (ICAD) 2008:21).

The role of gender is also critical in addressing HIV/AIDS, as some studies found 'women are more susceptible to HIV infection on each sexual encounter because of the biological nature of the process and the vulnerability of the reproductive tract tissues to the virus, especially in young women' (Dodds et al. 2001:4). Gender disparity exacerbates this situation because this generates gender-based violence, which further limits opportunities to negotiate safe sex (Ullah 2000). Biology also plays an important role in the transmission of the virus to women, because male to female HIV transmission is more probable than female to male. Women face a social burden in case of infection and may be subject to family rejection, contributing to a lack of care and treatment. At the same time, women bear the bulk of the burden of care when other members of the family become infected.

The gender implications of social perceptions are significant, as the perception remains that women are perceived as 'guiltier' than men when infected by HIV/

AIDS. The perception is founded in a belief that this disease comes from immoral sexual activities. Social status and source of infection are related to the degree of blame and rejection an individual faces. As a result of the social and community reaction towards HIV/AIDS infection, PLWHA fear exile, ostracism and rejection from the community, and this may prevent them from seeking treatment. Also, the burden of work loss and the lack of financial sources for meeting basic needs and caring for children lead people to deny their infection and avoid being tested (CPHA 2005; Lawson et al. 2006:23–25).

Acceptance and denial are often gendered. This means, according to Lawson and colleagues, the level of rejection or acceptance depends largely on whether the infected is male or female. Denial is also correlated to religion in Muslim communities where people tend to deny the possibility of any extramarital sexual relationship within their community and homosexual relations in particular (Lawson et al. 2006:28). Disclosure results in gossip, rejection, income insecurity and physical health problems. These circumstances by far lead PLWHA to be socially isolated and may be unwilling to be involved in social relations (see Chaps. 4 and 5).

HIV/AIDS is an extremely expensive disease, and there are direct and indirect costs involved. Direct costs refer to those of treatment and medical and support services presented to patients (Dodds et al. 2001:7). Indirect costs are related to income loss of infected individuals who are unable to work for health reasons (Dodds et al. 2001:8). It was estimated that new infections cost the healthcare system of Canada an average of $1.5 billion over a 5-year period (CPHA 2005:13). These costs need to be taken into consideration in formulating governmental policy and strategic plans. However, there are other costs that are generally not considered in government policy or strategic planning processes, such as social and personal costs (CPHA 2005:13). In planning and implementing health policies, it is necessary to consider intangible costs along with the tangible.

Under international law, governments are obliged to respect and protect the human rights enjoyed by all people (MacIntosh 2007:8). HIV is not only a health problem; it is also a social problem due to its direct link to several social factors like discrimination, poverty and overall vulnerability of the society (CPHA 2005:15). Due to these linkages, it is important to engage public personalities, religious leaders and government officials to find ways to confront stigma and discrimination and address public attitudes towards PLWHA (MacIntosh 2007).

Leadership is crucial in handling this pandemic. In order for leadership to be effective, it has to incorporate different segments of the society that deal with HIV either directly or indirectly, such as researchers, service providers and at-risk communities (CPHA 2005:15). The role of government can be critical in providing leadership through allocating adequate financial resources to healthcare budgets for HIV/AIDS. Vulnerable persons who are infected with HIV/AIDS need to be included in deliberations for policy and programme planning; this extends to both governmental and nongovernmental organizations that are engaged in addressing this epidemic (MacIntosh 2007:8). It can be achieved through meaningful participation of those infected and affected, because one way of reducing stigma and discrimination is to involve people who are at risk of HIV or are already infected. Such a strategy is expected to lead to the improvement of the care system and prevention of the spread of the virus. At the same time, the government needs to improve the accessibility to necessary services such as employment and housing for PLWHA (CPHA 2005:16). Early intervention is an important strategy in reducing transmission and providing appropriate and effective treatment. From the medical point of view, the earlier infected people are diagnosed, the better are the chance to maintain their health and get effective treatment and prohibit further transmission (CPHA 2005:16).

Chapter 4
Discrimination, Xenophobia and Stigmatization

> *...I wish I had cancer instead of this disease. I could have a dignified death. Now I have already died before my death. Cancer or other diseases would have brought me sympathies but this has brought hatred and shame, and made me isolated. (One of the participants)*

This chapter conceptualizes and analyzes multilevel discrimination, stigmatization and differential health outcomes. Discrimination and stigmatization contribute to trauma, complexities in relationships, dwindling levels of confidence and conflict in treatment regimes. This chapter also presents the findings of the research. Using a theoretical framework that outlines the hierarchies of discrimination and stigmatization, data is triangulated with the theories to better explain where and in what ways vulnerable populations are being discriminated against and stigmatized. The implications of xenophobia on treatment regimens and health outcomes are also explored.

Historically, individuals infected with sexually transmitted diseases (STDs) faced stigmatization due to their perceived involvement in sexual behaviour that was judged to be immoral. Moral judgments about the means of acquisition of HIV often result in the labelling of individuals as guilty, innocent or defenceless victims based on their perceived responsibility for infection. Regardless of whether the general public or healthcare providers are aware of transmission methods and outcomes of HIV/AIDS (Ullah 2011), the general tendency is to avoid any contact with PLWHA. This is compounded when the infected individuals are refugees or immigrants.

Although people living with HIV/AIDS are not considered a danger to public health or safety in Canada, they are expected to place an excessive demand on public health or social services (Aidslaw 2005). There are two exceptions to regulations defining restrictions on residence applicants for public health reasons: one for people applying for permanent residence as a refugee or as a person 'in need of protection' and another for 'family class' applicants (CIC 2011). Many theories related to identity, prejudice, stereotyping, group dynamics and social movements are relevant to the discussion of stigma. At the same time, historical and cross-cultural

A.A. Ullah, A.S. Huque, *Asian Immigrants in North America with HIV/AIDS*,
DOI 10.1007/978-981-287-119-0_4

contexts also deserve consideration, given that stigmas which are significant in a particular point of time or a society may be relatively insignificant in another society or at another point of time (MacIntosh 2007).

In this research, respondents were asked to provide demographic information such as age, level of education, monthly household income, ethnicity and histories of sexual behaviour, drug behaviour and migration experiences. This included the serostatus of their partners and diagnostics issues. Data were also collected about the treatment given by the healthcare providers and, whether they faced difficulty disclosing their HIV/AIDS status, the causes for not doing so and the immediate consequences of nondisclosure.

Stigma, Discrimination and Consequences

Chapter 2 conceptualized and defined stigma and discrimination, and data were analyzed to place this conceptualization in context. The definition of stigma can be articulated as 'prejudice, discounting, discrediting, and discriminating' (Herek and Glunt 1998:36). Prejudice, which is at the core of the definition of stigma, means 'to pre-judge or to structure a view on something before facts are revealed' (Goffman 1963:141). One approach to defining prejudice is the Social Learning Theory. According to this theory, prejudice is considered 'a consequence of our natural tendency to categorize the world to make sense of it'. Thus, prejudice is based on assumptions and not on facts (Ullah 2011:99). Stigma presents negative feedback which may be connected to social behaviour. This can be seen in reactions towards stigmatized persons (Lee and Craft 2002:6). The concept of stigma has been dichotomized into expressive and instrumental forms (Clay et al. 2003). For instance, despite the negative perception of an individual, he or she may act in consistence with that prejudice only in certain situations and not all the time (Ullah 2011:99).

Stigma is the result of discrimination, which is based on a prejudiced attitude. Consequently, the stigmatized person faces a wide range of discrimination and negative attitudes because of this stigma. One clear outcome of stigma is the isolation of the individual. HIV/AIDS is considered an issue that forms the foundation of stigma in many societies. Infected persons face harmful attitude from different sectors of society, including family, friends, colleagues and even healthcare personnel who are responsible for providing treatment and support. Stigma towards HIV/AIDS is present for many reasons. The most important issue in the degree of prejudice is the method of transmission, which, according to some social values, may be perceived as the result of 'immoral' behaviour. People look at PLWHA as deserving of their punishment due to their immorality. This is primarily the result of common misunderstanding that HIV/AIDS is primarily transmitted through sexual relations (Bharat et al. 2001:8).

For many people, HIV/AIDS is closely associated with homosexuality. This belief may be supported through the interpretation of religious texts suggesting that homosexuality should be punished (Fullilove and Fullilove 1999:1126). In most Asian societies, homosexuality is taboo. Personal religious beliefs are seen as powerful predictors of attitudes about homosexuality (Adamczyk and Pitt 2009). Religions in general consider homosexual behaviours as 'ungodly'. This has become both a social and religious construct which in essence discourages homosexual attitudes (Olson et al. 2006). The level of tolerance varies across religions. Some religions condemn homosexuality; some neither approve nor disapprove of it. While religious individuals may have more disapproving attitudes than nonreligious individuals, religions vary to a great degree in the extent to which they systematically condemn homosexuality. Considerable importance is attached to sexual morality in Islam along with Hinduism and Buddhism; people affiliated with these religions tend to disapprove of it. This may lead authorities to interpret religious precepts as proscribing homosexuality; for instance, in many Muslim countries, there are severe penalties for people found guilty of homosexual behaviour (Helie 2004). Under an Islamic system of government, all are exposed to the national religious culture. In this case, even if an individual is not personally religious, they may be less tolerant of homosexuality than residents of other countries due to their exposure to national religiosity (Adamczyk and Pitt 2009). Some religions, especially Islam, have already begun to spread the idea of abstinence as a way to limit infection among high-risk groups. Fullilove and Fullilove (1999) argue that this plays a significant role in stigmatizing homosexuality through the interpretation of the holy text which forbids these acts (Fullilove and Fullilove 1999:1126), but it is not clear whether adopting this approach reduces stigma or incidence of HIV infections.

The debate over the relationship between homosexuality and HIV transmission has gained significance due to the fact that homosexuality has been one of the primary routes through which the fastest transmission takes place. Another significant means of transmission is drug injection, primarily due to sharing of needles and other equipment (Fig. 4.1).

High-risk groups carry a higher level of stigma. Stigma towards PLWHA arises because of the fear that infection can be transmitted through superficial contact (Bharat et al. 2001:9). This stigmatization is layered on top of racial stigmatization when the infected individual is part of a visible minority (Chesney and Smith 1999:1168).

Profile Analysis

Most of the people interviewed for this research are either citizens or permanent residents of Canada. The process of refugee settlement is ongoing for some respondents. Under international law, those who become permanent residents or citizens have to give up their refugee status. In addition, a number of respondents

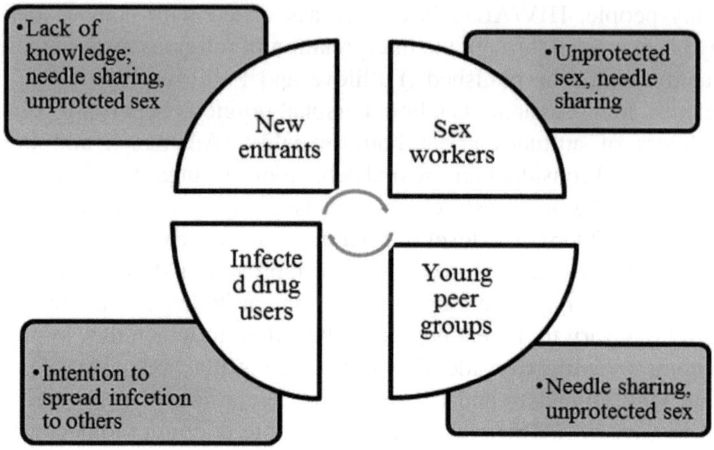

Fig. 4.1 Role of IDU in spreading HIV/AIDS infection

were second-generation immigrants. Respondents came from a diverse range of socioeconomic and cultural backgrounds. Socioeconomic status is characterized by education, current and previous occupation and income. The majority (57 %) was not working (either voluntarily retired or forced), while 29 % volunteer in medical treatment and service organizations, and 18 % were formerly employed in the fast food industry at McDonalds and Tim Horton's, while a few worked as sex workers or entertainers.

The age range of respondents was 17–49 years with a mean age of 31.6 years. Younger respondents, irrespective of gender, reported having higher education levels than older respondents. The majority contracted HIV from unprotected heterosexual sex, seven reported contracting HIV through homosexual sex, five reported contracting HIV through sharing injection equipment, and a small number were infected through blood transfusions and some claimed ignorance (Table 4.1).

Disclosure status of participants could not be clearly discerned. Some claimed that they had disclosed their status to a few people, such as their partners and healthcare providers. Some respondents claimed that only their parents knew about their status, while some were unsure if their status was known to anyone because they did not find any difference in treatment given to them. Some participants had not disclosed their status voluntarily, but their status was disclosed anyway. Respondents represented five countries from Asia, with the majority coming from India. Along with poverty, religious and ethnic violence have been displacing Indians since 1947, when the subcontinent was partitioned in 1947. The previous chapter reported on the trend among Indians to seek refuge in Canada. In addition, Sri Lanka experienced severe ethnic conflict which killed thousands and forced tens of thousands of people out of the country. A large number of Sri Lankan refugees came to Canada for escaping the conflict. Since the onset of the Maoist insurgency in the 1990s, thousands of people were killed and tens of thousands were displaced in Nepal.

Table 4.1 Profile of the participants

Origin	Sex	Sexual orientation[a]	Sexual history[b]	Perceived risk behaviour	Perceived reasons for infection
India	M	Bisexual	Mostly unprotected and travelled outside	MSM and blood transfusion	Unknown but the guess is unprotected sex
India	M	Gay [at some point of life]	Undisclosed	MSM and intravenous drug injection	Perhaps needle sharing from drug partners but unknown when it had happened. Maybe my partner was infected. Unprotected sex and Greeks could have transmitted this to me
India	F	Bisexual	Unprotected sex	Sexual abuse, intravenous drug injection	Unknown but may be blood transfusion Delayed detection, disclosure and treatment
India	U	Bisexual	Undisclosed	Substance use and blood transfusion	Unprotected sex and intravenous drug injection
India	M	Undisclosed	Undisclosed	Blood transfusion and unprotected sex	Barebacking might be a potential factor. Delayed detection and disclosure
India	U	Heterosexual	Unprotected sex	Substance use and lack of awareness	Unprotected sex and blood transfusion are primary reasons
Nepal	U	Bisexual	Undisclosed	Sexual abuse and substance use	Frequent bareback BJs might have caused this Anal sex could be another possible reason. However, whether this could be a source of this disease was not known
Nepal	M	Undisclosed	MSM and unprotected sex	Sexual abuse, blood transfusion and unprotected sex	Cannot remember but unprotected sex may have caused this. Delayed detection and disclosure
Nepal	M	Heterosexual	Unprotected sex	Intravenous drug injection	BJs and anal sex
Nepal	M	Undisclosed	Undisclosed	Blood transfusion, unprotected sex and intravenous drug injection	Barebacking but came to know about its impact only recently
Sri Lanka	F	Heterosexual	Undisclosed	Barebacking and intravenous drug injection	Blood transfusion
Sri Lanka	U	Bisexual	Unprotected sex	Lack of awareness about this disease	Unprotected sex and delayed treatment

(continued)

Table 4.1 (continued)

Origin	Sex	Sexual orientation[a]	Sexual history[b]	Perceived risk behaviour	Perceived reasons for infection
Thailand	U	Undisclosed	MSM and blood transfusion	NA	Blood transfusion and unsafe sex
Thailand	F	Undisclosed	Homosexuality		Delayed detection and treatment
Vietnam	M	Heterosexual	MSM and unprotected sex	NA	Using bathhouse, i.e. unidentified and unknown partners
Thailand	F	Bisexual	Intravenous Drug Injection	Same sex and unprotected sex	NA
Vietnam	U	Undisclosed	Unprotected sex	NA	Partner was infected. Delayed disclosed
Sri Lanka	U	Undisclosed	Unprotected sex	Blood transfusion and unprotected sex	Unknown but may be blood transfusion. Delayed detection, disclosure and treatment
Bangladesh	M	Undisclosed	Both protected and unprotected sex	Unprotected sex	Delayed disclosure and treatment. MSM is the primary reason

[a]Lesbian, gay, bisexual, transsexual
[b]Protected sex, extramarital sex, travel outside
U undisclosed, *M* male, *F* female

Further, statistics are available to suggest that more than 100,000 Vietnamese reside in Canada (Dorais 2003), the vast majority of whom were refugees created by the US–Vietnam war from 1969 to 1975. The Bangladeshi population in Canada is composed of refugees from the 1971 liberation war as well as migrants fleeing numerous natural disasters, political instability and escalating poverty.

Ethnicity, Gender and HIV/AIDS

The Public Health Agency of Canada (PHAC) warns that there is scope for misinterpreting aggregate data on HIV/AIDS because information on race and ethnicity is not available for all provinces and territories (PHAC 2011). In the early 1980s, only 21,681 AIDS diagnoses were reported to the Centre for Infectious Disease Prevention and Control (CIDPC). The number kept growing by around 2,000 cases per year until the early 1990s. After the launch of HAART, a decline in the number was observed from 1995 to 1997 (PHAC 2011).

It is important to note that during the late 1980s, when considered by ethnicity, AIDS cases in Canada was highest among Caucasian people, with approximately 91 % of cases occurring among this group. However, within one decade, this proportion dropped to 62 % of all reported AIDS cases (PHAC 2011). Methods of exposure vary within ethnic groups: Infected individuals from Aboriginal communities most frequently contracted HIV/AIDS through IDU; Afro-Canadians were most frequently infected through heterosexual behaviour; Caucasians were most frequently infected through homosexual behaviour (PHAC 2011; Avert 2012). Similarly, infection rates vary by gender. According to the Alliance for South Asian AIDS Prevention (ASAAP), there was a 10 % increase in the number of women clients who requested HIV/AIDS-related services and resources (ASAAP 2007). PHAC (2011) presents data on HIV infection (from 1998 to 2008): the majority of adult male cases were identified as Caucasian (66.4 %) and a minority as Aboriginal people (16.9 %) and Afro-Canadians (6.6 %). Conversely, among women, the highest proportion of reported cases self-identified as Aboriginal (42.9 %), followed by Caucasians (33.3 %) and Black Canadians (18.8 %) (PHAC 2011) (Table 4.2).

Table 4.2 Comparison of HIV case reports among women by race/ethnicity, 1998 versus 2008

	White	Black	Asian	Aboriginal	South/West Asian/Arab	Latin	Other	Total
1998								
Females	81	12	2	52	6	1	1	155
Males	348	22	11	68	16	13	0	478
2008								
Females	37	52	3	103	1	0	2	198
Males	265	43	31	93	8	28	6	474

Source: PHAC (Public Health Agency of Canada) (2011)

Initial Feelings and Reactions to HIV/AIDS

PLWHA experience stigma and isolation from various sources. Family members and friends may become reluctant to talk to them; doctors and nurses may become unwilling to treat them, contributing to feelings of stigmatization and discrimination (Ullah 2011:100). For example, although the role of family, as discussed later in Chap. 5, should be to support its members, psychologically and sometimes financially, this is often not the case for PLWHA; because of fear of infection, dishonour and shame, family members tend to disown them. For many, this comes as the first blow to the ability of PLWHA to live a normal life (Ullah 2011:101). This kind of treatment makes it clear to them that they deserve to be excluded and avoided. This is often justified by the fact that having an infected person within the family as a whole isolates the entire family unit from the society. Bharat and colleagues (2001) found that due to the fear in the family of the prospect of an infected person facing isolation and discrimination from society, they tend to conceal the illness from the society. However, the pain does not end here; rather additional stresses and depressions add to the burden of the family (Bharat et al. 2001:9).

What is the justification for such treatment from healthcare providers? It is believed that medical doctors and nurses are well aware of both the means of infection and the psychosocial trauma arising from infection, as well as the significant role they can play in instilling hope in PLWHA. However, regardless of their medical background, doctors and nurses have the same fear of becoming infected from association with patients. Physicians and nurses who view HIV/AIDS patients as responsible for their infections may treat them with less empathy. Further, there are arguments that stigma and discrimination extend to healthcare providers as well. Physicians and nurses may be stigmatized for treating PLWHA (for more see Ullah 2011; Chesney and Smith 1999:1168). Refusal to provide treatment, neglect of cases, testing of HIV without consent and violating privacy rights by disclosing patients' status are the manifestations of negative attitudes displayed by the medical staff (Bharat et al. 2001:10). This is extremely distressful for infected individuals and their families. Other examples of discriminatory attitudes practised by doctors and nurses include wearing masks while working and talking with infected people, maintaining a distance with the patients even while treating them, having their rooms identified in the hospitals and requiring extensive and at times unnecessary testing at the patient's expense. Such practices have significant implications for the willingness of at-risk individuals to get tested or disclose their status (Ullah 2011:101). Stigma and discrimination are also passed on vertically, meaning that children of PLWHA and medical staff working with PLWHA face almost the same level of stigma (Ullah 2011:102).

Most countries lack policies to protect the right to work or to ensure job security for infected persons. Therefore, job security rests entirely in the hands of the employers. In South Asia, especially India, dismissal of infected persons from jobs happens frequently (Bharat et al. 2001:10). Job loss has a direct impact on the psychological well-being of an individual, particularly those suffering from HIV/AIDS. It has a catastrophic impact on their financial stability.

HIV/AIDS-related stigma and discrimination are also gendered. The long-standing notion that this disease is transmitted 'only' through sexual relations puts women, sex workers and homosexuals in the position of being seen as responsible for the disease. Gender roles are not limited to home only but rather are widespread from workplace to schools and medical facilities. Bharat et al. (2001:19) found that the notion HIV is infected through only promiscuous sexual practices is very strong and leads people to act negatively towards women and MSM.

A positive diagnosis of HIV/AIDS completely alters the life trajectory of an individual. It is, therefore, understandable that infected persons would seek to conceal their status and even refuse to admit to having been tested for HIV (Chesney and Smith 1999:1165). After being tested, an individual may actually be able to predict the level of stigma they may face (Lee and Craft 2002:3). Also, they usually are concerned about their family and friends and are concerned about their perception of the disease, and this may prompt them to hide their status. Specifically, women become very sensitive to this issue as they may be perceived as either a sex worker or drug user, resulting in many adverse events including losing custody of their children (Chesney and Smith 1999:1166). The big dilemma they face in concealing their status juxtaposes exposure to shame and seeking treatment (Lee and Craft 2002:3). Overcoming this dilemma is important for PLWHA because being indecisive about disclosure can only delay their treatment.

Concealing HIV status has consequences for both the patients and the community. The primary burden of concealment is psychological. One participant who took about six months to disclose his status stated that 'carrying this news in secret is the heaviest burden in the world. I almost went mad as I felt it should be disclosed to someone. I guess I have lost a few years from my life in those six months by not disclosing it. Better to face whatever comes due to the disclosure'. The inner struggle over disclosure can contribute to loneliness, isolation and depression (Chesney and Smith 1999:1165). Concealment produces anxiety and frustration among the infected persons. In addition, they are concerned that seeking treatment may result in unintentional and unwanted disclosure and place them in embarrassing positions. Another damaging outcome of concealment is evident in sexual relationships. The potential of passing this infection on to loved ones through sexual encounters is particularly frightening. In such circumstances, PLWHA lose the courage to negotiate safe sex because the justification may not make sense to their partners and the consequences are unknown.

One participant stated:

> it is the most difficult situation in a relationship. To me, this was not morally acceptable. I was asked a number of times about my reasons for becoming suddenly conservative in our sexual relationship. I tried to explain, but felt that I was cheating myself.

Chesney and Smith (1999:1166) suggest that refusal to reveal their status requires PLWHA to live their sexual life without telling their partners in order to keep their status secret. This results in transmitting the virus to their partners, delays HIV testing, restricts use of preventive programmes and hinders the adoption of preventative behaviours.

The delay could happen for many reasons. Some people delay because they cannot accept the reality of being infected, do not know how it happened to them or do not trust the result of the tests. 'I thought I would rather carry the pain alone. What is the point telling this to others? Bad news begets bad news.' Fear of stigma is particularly prevalent among certain risk groups, such as MSM. This, in turn, conveys the fear of having the same stigma by just admitting to HIV testing (Chesney and Smith 1999:1164). This means specific groups carry the burden of double sigma which has double impact. Healthcare professionals who work directly with HIV patients can be another source of delay in providing care; for example, treating HIV sufferers may confine their career path, making it difficult to switch from HIV treatment to another branch of healthcare.

How long can an infected person conceal the status? Although at the onset of the disease patients can hide their status, eventually their physical appearance is affected and they cannot hide it anymore (Chesney and Smith 1999:1168). At this stage, friends, parents and partners may react violently for two reasons: 'anger' for hiding the diagnosis and 'guilt' for contracting HIV. This suggests that the earlier the disclosure happens, the better. HIV/AIDS sufferers need to be supported but not subjected to discrimination. Cooperation and empathy will help them sustain their life and deal with the disease.

The feelings of our respondents are measured with the help of the 5-stage model developed by Kübler-Ross (1969): denial, anger, bargaining, depression and acceptance (for details, see Chap. 2).[1] These stages represent the feelings of PLWHA after their diagnosis. These five variables are connected to self-esteem which is, in turn, connected to stigma. Negativity in emotions occurs when individuals' roles are affected (Lee and Craft 2002:7). Positive feelings can be effective and useful in preventing HIV/AIDS-related stigma. The feeling of empathy has a profound impact on attitudes. Directing empathy towards vulnerable groups is a valuable and effective method to change attitudes about these groups and consequently diminish stigma (Batson et al. 2002:1656). Individuals are likely to use three major psychological and behavioural patterns in coping with a life-threatening illness: retreat and conversion of energy, followed by exclusion from the threat of death and ending

[1] *Denial*: a defence mechanism postulated by Sigmund Freud, in which a person is faced with a fact that is too uncomfortable to accept and rejects it instead, insisting that it is not true despite what may be overwhelming evidence. *Anger*: Anger is an emotional state that may range from minor irritation to intense rage. Anger can raise the heart rate, increase blood pressure and increase the levels of noradrenaline and adrenaline. Often includes feelings of wanting to fight back or get even. *Bargaining*: Attempting to make deals to avoid the loss or attempting to make deals to stop or change the loss. Begging, wishing and praying to avoid the loss. *Depression*: overwhelming feelings of hopelessness, frustration, bitterness, self-pity, mourning loss as well as the hopes, dreams and plans for the future. Feeling lack of control, feeling numb or perhaps feeling suicidal. *Acceptance*: usually refers to the experience of a situation without an intention to change that situation (Kübler-Ross 1969)

with attempts to master the threat of death (Kübler-Ross 1969). Doka and Martin (2010) and Charles Corr et al. (1999) offered additional insight on ways in which humans go through different emotions in order to deal with death.

The Initial Feelings

When asked about the initial feelings when respondents first learned of their HIV status, most replies were identical: it was a heart breaking feeling, a heavy burden and almost indescribable:

> I wish there were languages to explain the feelings. I wish there was something or someone to understand the feelings. I wish I could explain what that feeling was like. I believe I keep carrying a feeling almost similar to the initial feeling. No difference. Of course, initial feelings were the beginning.

Many of the participants initially did not believe the result of the diagnosis. They rushed to be tested multiple times; some of the respondents went for six or seven opinions, in the hope of receiving a negative diagnosis:

> It is not easy to accept the fact that one was diagnosed with a deadly disease. I want to believe that HIV did not exist. Scientists arrived at this conclusion by mistake. They have now come up with new ideas. Or, I want to know that this is a disease like fever. We get this disease and purchase some medication available on the shelf and get well.

A certain framework of lifestyle becomes predominant. Within this framework, only a few activities are accommodated: medication, meals and mobility (3 M's).

Some participants who disclosed their status to their families received consolation, cooperation and promise about future support of all kinds. However, as time passed on, attention diverted to other issues and PLWHA became despondent:

> I was a normal person a few days ago. I used to go to work and shops, the bank, and had coffee with friends. The number of calls from friends became less frequent than before. When I make calls they are not received. Even if they answer the phone, the conversation time has shortened dramatically. All these changes happened very so fast! So painful! These, I guess, push me toward my last breath… Can you imagine how the world gets changed?

The damaging shame is exacerbated by the popular impression among people that HIV is transmitted by indiscriminate, unsafe sex with sex workers and men:

> I always pray to God. I ask what was the big crime I committed to have such a punishment? What can I do to get rid of this? What do you want me to do? I have not been a sex worker, nor a client. How do I let the whole society know that I have become a part of this group? I can't.

A different picture appears from the opinion expressed by the participants about their feelings. Interestingly, some respondents felt that they were somewhat relieved after the positive diagnosis, as they now had confirmation of why they were suffering from multiple symptoms for months and why no medication could relieve those symptoms. In a way they experienced some degree of relief, at least by the fact that they knew which direction to take regarding their treatment regimen.

After they were informed of their status as HIV positive, most respondents had to wait for 2–3 months before they were able to consult infectious disease specialists. Many admitted that they were reluctant to take medication, as they were losing hope about life. However, some doctors, according to participants, generally helped to change their way of thinking about life. '...very surprisingly, doctors talk about saving life! I wonder how this modern medical science miserably failed to give hopes to people living with this disease.'

A wide range of reactions from family members, friends and employers were expressed in different ways, ranging from hatred to sympathy. Extreme shock, nervousness, sadness and depression were primary reactions; a few handled the disclosure very well and gave the impression that they are seen no differently from before and treated the same way as others. Some were assured that friends and family would always be by their side.

A person diagnosed as HIV positive is confronted with a perceived threat to his or her physical health as well as the possibility of death. This challenge also offers opportunities for practitioners who are trained in the field of narrative therapy to make use of their unique knowledge and skills to offer support to people living with HIV/AIDS. Narrative practice is based upon the belief that our sense of self is socially constructed and exists in relationship to other people (Carey and Russell 2003:68), and is based on the idea that the notion of the socially constructed self and the ideas that one's sense of self is relational and contextual (Bird 2002).

Participant A is a 37 year old (from Bangladesh), who was tested for HIV after an unprotected sexual encounter. He was the eldest of four children. His family in Canada and relatives in his country of origin were financially dependent on his income. His test indicated that he was an HIV sufferer.

> I jumped out of my chair and started crying, lamenting loudly, slapping myself. I sat on the floor in the corner of the clinic and pulled my knees into chest and continued to cry. At that moment I realized that this devastating pain is something that nobody else can share. Hopelessness and despair began to engulf me, and I started to think I am different from all others around me. I would continue to think and act differently from how and what I used to do before.

Understandably, his positive diagnosis presented a perceived threat to his physical health and the financial stability of his family. The feelings of living with HIV for the rest of his life rendered him inconsolable. Asian communities living abroad interact more with one another than they do in their country of origin. Therefore, the biggest concern of Participant A was related to the stigma associated with HIV/AIDS. This condition is perceived as contagious and threatening to the community (Alonzo and Reynolds 1995). HIV-positive people experience 'their lives to be single storied, perceiving themselves trapped in a single dimension of living, one that predominantly features a sense of hopelessness, futility, emptiness, shame, despair and depression' (White 2004:60). As Participant A stated, 'I cry my own tears of despair and hopelessness and think about the unfair situation. But the reality is that what I learned from reading and from counseling sessions that "I've got the virus but I'm not the virus"'.

The value that he places on people and relationships appears to be his lifeline, his hopes and dreams and principles of living and 'intentional states of identity' (Carey and Russell 2003:9). These intentional states of identity include the following: (1) intentions or purposes that shaped a particular action, (2) the values and beliefs that supported the action, (3) the hopes and dreams associated with these values and (4) the principles of living or commitments represented by these hopes and dreams (Carey and Russell 2003:65).

Vertical and Horizontal Stigma: Is It a Contagion?

Approximately, a million children under 15 years were newly infected with HIV in 2005, and about 90 % of these newly infected children were born to HIV-infected mothers and acquired HIV during pregnancy, labour and delivery or via breastfeeding (UNAIDS 2005, 2006).

Vertical transmission from infected mothers to infants continues to be a source of high risk for the infant, even with the treatments for these groups that are now available. In addition, a variety of other special settings and subpopulations are at increased risk, including incarcerated youth and adults, and individuals with chronic mental illnesses, and they deserve more attention.

What are the implications for this bi-directional transmission? Communities generally blame individuals for their infection in the case of horizontal transmission. In the case of vertical transmission, who should be held responsible for infection? Children who are infected by their parents are not responsible for getting the virus. This is medically proven and socially acknowledged. However, studies, theories and empirics bear out that stigma travels through multiple generations who were infected through vertical transmission, to varying degrees. The following figure in line with the theory of double discrimination (discussed in detail in Chap. 2) suggests that the degree of discrimination depends on the status of the individual in their respective countries.

The concept of 'stigma contagion' is introduced here to explain the power of stigma to impact the lives of people, irrespective of the 'guilt' and 'innocence'. As one participant stated:

> I got it from my parents. Fortunately, I have been surviving due to the HAART. This does not necessarily mean that I am not in pain. This is not just physical pain but also continued psychological pain. It is just unbearable pain. Some of my relatives and I know that I am not responsible for this. But how could I make the whole society understand that I am innocent. Being blamed for a crime that you did not commit is the most painful thing, isn't it? What is more painful you know, I cannot ask my parents what was my fault. They passed away.

Obviously, not much research has been conducted on disclosure to children of HIV infections, their mental state, how they face the consequences and how resilient they are to it. This issue merits deeper investigation on the debate over whether concealment or disclosure protects children infected through vertical transmission, and the

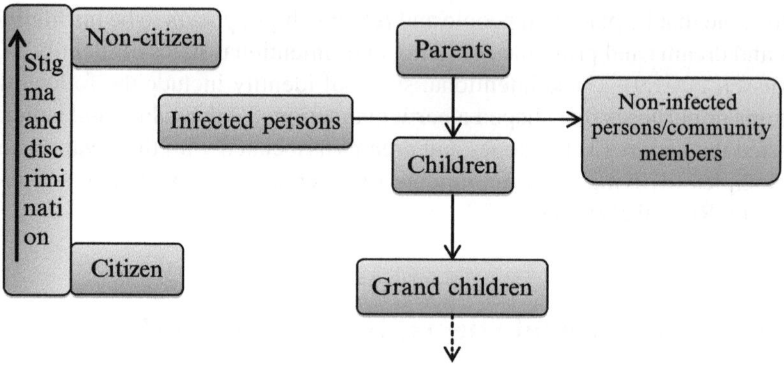

Fig. 4.2 Showing vertical and horizontal transmissions

Fig. 4.3 Status of disclosure

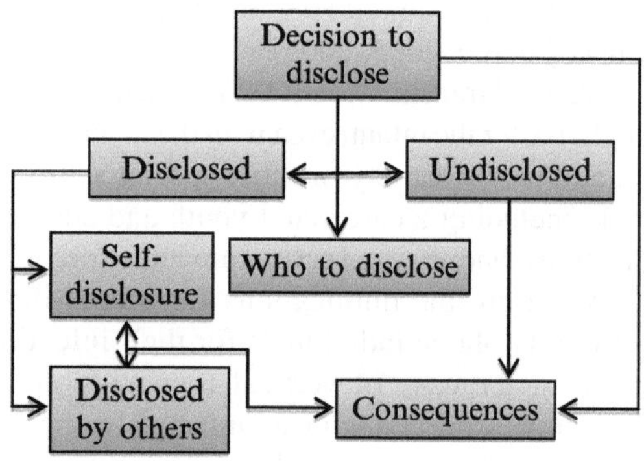

benefits of concealment or disclosure (Fig. 4.2). How would one expect children to deal with their infection? If disclosed to them, it may jeopardize their childhood and education prospects and cause permanent mental trauma. Some studies point out that disclosure to children may have serious negative outcomes, such as heightened family problems, diminished quality of family relationships (Lee et al. 2002), lowered self-esteem and painful memories (Kennedy et al. 2010). Other studies show that the initial negative effects of disclosure dissipate over time (Lee et al. 2002).

In order to maintain family relationship within the family, it might be better for parents to disclose their status to their children. Disclosure has different outcomes depending on whether it is intentional or unintentional (Fig. 4.3). Some parents obviously plan to keep it concealed intentionally. Kennedy et al. (2010) found that some parents wait for their children to be mature enough to understand and handle this issue before disclosing. Sometimes, parents wait because they are not sure about the proper way of disclosing their status. Unintentional disclosure is not uncommon. In developing or underdeveloped countries, most frequent avenues through which unintentional disclosure occurs are clinics, diagnostic centres and care givers. Often, dramatic deterioration in health condition provides clear indication of the infection. Kennedy and colleagues revealed that children can understand that their parents have health problems from some changes in their parents' routine, such as the behavioural changes and more frequent visits to doctors than before and consumption of unusually high amount of medication. Disclosure among children and adults may generate both positive and negative reactions. Sometimes children understand and think that nothing could revert the situation back to normal and become more involved in family affairs than before in managing the consequence. In many cases, children were found to become more religious, praying for their parents. Some children experienced intensely negative reactions immediately after disclosure. The most common reaction for children was continued fear for the parents' health and life.

> My parents invited some of my relatives because they did not see them for a long time. We were also longing for having a good time with them. At the last moment, they declined the invitation saying they got some urgent errands to finish. My parents told us later that they declined because of the fact that they knew our sero statuses.

This is how fear and stigma spreads beyond family boundaries, from individual to the families and the community.

Disclosure and Consequences

The consequence theory of HIV disclosure suggests that the interplay between disclosure and disease progression is moderated by the consequences one anticipates to result from the disclosure. Stresses accumulate as the disease progresses. Thus, it is necessary to think about the costs and benefits of disclosure. Individuals disclose when the rewards outweigh the associated costs (Serovich 2001). The vulnerability of an HIV sufferer to mistreatments from individuals and society emanates from disclosure. There is dearth of research on the potential impact of disclosure on the overall well-being of PLWHA. This inability to disclose often results in extreme stress and depression. The above section outlines potential factors that may prevent people from disclosing the status. These factors are often deeply socially rooted; therefore, it remains difficult to disclose. These factors are responsible for delaying disclosure.

Before going into a detailed analysis of the consequences of disclosure, it is worth discussing what exactly is meant by disclosure in the context of HIV status. Sandelowski et al. (2004) and Chandra et al. (2003) refer to three types of disclosure: managed disclosure, voluntary disclosure and disclosure without consent. In managed disclosure, PLWHA maintain control over the decision to disclose, selecting disclosure styles ranging from full to selective. Voluntary disclosure has two different dimensions: voluntary disclosure as a positive desirable act and voluntary disclosure where there is no other choice. Disclosure without consent is seen as revealing the status without their consent (Greeff et al. 2008).

Obviously, neither of the categories of 'disclosed' and 'undisclosed' offers guarantees against vulnerability to abuse. However, the category of 'disclosed' may have immediate consequences and the 'undisclosed' could have secret and long-term consequences. The discourse of whom to disclose to remains an important issue due to the fact that this is shocking news to all. There are differences in the level of potential abuse and manifestations of stigma depending on the relationship between the individual disclosing their status and the individual to whom the status is disclosed. Generally, there could be misinformation and disinformation about the infection should this be disclosed by others. In this case, it may not be possible for the disclosing individuals to defend themselves. Prejudice towards PLWHA begins before confirmation is made about the level of CD4 count or the means of infection. Decisions to disclose may be affected by many factors. However, the number and severity of the factors depends on the society and family one lives in. The general assumption is that people at the outset disclose their status to their partners. However, what happens to those who do not have partners? To whom do those without partners disclose their status first?

The consequence of disclosure varies, depending on the level of knowledge and awareness about the infection. Related to disclosure, confidentiality is a significant factor in the context of healthcare system. However, due to its practical context, serostatus should be known to those who need to know such as doctors, nurses, care providers and psychosocial counsellors (Fig. 4.4).

Consequences could be both negative and positive. A key question is related to the comparison of costs over the benefits. Greeff et al. (2008) found that people disclose their status because sharing experiences and psychological support during group therapy meetings is helpful. Another important question is related to the factors that promote disclosure. According to Marks et al. (1991), disclosing to at-risk partners may encourage the use of safe sexual or drug-sharing behaviour. Derlega et al. (1993) documented that since disclosure is effectively a prerequisite for social support, revealing one's serostatus becomes an important mental health issue. This implies that disclosure provides relief to the person, while nondisclosure leads to the suppression of feelings that can increase the likelihood of stress-related problems (Pennebaker et al. 1990). It also has an impact on 'individuals disclosing to friends and family who provide helpful links to education, health care, and the needed social support demonstrate improved physical health' (Fennell et al. 1994:102–103).

'There is a heightened sense of self-understanding, healing, and authenticity in their relationships with others; an enhanced sense of accomplishment and pride, empowerment, and purpose; a welcome relief from the burdens of secrecy and rumors; and the ease of further disclosure and support' (Greeff et al. 2008). The same study further asserts that there are other positive consequences of disclosure. For example, this alerts those who intend to engage in unprotected sex with a seropositive, serves as a psychological shield to oneself not to indulge in unprotected sex, helps to clear one's conscience and helps to encourage others to go for VCT.

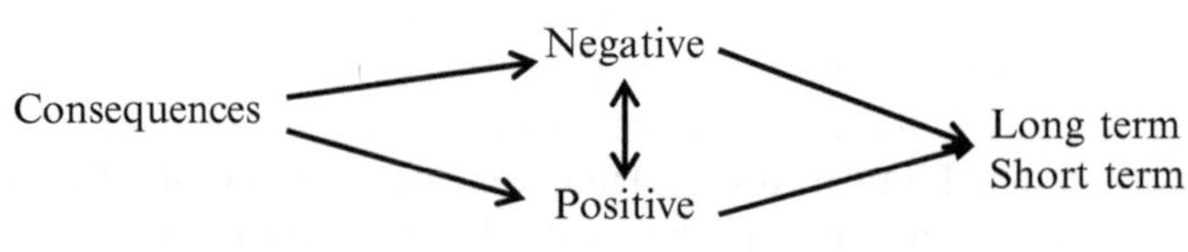

Fig. 4.4 Consequences of disclosure

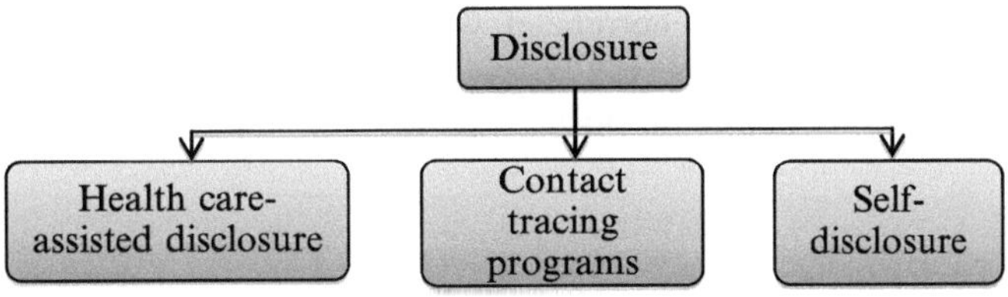

Fig. 4.5 Showing ways to disclose

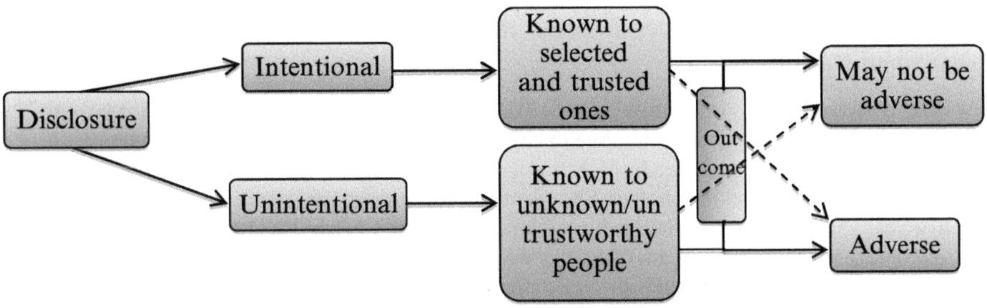

Fig. 4.6 Disclosure and potential outcome

Zea et al. (2005) explored disclosure and post-disclosure life with the help of a three-stage model in the US context. They have highlighted the mechanisms through which the status is disclosed (Fig. 4.5). Healthcare-assisted disclosure takes place with the assistance of both the healthcare providers and the acceptance of the infected during disclosure to a partner or others. In order to trace contacts, healthcare providers ask HIV sufferers for the names of their current and past partners (sexual or needle sharing, etc.). This information is then passed on to the public health department. This obviously raises confidentiality and privacy-related issues. This is why a clear understanding of the consequences of disclosure is vital.

A study of women diagnosed with HIV found that while in some cases disclosure was positively associated with increased emotional and personal support, this was not so for the majority of cases (Zea et al. 2005). The study showed that in most of the cases, disclosure was associated with negative reactions, including rejection, hatred, assault (physical and verbal) and abandonment. It is clear that, generally, society is not yet prepared for a hassle-free disclosure (Fig. 4.6).

Among men, disclosure of HIV status frequently leads to rejection from peers. Data shows that HIV sufferer gay men reported self- or externally imposed social isolation based on a fear of rejection or stigmatization by HIV-negative men. Lack of disclosure due to fear of stigmatization has been associated with significant mental health consequences among gay men, particularly depression, highlighting the importance of this process (Frost et al. 2007). Fear of the negative social consequences caused most of the participants to avoid being tested (Kellerman et al. 2002; Imrie and Macdonald 2009). On the other hand, awareness about HAART and intention to disclose are correlated with neutral or positive mental health outcomes. When the infected person knows that HAART can be an effective treatment, they are more willing to disclose.

Rejection in Relationships

One of the primary concerns of PLWHA is the likelihood of being isolated and rejected by their own community. Rejection by sexual partners, family members, peers, friends and colleagues is often the principal barrier to disclosure. As one participant stated:

> I did not want to lose my family and my friends. I thought they would leave me. My wife noticed my consistent decline her urge to engage in sex and asked me if I was tested positive. I nodded. I saw how hard her heart was pounding. She spent a few days and night without eating, sleeping and taking shower. She seemed to be getting over it in a month… However, in a year she developed a relationship with another man, I guess. She began to return home very late. I used to ask her if anything was wrong. She tearfully replied that her entire life has gone wrong. It was obvious that she was referring to my status. I felt helpless. While I understand her pain, I guess being helpless is more painful. She has choices but I do not have any.

Nearly every participant experienced rejection by potential sexual partners due to HIV status. The harm this caused to their self-esteem and self-confidence was long-lasting. Some men reported subsequently developing significant social and sexual distance from other men with HIV, whom they frequently characterized as morally inferior.

People in general do not accept food prepared by someone living with HIV/AIDS. This again depends on the knowledge, understanding and information the person has about it.

> …I shared a can of coke with one of my friends. He perhaps was shy of declining my offer. It was so painful when I knew later on that he went to laboratory to get tested.

Mental and Emotional Well-Being

Is it possible to ignore stigma? Stigma leads to human rights violations, fuels the epidemic and impedes care efforts. This has long-standing implication for society: ‘AIDS is not killing people anymore. What is killing us is the stigma. The way we are scowled upon kills us’ (one respondent).

Adherence to HIV Medication

Can awareness and proper knowledge about HIV/AIDS mitigate stigma? It can be argued that awareness, knowledge and information have little to do with mitigation of stigma. Rather, information about and access to HAART is more effective.

Adherence to HIV treatment is important for the medication to work effectively for reducing the amount of viral load. Skipping medications, even occasionally, allows HIV to multiply very fast. Perceived levels of HIV-related stigma can have direct consequences on medication adherence. Stigma and the associated adherence difficulties are more common among people who disclose their HIV status to a broad range of social contacts (Mao et al. 2009). Reduced rates of adherence to treatment are also seen in people with physical manifestations of HIV (Mao et al. 2009; Vanable et al. 2006). Rintamak and colleagues (2006) found a direct correlation between adherence and social stigma. However, characteristics such as regimen complexity, forgetfulness, desire to avoid side effects of medication, inadequate patient knowledge, family/work responsibilities, depression, medication availability or a desire to simply have breaks from the endless routine of taking pills have association with poor adherence. As one participant stated:

> The amount is too high. This makes me very weak. I have never been used to doing anything on a routine. I have been a free person, free thinker. Getting my medication feels like a big imposition. Family members around me sometimes seem to be disturbed. I sometimes think I should give up. I know I will die soon, then, what is point?

There is no doubt that the complex treatment regimens pose a burden for patients. One may naturally forget to take medication sometimes. In many cases, they cannot ask anyone to remind them to take the medication, while family members or partners may be hesitant to remind them to take medication. Stigma may be embedded in the way they are reminded.

Criminalization of HIV Transmission

> There is no evidence that criminal laws specific to HIV transmission will make any significant impact on the spread of HIV or on halting the epidemic. Therefore, priority must be given to increasing access to comprehensive and evidence-informed prevention methods in the fight against HIV/AIDS. (Excerpt from the conclusions of the 1st Global Parliamentary Meeting on HIV/AIDS, Manila, Philippines, 2007)

Enforcement of such laws will have a strong impact on the disclosure issue. However, intentional spread of the virus to others is a criminal act in many countries. Applying criminal law to those who intentionally transmit or expose others to HIV infection could be justified. Criminalization of HIV transmission may reinforce 'HIV-related stigma, spread misinformation about HIV, hinder HIV testing and counseling support and, importantly, create a false sense of security by encouraging HIV-negative men to indulge in risky behaviors, believing themselves legally protected from transmission' (UNAIDS 2008; Mao et al. 2009; Vanable et al. 2006; Peretti-Watel et al. 2006).

The Open Society Institute (OSI) expressed concern over the recent creation of HIV-specific laws that criminalize HIV transmission and exposure in many developing and underdeveloped countries. Existing criminal laws are increasingly being used to prosecute people for transmitting HIV or exposing others to HIV infection in countries in Europe and North America. Jürgens et al. (2009) articulated ten common rationales for why criminalization of HIV exposure and transmission is unfair:

(a) Criminalizing HIV transmission could only be justified when individuals purposely or maliciously transmit HIV with the intent to harm others.
(b) Evidence suggests that application of criminal laws does not reduce the spread of HIV.
(c) Criminalization undermines HIV prevention efforts.
(d) Criminalization may promote fear and stigma.
(e) Criminalization may be biasedly applied to women and aggravate oppression.
(f) Criminalization is often drafted and applied too broadly and often punishes behaviour that is not blameworthy.
(g) Criminalization is often applied unfairly, selectively and ineffectively.
(h) Criminalization ignores the real challenges of HIV prevention.
(i) Legislators may reform laws that stand in the way of HIV prevention and treatment.
(j) Human rights-based responses to HIV are most effective.

Cultural Sensitivity and Social Segregation

Cultural sensitivity largely determines when and to whom HIV status should be disclosed. Asian communities are known for their collectivist orientation. This means that individual behaviour casts a reflection on the larger family and/or community group (Yoshioka and Schustack 2001). Therefore, disclosure for Asians is influenced by the fact that most Asians intend to protect the family from shame. Asian cultures do not endorse talking about personal or emotional topics owing to the potential for embarrassment and discomfort. Homosexuality and bisexuality are viewed in many Asian cultures as deviance, contrary to values of family, and are considered to be the result of moral erosion. One study conducted in mid-1990s in Bangladesh on high-risk groups (commercial sex workers and their clients) can be considered for understanding the level of knowledge about HIV/AIDS. Respondents were asked about the key risk behaviours for the spread of HIV (unprotected anal and vaginal intercourse, having multiple sex partners and using non-sterile drug injection equipment), and only two per cent were able to reply correctly (Ullah et al. 1999). Nasreen (2005) argues that the low level of awareness about HIV/AIDS in South Asia, especially in Bangladesh, relates to cultural mores. As one Bangladeshi participant stated:

> After I came to know my serostatus, I decided not to disclose to anyone in my family. I maintained that position for a few months. At some point I felt it is too much for me to carry this burden. I should share and I did knowing that it might bring more pain to me and to the family. I was quite aware that it is not only me but also the whole family will be labeled-like oh this family is a HIV family.

If discrimination was a factor in job interviews, there is a need to identify why one was targeted. Was it because they were HIV sufferers, or they belonged to a particular gender or race? A major complaint ethnic minorities have about racism is that it is more likely to be covert than overt, at least at institutional levels. That means a prospective employer is not likely to say outright that a particular ethnic group need not apply for a job at that company. However, a prospective employer might ask questions during interview about race, colour, sex, religion, national origin, birthplace, age, disability or marital or family status. A good example of discrimination is, most job announcements in Canada emphasize that 'all qualified candidates are encouraged to apply; however, Canadians and permanent residents will be given priority. … [the organization] is actively committed to diversity and the principles of Employment Equity and invites applications from all qualified candidates. Women, Aboriginal peoples, members of visible minorities, and people with disabilities are especially encouraged to apply and to voluntarily self-identify as a member of a designated group as part of their application'. This does not overtly say that Canadian citizens will be given priority over immigrants or both will receive equal treatment, regardless of what credentials the applicants possess.

During the mid-1990s, the South Asian community was not much aware of HIV/AIDS. Now that they have more knowledge, the stigma has increased, and stigma against PLWHA within the South Asian community in Canada is much greater than among other communities. The level of stigmatization depends on how people think an individual contacted HIV. If it was through sexual activity, then stigma is worse than if it was by blood transfusion. But once one is infected, it is rarely possible to determine what caused this infection.

On the individual level, stigma is imposed in a more destructive manner:

> I called my long lasting friend and wanted to offer coffee. He declined while swearing profanely. He stated that he was not peer of mine. Another participant stated that his friend called him 'a prostitute' in public. Maybe I am, but I knew she was pointing to my HIV status. This is verbal abuse. To me that treatment was too harsh. Those who hold a tendency of rejection can manifest it bit by bit. Then we don't get shockingly surprised.

Infected people generally disclose their status to the most trusted person. However, some people abuse this trust. One participant had to leave the house where he was staying with his friend soon after he revealed his status. People are now more aware of this pandemic than a decade ago. Therefore, misconceptions apply more in the case of older generations. First-generation, Canadian-born South Asians are not hesitant to talk about HIV/AIDS. This could be due to the fact that they attended Canadian schools where sex education and HIV/AIDS education are offered. However, they cannot talk about sex and HIV issues with their parents due to imbalances in power relations and cultural barriers. This again depends on the relationship one has with the infected person—for example, whether they are considered a friend as opposed to an acquaintance. Stigma and taboos around sex are strong among South Asians, and parents still cannot accept that their kids have sex before marriage. Overall, this has not had a significant impact on the actual reduction of stigma.

To Whom to Disclose?

Once the person decides to disclose, the first task is to identify a person for disclosure. Most research confirms that the overwhelming majority of PLWHA first chose their partners, followed by family members and close friends. The spouse is the first person with whom they shared this information, followed by mothers, fathers, sibling and children. Beyond their own family, healthcare providers and then friends were informed first, followed by other HIV-infected neighbours.

In choosing who to disclose to, the PLWHA take numerous factors into considerations, for instance, how close is the person to the infected individual, how trustworthy and sympathetic he or she is going to be, how comfortable they are with knowing and how safe disclosure is in terms of concealability. Some respondents said they trusted the person to whom they disclosed their status because they were the ones who took them to hospitals for diagnosis and treatment. Many respondents thought that healthcare providers should be the first to know about their status. The time taken to disclose ranged from 1 week to 3 years. Those who took the longest time to disclose indicated that shame, uncertainty, fear and lack of reliable persons to disclose were the major impediments to early disclosure.

Disclosure and Serosorting

'Serosorting' occurs when both HIV sufferers and HIV-negative people screen prospective partners for similar HIV status before associating with them socially or sexually (Eaton et al. 2009). Studies of 'serosorting' demonstrate that it extends to individual relationships and communities. Serosorting may be protective among certain groups, for example, reducing transmission among high-risk HIV-negative gay men (Philip et al. 2010). However, HIV-negative MSM who serosort are inadvertently placing themselves at risk for HIV through infrequent HIV testing, lack of HIV status disclosure, acute HIV infection as well as co-occurring sexually transmitted infections. HIV-negative and HIV sufferers may be practising seroguessing or serosorting based on perceived rather than actual HIV status (Eaton et al. 2009; Wilson et al. 2010; Zablotska et al. 2009). As one respondent stated:

> Initially, I planned not to disclose to any of the family members and relatives. My impression was that there would be no benefit from disclosing this disastrous news to anyone. This would put me in a more vulnerable position. At one point, I realized that I needed mental support. I had difficulty deciding who to share information on the tribulations and trauma I was going through. My parents are old. How they are going to take this news? What would be their reaction? How would it affect their wellbeing? Should I share this with them only for my sake at the cost of causing them additional burden of tensions and mental agony?

It was possible to identify one of the main reasons for disclosing to their parents that in any treatment they won't serosort:

> It took around six months for me to make the decision when, who and how to disclose my serostatus. Then I did to my parents. I thought my heart would be lighter after disclosure. It was a heavy burden and felt like living in an air-tight compartment. I found out that disclosure was not the best strategy for me. I witnessed how hurt my parents were by the news. It was really stressful. I regretted my decision to tell them of my status. At this stage of life, they do not deserve to carry this kind of burden of pain. I understand this is very difficult for parents to see their children die a slow death. At the outset, they were most concerned about my life. Later, they became more concerned about the reaction of the community and stigma attached to this infection.

At some point, shame becomes more important than life:

> The fact that I am dying is no more a concern for many, the concern is the shame I brought to the family. One day, my parents came to me to ask how I was infected. I begged them not to ask because the reason will not give my normal life back nor theirs. I could not think of any answer that might have calmed them down. They left my room crying. Another day, they asked me if anyone else knows about my status. They warned me not to disclose it to anyone, not even to a relative or a close friend. If anyone else came to know, our social life will come to a total halt, and we will not be able to show our face to anyone. I wanted to tell them, it is a disease and I myself am infected, none else, why can you not show your face. It is me who is suffering. But I did not say it, because that would be disrespectful to my parents. I did not want to add to their agony.

The participant said he became angry with his parents due to their excessive concern about the society and the family. However, he clearly understands that stigma extends both vertically and horizontally rather than being an individual issue: 'I regret disclosing my status to them. It pains me to see how hard it is for them. I see how much change took place in their attitude and the way they talk and serve food to me. It is a big change from the past.' This participant understood that his parents had been trying not to hurt him: 'I feel it would be better to keep my own pain to myself. I disclosed with the hope that sharing the agony with them will lessen my pain and reduce the burden in my heart. It turned out the other way round. I cannot blame them either.'

> Within a year, manifestations of my infection began to appear. Frequently, I was being asked by my friends and relatives and neighbors if I was infected with something and advised me to consult a doctor. I had no answer for this. My silence indicated to them that I was infected. I cannot conceal it or deceive people anymore. As result, I have lost my social life, my family, my love, my friends, my relatives and my job and lastly my will to live.

It is difficult to conclude however that disclosure is good or bad for the psychological well-being of PLWHA. From ethical and medical points of view, disclosure is an essential part for determining treatment regimens and for ensuring safe sexual behaviour in the future so that further transmission does not occur. Participants offered varying insights:

> One of my family members back home wrote a letter to my parents to inform them that their son is infected with HIV. It cannot be hidden and God is punishing you because you betrayed us. You fled and thought there would be no God in foreign country. But God is everywhere. I got to read this letter because I found it on my mother's desk, and decided to commit suicide I reconsidered it later.

> My family members are not aware of my status yet, but some of my friends already know it. I trusted one friend and disclosed it to him. However, he failed to uphold my trust. He, I guess, spread the information about my status to other friends. I realized later when I found them avoiding me. I am often asked by my family members why my friends do not visit me as frequently as before and if I have strained relationship with friends. This situation is in fact very difficult because I have no answer to such questions. I told them it was their decision.

If a person's identity and HIV status have been released to the public, it is a direct violation of their right to confidentiality:

> Sometimes I feel I should disclose my status. This feeling comes from my frustrations about being asked over and over again about my behavioral changes. They keep asking what happened to me, because I forget instructions and requests. How could I tell them that my mind is always occupied with the thought of this infection and its consequences. I am not sure what behavioral changes they are referring to. I do realize that I am no longer as cheerful and alert as before. I prefer to spend time alone in my room. I have been a happy person all along. Suddenly, the cloud of sadness engulfed me.
>
> Just a few days ago, we had an invitation to a relatives' wedding. I thought I would be able to attend. Everything was set. But on the day of the party, I felt sick and could not attend the party. I have later heard that there were gossips about me in the party and afterwards. I felt very bad because my parents are facing unpleasant experiences because of my infection.

In principle, disclosure should be voluntary; however, some manifestations of the diseases and reaction to the HAART are so distinct that people at some point would easily identify the symptoms:

> I understand this will be disclosed one day. It is natural. I am preparing for that day. [Interviewer: What are you afraid of?] I am not sure but anything can happen. I may be expelled from my home. I may be beaten or even killed. I may be confined for life. My food may be cut off. Who knows?

Another participant had a similar view about disclosure:

> Disclosure is not something you have to do; truth automatically comes out at some point of time. The nature of the infection makes it easy for people to know. It cannot be hidden. It may take longer or shorter time before it is known. Changes in behaviors and life style will make people suspect that something is going wrong. Visiting clinics is one of the easiest ways to have it disclosed. People look differently at the visitors to those clinics.

Rejection from the family is difficult to accept for those who are still financially dependent. Family ties are important in Asian culture. As one participant stated:

> Actually, I am not sure about the reactions from the family and the society as well. But, I have heard that a family disowned an infected person after they knew about the status. I am not sure if I can take such brutal treatment from my family'. [Interviewer: How are you preparing yourself, like you mentioned?] I am preparing myself for any eventuality. If I am shunned by my family, I will have to accept it and live on my own. That is what I meant. [Interviewer: How was your status disclosed?] This is a surprise even to me. I have no idea how it was disclosed. My intention was to keep it undisclosed as long as I can. However, I began to realize that my community already has an idea about my status. How did you realize? Well, you can imagine, right? You can see people are keeping away (as if keeping safe distance) from you. This has never happened before'. [Interviewer: What is your guess about the disclosure?] May be from the clinics or partially based on assumptions.

> One of my closest friends early in the morning knocked on my door. I found him nervous, and asked the reason. He asked me what was happening to me, and replied that there was nothing new. He shouted 'nothing new' you liar? I said honestly, nothing new. He roared at me. He kept saying 'you wanted to pass this infection to us? Then why you did not tell your status to me? I have known you got this long ago'. I remained silent. I was afraid of his ferocious face- a new face I never saw in him. He left without saying a 'good bye. I expected sympathy from my friend. However, it is my destiny. He ended the long lasting friendship. I understand we had coffee together a couple of days ago. He might have thought he could be infected from this companionship. I understand his position but he could have been polite while confronting me. I believe that the infection is responsible for ending this friendship, regardless of whether I am responsible for this infection or not. This is obviously very painful'

Some participants have positive attitudes towards disclosure and the disease itself. A few participants seemed to perceive this disease to be like any other disease. Some said they believed that family and society would take it as easily as they did. However, with time, this perception changed. They said that they could contribute to the society if they received support.

> I cannot understand why there are barriers to disclosing our status. It is a disease, it is an infection. We do not hide when we get fever or cough. I honestly disclosed my status to my wife and sought her cooperation. She was sympathetic initially. She eventually started to change. But this is the reality. We have to accept this. She used to come back home late. I used to receive so many calls from her male friends. She got her new mobile phone. Within a few months she started to sleep in a separate bed room. I regret disclosing the status to her. I began to realize it was a mistake to do so. I knew I was going to be deserted soon. It happened sooner than I thought. Fortunately, we do not have children. This would have made their life very difficult. She perhaps volunteered this information to all our relatives to justify entering into a new relationship. Some of my relatives and friends came to see me afterwards to make sure if the information they got was correct. Some behaved normally, while others left immediately with an impression that it was my fault and I was a bad person.

As discussed, nondisclosure adds a significant amount of psychological stress. This respondent internalizes other peoples' assumptions:

> My employer and my colleagues did not know about my status for a long time. However, my supervisor noticed that my performance was declining. He asked me take leave for a few days, if needed. I asked the reason for his offer. He said that he noticed my lack of concentration that was affecting output. I was really scared that time because I thought they already knew about my infection and this was a prelude to dismissal. I cannot afford to lose my job. It would mean putting me into further isolation and will make me broke.

Stigmatization and discrimination can occur anywhere; perpetrators do not choose a suitable place to practise stigmatization or discrimination. However, the location of stigmatization or discrimination—for example, schools or work places—is very significant for the stigmatized. Depending on the place, the impact of stigmatization and discrimination can have serious consequences. By this reckoning, workplace discrimination is most damaging because it may lead to job loss, along with other direct impacts. Discrimination in the workplace may occur in the recruitment process, as the terms and conditions and benefit packages may be offered differently from other employees. Transfer, promotion, dismissal or other personnel decisions may be influenced by it. Another impact of stigmatization is harassment, which could encompass different kinds of behaviours such as sharing offensive jokes, sending suggestive emails or texts, displaying or showing pornographic images, taunting about religion and race and asking about personal life. In the workplace, abuse resulting from stigma ranges from verbal to physical, yelling and using offensive language, isolation, intimidation, assignment of more difficult jobs than before, unfair changes in work roster and undermining of performance. One participant described the way she lost her job:

> After the second month, I was called by my supervisor. He was, I would say, a good person, and had a good heart. He said, he somehow knew my status as did others in the office, and there are some issues related to it. The company would like to give you a month more and would be grateful if you quit the job. I did not take that month. That day was my last day at my work. How could I go again where I have been asked to leave due to my serostatus. It was so humiliating, disgraceful and painful. I remember I spent 2 days without any food. I wanted to cry loudly. But no strength was left to cry out. There was a number of times, I planned to commit suicide. I changed my decision. I knew PLWHA can live long life.

This participant described multiple burdens, one of which was her financial situation. With no savings, she lived without a job for a few months. A community service organization recruited her with full knowledge about her status. However, prior to obtaining this position, the participant described internalization of stigma practised against her:

> You know how expensive life here is. My friends and relatives already knew my status. One of my friends came to collect money I owed her. She needed that money. I think she hurried because she thought I would die soon before I repay that money. One morning I opened my refrigerator, and it was empty. I was hungry. I was afraid to go out for groceries. I waited until it was dark before I went out.

Studies suggest that disclosure often leads to violence against PLWHA, and it often escalates because of gender. Females in most Asian countries have a lower position in the family hierarchy. Therefore, the dominant position of male members makes it possible to perpetrate violence against them:

> It was even more shocking to me. I thought my husband is the one most nearest to me on earth. As soon as he knew my serostatus, I felt the distance growing between us. He just pushed me back and shouted: what? What? What did you say? This is not the first time he treated me this way. I always thought husband is the best friend, the closest one who you can share everything with. Now I realize he is ready to hear only good news …anyway life is like that. My life is mine and his is his. I have to live long.

When asked about a mark on her forehead she said:

> 'One day I was feeling very bad. I cooked for him. I held his hand and asked him to dine together. He threw me on the wall. I was bleeding from my forehead. He did not look at me even'. [Interviewer: would you say that was a physical abuse? Not now?] 'I am no longer with him. Every day, he used to physically abuse me. This has forced me out of his home. You know, his physical violence in fact is less painful than his verbal abuse. His verbal abuse is so sharp and loaded. This would induce you vomit. I cannot bring them to my tongue. They were so disgraceful, painful and unthinkable for a human being, for a partner who you have lived so long together. I am now at least free from those times. I waited for him to be normal. My understanding was that the suddenness of the news made him sad but as time would pass he would be fine. But it was never the case. He never came back to normal. I thought I should set him free and I die alone. That is what he wants in his mind, I believe'.

Many studies recommend that when facing difficulties with disclosure, those receiving the news should stay calm and take time to consider the implications. However, sudden bursts of emotion are often difficult to control. PLWHA should receive counselling on how to disclose, and parents, partners and friends should have adequate information on the strategies to react:

> I was told from the clinic that I should share this with my family members, primarily with my mother. I attempted a number of times to share this with my mother. I failed. I did not sleep the whole night. I made 5 to 6 attempts. I leaned at the door of my mum's room many times when she was even sleeping. I returned my room without saying anything. I really did not know what and how to say. How to say, your son is dying soon of a disease everyone hates about. I did not sleep for 3 days in a row, I remember. My mum realized I might have some difficulty that I am going through. She came into my room asked what was wrong with me. I immediately decided to disclose, that is the time. She started slapping and kicking me with her voice raised. What *harami* (illicit activity) you committed, why did you do this. This disease does not infect innocent people. We have in our knowledge not done any wrong to God. Why are we punished so brutally? I looked at my mum's shivering face. I got scared rather. I felt bad for my mum and felt helpless for myself either.

Circumstances often determine the opportunity for disclosure:

> I did not disclose because I knew we had a number of sexual encounters after I was diagnosed. If he knew that we did even I was detected, he would simply kill me. He would think that I also wanted to kill him by passing this infection on to him. It was so unbearable not to tell him. I decided to go another clinic to get tested. I told him that I got something serious to tell you. He stared at me. I got scared. I said, nothing, I was just joking. It is now 5 years, I have been hiding the status from my nearest family members. However, my husband came to know my status. I asked him how he knew. He did not say anything. He seemed very frustrated. Natural!

Managing post-disclosure situations, stigma and discrimination is important for PLWHA. Many participants expressed hope that HIV/AIDS will soon be treated as any other diseases—with acceptance and understanding:

> I don't want to remain being ashamed of myself; denying myself. Secrecy with my status in fact declines my confidence. I do not want to be afraid of anything. But I cannot. I do not want to live in confinement anymore. I want to be as I was; I do not want to live in a split personality.

The feelings PLWHA experienced before disclosing are mixed: doubt, worry, hurt, acceptance and courage. There is doubt about the decision to disclose or not to disclose, who to disclose to and when. The worry is about whether they should speak out and what people were going to do with the information. The experience of being hurt sometimes motivated them to speak out. However, when acceptance takes place, they are more prepared to talk. Many of them stated that they had accepted their situation, irrespective of the complications attached to being diagnosed as HIV positive.

Primarily, personal reasons were the principal factors that influenced the decision to disclose. Some participants disclosed their status because they realized that they should break the silence: 'Until or unless we disclose, we do not know about the reactions from the family members, community members or relatives. This is why we have to disclose. Hiding things won't provide any solution.' Economic factors often also influence decisions: 'We have to seek medical treatment here. We cannot go out of the country. We have to confess to the doctors about our status, otherwise we cannot get medical treatment'. Some considered disclosure as a learning opportunity, as it helps others to be careful about their behaviour and not to make the same mistakes.

On the other hand, refusal to disclose was a result of previous experiences about how others were treated. Anxiety, denial and comfort in keeping their illness a secret were stated as reasons for not disclosing. Many expressed concerns about confidentiality, believing that once they disclosed to one individual, the information would be given to others without their consent. The fear that their families would be stigmatized by the community also influenced this decision. Fear of being ridiculed, rejected and blamed for having the disease creates a strong barrier to disclosure.

Disclosure in the Asian context poses additional challenges, due in part to cultural barriers. There are fundamental differences in the factors that influence the decision to disclose, such as collectivist versus individualist notions. In the West, researchers generally find that infected persons decide to disclose primarily for individual reasons, whereas in the Asian context, PLWHA do not disclose their HIV status for collective reasons, such as the fear that this would bring disgrace and shame to the family. Further, in the South Asian context, health issues are not frequently discussed within families. In addition, the decision to disclose is also influenced by the emotional need for self-protection.

Fear of stigma and internalization of stigma are not visible elements. When PLWHA feel shame and guilt for their infection and blame themselves, this means they have internalized the stigma. This is, of course, a social construct and may lead PLWHA to have low self-esteem or believe that they should be punished. As a result, they may choose not to attend social gatherings, take counselling or adhere to medication and stick to self-imposed isolation. These circumstances generate frustration which leads them to consider quitting jobs or becoming reluctant to apply for a promotion. There is evidence that they avoid going to hospitals and decide to remain single. As one participant stated:

> I am not a Canadian, my color is different from them, I am infected with HIV, I am poor. I feel I am nowhere in the world. I am scared of people. I was chased one day by one of my neighbors. I reported to the police. But nothing happened. Nothing changed, nothing.

Disclosure: Exemplar of Consequences

It is legally binding for a person to disclose their serostatus to sexual partners before engaging in unprotected sex that may pose a 'significant risk' of HIV transmission. What does 'significant risk' mean? A combination of police and crown attorneys has applied a variety of existing laws to HIV sufferers for not disclosing their health status, since there are no HIV-specific crimes under Canadian law. Debates about disclosure and the law are ongoing. The Supreme Court has been going through the legislation involving disclosure laws. This process was initiated following two cases in Quebec and Manitoba where PLWHA were acquitted of criminal charges after concealing their statuses from partners. Canada has witnessed one of the highest levels of prosecution for nondisclosure (Grant 2011). The case of Cuerrier has sparked the debate:

> Cuerrier tested positive in August 1992. He was advised by the public health nurse to practice safe sex and disclose the status to sex partners. He lived in a small community and declined to disclose. He was in a relationship, and began unprotected sex frequently. His partner did not ask specifically about HIV but they discussed about STDs. Cuerrier mentioned about his previous HIV test that came out negative and he hid his latest test result. The partner said at trial that she knew the risks of unprotected sex, including HIV and other STDs. A few months later, both Cuerrier and partner had HIV-antibody tests. He tested HIV-positive; she tested HIV-negative. Both were told of Cuerrier's infection, and advised to use condoms for sex. They continued having unprotected sex for 15 months. The partner later testified that: (i) she loved Cuerrier and did not want to lose him; (ii) as they had already had unprotected sex, she felt she was probably already infected; (iii) however, she would not have had sex with Cuerrier had she known his HIV status at the outset. At the time of trial, she tested HIV-negative. A few months later, Cuerrier began a sexual relationship with another one. After their first sexual encounter, she told him she was afraid of diseases, but did not specifically mention HIV. Cuerrier did not tell her he was HIV-positive. No condom was used for about half of their 10 sexual encounters. The new partner then discovered that Cuerrier was HIV-positive and confronted him, at which point he said he was sorry and should have told her. She was not infected. (Aidslaw 1999)

In 1998, the Supreme Court ruled that those who do not allow an opportunity for informed consent by hiding their viral infection expose their sex partners to 'significant risk of serious bodily harm', even if transmission does not occur. As a result, infected persons could be held criminally liable on a range of charges including assault, aggravated assault, sexual assault, attempted murder or even murder. Counterarguments suggest that with regular antiviral medication or use of condoms, the risk of infection could be lowered. There are further arguments over whether an infected person who is not sexually active should be treated the same way as a sexually active person. Grant (2011) argues that in R. v. Cuerrier, the court could not have foreseen all possible factors that could determine whether a risk of serious bodily harm is significant or did it foresee the extent to which any threat of transmitting HIV could be seen as significant in future cases. Some factors such as viral load and the type of sexual activity have come to play a significant role in such cases. Condom use was the primary means of decreasing the likelihood of transmission (HIV/AIDS News 2007); in recent cases, the courts have considered viral load in assessing the degree of risk presented by an accused. Thus, viral load should not be taken into account until a full understanding of its effect on rates of transmission has been acquired (see Chap. 2). The nature of sexual activity is another important risk factor. Oral sex, for example, is considered low risk. In case of Cuerrier, the crown acknowledged that charges would not have been laid for oral sex alone (Grant 2011).

In 1998, the development of the law of assault in Canada took an interesting turn. In that year, the Supreme Court ruled that disclosure of HIV status is required by criminal law before a PLWHA engages in sexual activity that poses a 'significant risk' of transmitting HIV (Symington 2010). While every HIV infection is regrettable and it is always desirable to avoid exposing others to this risk, whether the criminal law of assault can appropriately be applied to the issue of HIV exposure is a controversial question. Is it helpful to categorize otherwise consensual sexual activities as assaults when disclosure does not take place? What impact does the criminalization of HIV exposure have on PLWHA and on HIV prevention, treatment, care and support? Does the criminalization of HIV exposure protect women from harm? Is the trend towards criminalization of HIV exposure an appropriate response or an extreme manifestation of 'AIDS panic'?

In the decade since the Supreme Court issued its judgment in the Cuerrier case, at least 110 persons in Canada have been charged for failing to disclose their HIV-positive status prior to engaging in sexual activities (Grant 2011). From the mid-2000s onwards, there has been a marked escalation in the use of criminal law with respect to nondisclosure. Today, the central question is whether the legal obligation to disclose applies with respect to protected sex and lower-risk sexual activities (i.e. protected sex, oral sex) or only to unprotected intercourse. In several cases, trial courts have considered whether a 'significant risk' of HIV transmission existed in circumstances where condoms were used (Grant 2011).

Twelve years on after the Cuerrier case, there remains little evidence to support the claim that criminal charges for failing to disclose HIV status contribute to prevention by deterring PLWHA from nondisclosure or practising unprotected sex. Any preventative effect that criminal prosecution can have is minimal. Rarely are charges made in an ongoing relationship; rather, they are generally made only after the relationship ends. Therefore, the only realistic possibility of some prevention benefit from criminal is through deterrence. That is, it is hoped that the fact that nondisclosure is a criminal act where there is a significant risk of transmission will cause PLWHA to disclose their HIV-positive status or—in the absence of disclosure—to take steps to ensure they do not put their partners at a significant risk of HIV infection. However, embedded in this hope is an assumption that disclosure of HIV status leads sexual partners to change their sexual practices and either engage only in lower-risk sexual activities, consistently use protection or refrain from sexual activity altogether.

Chapter 5
Vulnerability and Resilience in Living with HIV/AIDS

The previous chapter analyzed the respondents' experiences about stigma and discrimination. This chapter describes the structures, processes and circumstances in which stigma is endured. The discussion emphasizes mental health outcomes when discrimination, stigmatization and xenophobia combine to humiliate PLWHA and analyzes their strength of resilience and coping mechanisms while facing stigma and discrimination.

It is pertinent to begin with the dynamics of vulnerability to abuse at different levels and demonstrate how resilient PLWHA are in the face of these difficulties. Before we analyze the resilience and the vulnerabilities generated by stigmatized treatment, we conceptualize the terms by putting stigma into context. Edward and Warelow (2005) discuss resilience as people's coping skills that foster the adaptation of adverse events, such as those associated with the problem of mental illness. According to Edward and Warelow (2005), emotional intelligence is often discussed in the context of resilient behaviour demonstrated by individuals in the face of adversity. Emotional resilience is the ability to 'identify, express, and understand emotions; to incorporate emotions into thought; and to normalize both positive and negative emotions' (Matthews et al. 2002). Resilience provides a person with self-confidence to handle complex issues, develop self-reliance and remain committed to a particular goal. This is particularly important for a person facing stigmatization or discrimination. In line with this, Brodkin and Coleman (1996) note that a person who is resilient has intrinsic power to bounce back from a problem that might otherwise lead them towards depression. However, resilience, according to Tusaie and Dyer (2004), rests on the interplay between the individual and their broader environment.

Coping strategies are temporary responses that individuals, households and communities adopt in order to avert a negative effect. In the AIDS literature, coping strategies aim at maintaining or improving household food security, raising and supplementing income and alleviating the loss of labour (Mutangadura et al. 1999). The level of resilience to the impact of AIDS differs across households and is influenced by several factors. These include the livelihood system, available production

A.A. Ullah, A.S. Huque, *Asian Immigrants in North America with HIV/AIDS*,
DOI 10.1007/978-981-287-119-0_5

options, resource endowment at the onset of the crisis and the households' capability to exploit these resources (Davies 1996). Gender is another important factor determining differences in the capacity to persist or adapt (Moser 1996). Women are particularly vulnerable to the impact of AIDS because of their limited access to assets and resources, bargaining power, lower levels of education and weaker economic status in general.

Actual levels of resilience are difficult to measure in absolute terms and can only be studied through proxy indicators. Because different factors contribute to resilience, no single proxy indicator can capture the totality of resilience (Carpenter and Brock 2004). A variety of different indicators are thus needed to adequately represent resilience to AIDS impacts, such as stability in livelihood assets, outcome, the capacity and level of interest in change or adapting to a new situation.

Judgment on resilience to AIDS impacts is often made by comparing quantitative snapshots of the household asset-base and household livelihood strategies before and after the death of a core adult member. Several household surveys undertaken in the mid-1990s (see World Bank 1997; Ainsworth et al. 1998) indicated various degrees of household resilience and recovery of consumption levels following an AIDS-related death in the household. 'Vulnerability is the flipside of resilience and attempts to describe the proneness of people, households and communities to an acute fall in the level of certain variables or livelihood outcomes' (Ellis 2003). Generally, vulnerability is the likelihood of having a negative impact on the overall well-being of an infected person or their family (Barnett and Whiteside 2002; Loevinsohn and Gillespie 2003).

Resilience Factors and Stigma

Vulnerability can be broadly categorized into two streams: social and biological. Social vulnerability refers to multiple stressors such as abuse and exclusion to which people are exposed. Biological vulnerability refers to the possibility of contracting additional infections, such as tuberculosis. Resilience has various meanings, but often refers to the ability to withstand external shocks and recover from it (Adger 2000). However, it has two distinct connotations when put in the context of HIV/AIDS. 'From an emotional or psychological dimension, resilience to AIDS means the ability to accept one's status, endure pain, stay positive and see beyond the illness' (Kotoh 2008). From a material or economic perspective, resilience refers to the responses adopted by individuals in order to avoid the worst impacts of AIDS (Loevinsohn and Gillespie 2003). Resilience is important in the face of adversities. Individuals may enhance their ability to overcome adversity by being able to share challenges with family members. 'The tendency towards shame and blame is reduced if the family is able to view a dilemma as 'normal'' (Walsh 2003).

The conceptualization of resilience continues to evolve. This emerges in the face of adversity and challenge (Hawley 2000; Block 1971; Block and Block 1980; Garmezy 1991; Garmezy et al. 1984; Patterson 2002). Many studies describe resilience as a 'personality trait of an individual, however some researches define resilience from a process-oriented perspective' (Ganong and Coleman 2002; Walsh 2003:23).

Resilience is fostered by shared facilitative beliefs that increase options for problem solving, healing and growth (Walsh 2003). A large number of researches suggest that a positive outlook has a significant role in coping with stress, recovering from crises and overcoming barriers (Seligman and Csikszentmihalyi 2000). Highly functional individuals were found to hold a more optimistic view of life than those with a negative outlook on life. An individual with a positive outlook can accept what is beyond their control and cannot be changed and understand the difference between what is and what is not possible (Walsh 2003). 'Resilience is strengthened by connectedness which is manifested in mutual support, collaboration and a commitment to face challenges together' (Walsh 2003). The role of the family in this regard is crucial because, according to McCubbin (2001), family connectedness (bonds of unity in a family system, trust, support etc.,) and family cohesion are significant factors in enhancing resilience.

The experience of shock, pain and loss is an inevitable part of life. The consequences can be both short and long term. The way they are dealt with has a significant impact on long-term life experiences. In our practical life, we see that some people can maintain complete tranquility in the event of a huge mental shock, while some fall apart. In order to be resilient, an individual must possess certain qualities such as intelligence, self-confidence, trust, self-image, self-esteem, communication skills, courage, competence and capacity. This is particularly important because the ability to cope in the face of adversity depends on the resilience of an individual. It does not alleviate stress, but it reduces psychological distress. Some individuals are naturally endowed with these abilities, while others develop resilience from the environment in which they face adversity (Friedli 2009).

In countries where the HIV/AIDS epidemic is widespread, populations considered to be the most at risk of infection are generally groups neglected from social, economic and epidemiological point of view. Consequently, very little effort has been made to provide HIV interventions for these groups who, in turn, are often excluded from mainstream HIV prevention services. Transmission rates and HIV prevalence among the high-risk groups can be up to 10 times higher than other groups in society. This can be explained to a large extent by the extent of discrimination, stigmatization and even hatred perpetrated towards these groups. Mounting social and political rejection has magnified the notion that particular groups, such as MSM, are a class apart from the rest of society. The same pattern is reflected in public policy and legislation in the form of sodomy laws or the criminalization of homosexuality and has fuelled acts of violence against specific groups in many countries.

The level of isolation and vulnerability of refugees is multiplied if they become HIV positive. They will suffer the stigma and rejection reserved for other at-risk populations both from society and within their own households. Ultimately, as stigma and discrimination against them continue to grow, access to HIV prevention and treatment decreases, leaving both refugees and society at large increasingly vulnerable. The sheer scale of the HIV/AIDS pandemic with its progressive impacts on refugees is the basis for targeted funds, policies and national strategies. However,

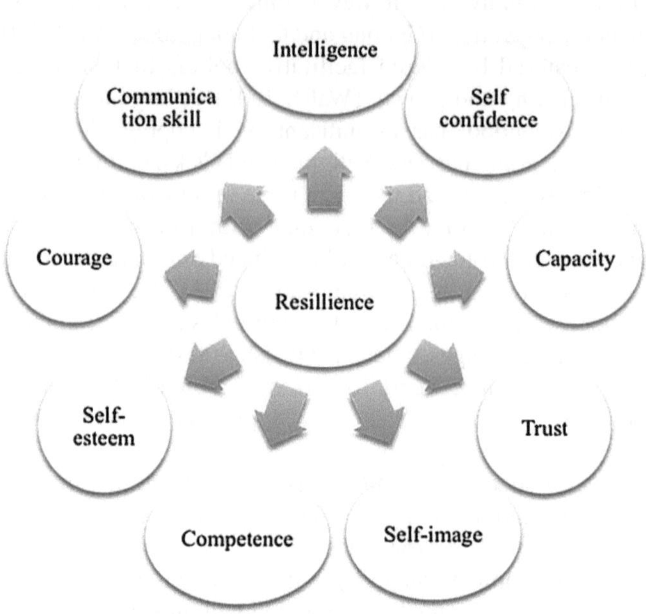

Fig. 5.1 Components of resilience

preexisting and ongoing comorbid conditions such as poverty and violence continue to affect this community and adversely influence the outcome of interventions targeted for HIV/AIDS care, treatment and prevention (Fig. 5.1).

Mainstreaming an approach to the measurement of vulnerability and resilience of refugees affected by HIV/AIDS allows us to track the impacts of their contexts on the key domains of their functioning and surviving. The incorporation of the psychosocial indicators in the study of HIV/AIDS and refugee populations underscores the importance of psychological functioning and social inclusion as critical measures of the response of governments to the welfare of those affected by HIV/AIDS, particularly children. HIV/AIDS infection often coincides with a decline into worsening poverty, with the loss of economic safety nets and adult wage earners, forcing many children to withdraw from school and take up increased adult responsibilities for home care and work. Although families and communities remain the front line of support for PLWHA, increasing strains on social networks and community resources due to the pandemic leave many PLWHA abandoned and vulnerable to exploitation.

A wide range of emotions could be observed among the participants. Some were falling apart, while many others were very resilient. Many infected persons have devised techniques to endure the challenges they encounter relating to their infection. It was in fact clear from the interviews that a resilient person can lead a better life than a non-resilient person. The ability to manage their livelihood makes a person more tolerant, patient and capable of overcoming trauma and hardship.

> I was not mentally prepared about how our society treats me in this case. I was thinking about my life only: how short or how long etc. As time passed, I realized, the society I am living in is not so simple, not so easy, nor so sympathetic and aware. I became a foreign element in my own society, my own community. I broke down mentally. I was trying to figure out the best options for me. Is suicide the best option as opposed to staying isolated or leaving the community for another? I decided that it was my life, and I have to take care of my own life. There will be difficulties in life; we are human being we can face it. We have to face it, this is why we are humans and not animals.

Another participant shared his thought:

> I believe I am not alone. All the people may leave you, still you are with yourself, and your God. God will never leave you. If you can hold on to your belief, you feel that you are the strongest one in the world. God is testing us by giving this disease and sufferings. This is given to us, not to animals.

It appears that the participant turned to spirituality as a source of courage. This may be an effective technique for resilience, and in this way, religion is receiving growing attention in efforts to manage psychological distress.

Resilient people generally look for alternatives, options and solutions rather than resigning to distress:

> I was surfing the internet, and found some useful information posted there. Obviously, there is some useless material, but most of it is useful. I would call the internet a 'secret doctor or counselor'. I have learnt how to manage trauma, stigma and discrimination. I learnt that there is stigma in every corner of the world. We cannot flee them but we can manage them. I realized that the infection is my problem, not of others.

While this participant seemed to be resilient, he/she chose to stay at home and search the Internet rather than going out and seeking counsel from a medical practitioner. He/she demonstrated both resilience and non-resilience, by attempting to increase her/his knowledge and understanding and also by confining herself/himself at home. Family and community support are very important in providing buffers against negative outcomes.

Conceptual Frameworks

Not much research can be found that deal with manifestations of resilience among people living with HIV/AIDS. This study was informed by a conceptual framework which incorporates resilience theory. While there is no universally accepted definition of resilience, 'it is seen as successful adaptation to negative life events, trauma, stress, and other forms of risk and as having the capacity to cope with significant change' (Greene and Conrad 2002). Emlet et al. (2011) has offered an interesting framework to measure and explain resilience. Acceptance by self, optimism, generativity and a will to live are primary components of Emlet's framework.

Very few infected persons acknowledged that acceptance was central to overcoming the negative effects of HIV/AIDS. As stated earlier, not all respondents demonstrated acceptance; however, many of those who did were generally more resilient. 'I try to realize that it is my life and I have to take care of myself and enjoy life as long as I can. I really have to value my life. I see no problem seeing myself as what I am. I accept it'.

Resilience is about maintaining future-mindedness, feeling upbeat about life and remaining hopeful about one's continued well-being (Emlet et al. 2011). How is it possible to maintain one's optimism when society rejects an infected person? Many studies point out that health and successful coping with depression, despair and hopelessness are inextricably linked (Taylor 1991; Snyder et al. 1991). According to Scheier and Carver (1987), optimism can be described as a generalized belief in good outcomes. Optimism, as conceived by Scheier and Carver (1987), is related to ego strength and internal control (Pruyser 1986).

> I had a lot of plans. I will pursue my plans no matter what happens in my life. There are many elements in the society that causes morale to decline. However, it is the person who has to turn his/her life for the better. I always think that there may be many people living in worse condition than mine. This is also a huge motivation for going ahead. I know hope is only our medication. This hope could not be borrowed; we have to generate it from within.

Proactive approaches and positive attitudes towards life are very significant in managing stigma. A positive attitude towards life can give fresh hope to the PLWHA. 'If we undermine ourselves, how can we expect to be respected by others? We have to be strong, and believe that we are part of the society and the world. What we are carrying is also a part of the social phenomenon.'

Many of them said when they lose hope, it feels like they have lost the battle:

> No part of life is problem-free. We just have to be able to get over those problems. Mutual respect and love are important. In most cases we do not see it, which is obviously painful. I understand that frustration kills a person. We should just wipe off our frustrations from life. I guess I will be alright. I always think I am the same as all others around me. I am no different.

The desire for a long life is particularly important for those who become frustrated. The majority of respondents were found to cherish their will to live long. One participant used this to develop a positive outlook towards the infection: 'Look, people try to survive in wars, natural disasters, flood, famine, then why not us? This is less than a cyclone or flood. Cyclone washes away lives in moments. This disease progresses slowly, gives option to have medications, give option to live a healthy life, then you can stay strong for long'.

Another participant stated:

> The world is like a cycle. People will pass away to offer space to those who are coming to the world. But the only question is how graceful or disgraceful is the death. This is obviously determined by the society. Therefore, we have to make changes in the society. If we can take this disease as normal, why can the others not do the same, especially when they are not the direct victims.

Generativity is one of the most significant contributions made by Emlet and colleagues (2011) to the study of HIV/AIDS. This phenomenon emphasizes the role

PLWHA can play as educators. PLWHA know how heavy the burden of this disease is, and therefore, they can be the best educators for others in the same situation. The feelings of responsibility and empathy for others come from generativity (Emlet et al. 2011).

Some of the respondents feel that they should do something for the next generation. One of the participants said: 'We are the people who can pass accurate information on to them. Nobody else can understand the situation as well as we do'. Some think that they should be recruited as educators. However, many of them showed no interest in taking up the role of an educator. When asked why, they said, 'Who will listen to us? Who will respect what we say? We know most people look down upon us'. When asked what the younger generation should understand about the difficulties PLWHA experience, participants suggested, 'nobody knows the woes we are going through better than us relating to this infection. We can help make them understand'.

Emlet and colleagues (2011) also highlighted the concept of self-management. It involves self-care, which includes 'taking medications as prescribed on time, making regular doctor visits, maintaining a healthy balance of diet and exercise, personal responsibility (i.e. refraining from drugs and risky sex and too much alcohol), and practicing self-control' (Emlet et al. 2011). Self-management is crucial for living a healthy life. In case of HIV infection, people experience isolation and stigma first. In the face of such exclusion, self-management helps to start life afresh. Obviously, counselling and appropriate management techniques are required after the diagnosis. Therefore, proactive efforts by PLHWA are extremely important.

According to Emlet et al. (2011), another aspect of self-management relates to efforts to exert control over the disease condition. This includes knowing more about the disease and becoming involved in health promotion activities to be able to cope physically at a higher level. 'I do jog almost every day. The day I cannot go out I try to do some light exercise at home. This gives me a lot of confidence.'

Support systems including close personal relationships, memberships in recreational activities and/or HIV/AIDS-related support groups/organizations are critical for living with HIV. In some cases, the family has been a major source of support in managing the challenges of HIV/AIDS. Some families had difficulty accepting a member's HIV diagnosis. This apparently depends on the ties and bonds that exist among family members. There are cases where spouses abandoned their partners after learning of their partner's diagnosis.

> I believed family is my first and last resort. I can share everything. Still I was not sure if I should disclose my status to them. In fact, my parents knew it before I disclosed. I guess it was from my doctor. I was surprised. My parents reassured me that I should not worry. This is part of life. But we have to know how to live with it. That gave me so much consolation and confidence.

For some of the sufferers, their HIV status provided an opportunity to reshape problematic relationships. However, one has to be very optimistic to expect that relationships will improve after disclosing HIV status. Emlet and colleagues (2011) go on to add that 'although relationships with family and partners were a profound source of support, the informants' remarks revealed that relational living extended beyond individuals with close emotional ties'. Social connectedness with sexual partners, friends or groups gives meaning to the lives of PLWHA and makes them feel valued as individuals. This enables them to engage in relationships on an equal footing. Many researchers emphasized that involvement in some kind of support group is very helpful because it broadens the social network available to PLWHA.

Intersectionality and the Implications

Women from visible minorities may experience discrimination in a different way than men from the same minority group. Similarly, men from racial minority groups may experience discrimination that would not be faced by nonminority males or women of the same background. This happens because people may experience distinct forms of stereotyping based on a combination of race and gender. An intersectional approach takes into account the historical, social and political context facing an individual and recognizes their unique experience based on the intersection of all relevant grounds. It concedes the complexity of how people experience discrimination and recognizes that it may be unique.

Conceptualization of the term intersectionality and the intersectional framework are important in this study because this book aims to review the intersections of race, class and gender. It is relevant because the level of stigma and discrimination varies across race, class and gender (Ralston 2012; Steinberg 2007). According to Crenshaw (1996) and Phoenix and Pamela (2006), intersectionality as a concept has occupied significant space in the study of culture, gender and psychosocial realities. It was first evoked by feminists to challenge singular categories of oppression. For instance, black women were oppressed in different ways compared to white women. People living with HIV/AIDS can be thought of as living with multiple forms of stigma, rather than one, that serve to marginalize them in different ways. Understanding race, class, origin, sexuality and gender orientation as social structures implies that PLWHA are placed on a power hierarchy. The idea that power causes inequality is a major element in conceptualizing race, class and gender as social structures (Andersen and Hill Collins 2010).

The traits of discrimination and stigma are social constructs. For example, the construction of the masculine identity differs according to race, class and sexuality. The intersectional approach to understanding stigma produces a certain construction of masculinity that helps people formulate certain views of those they see as different. Therefore, race, class, gender and sexuality matter because they influence the social construction of attributes, thus determining what traits are to be stigmatized. Stigma and intersectionality are closely intertwined. Masculinity is also socially constructed and may mean something different for a Caucasian upper-middle class male than a Caucasian working class male. The construction of masculinity for the gay Caucasian upper-middle class male might be significantly different than that for a heterosexual Afro-Canadian male living in poverty (Ralston 2012). Further, the stigma that is created by being a male victim of sexual assault could differ across race, class and sexuality categories because the construction of masculinity could ultimately be different. It is therefore important to examine how masculinity is constructed based on race, class, gender and sexuality in order to see how the stigma created against a male victim of sexual assault varies depending on the construction of masculinity.

Xenophobia and the Role of Resilience

Xenophobia is one of the most damaging vulnerabilities migrant and refugee population face. In the Western world, xenophobia may not be visible in the public sphere, but this does not necessarily mean that xenophobia or xenophobic violence does not exist. It exists everywhere in different forms and scales and is not always visible. Xenophobic violence is one common form to which refugees, asylum seekers and migrants fall victim. They may also be victims of related forms of violence, such as that motivated by race, religion, sexual orientation or gender. How does this relate to HIV stigma? Gilmour (1994) argues that Canada has a long history of hate-motivated violence towards racial or ethnic minorities and raises questions about incidents of hate-motivated violence directed against members of visible minorities because of their race or colour of their skin. Similar to Lewis (1992), Gilmour emphasizes that systemic discrimination against members of visible minorities exists in Canada. After the riots in Toronto in the spring of 1992, the Ontario government realized that 'while every visible minority experienced the wounds of systemic discrimination throughout Southern Ontario, the root kind of racism to be dealt with was anti-Black racism' (Lewis 1992:2). Statistics Canada (2012) reports that the rate of hate crime in Canada increased substantially, as shown in Fig. 5.2.

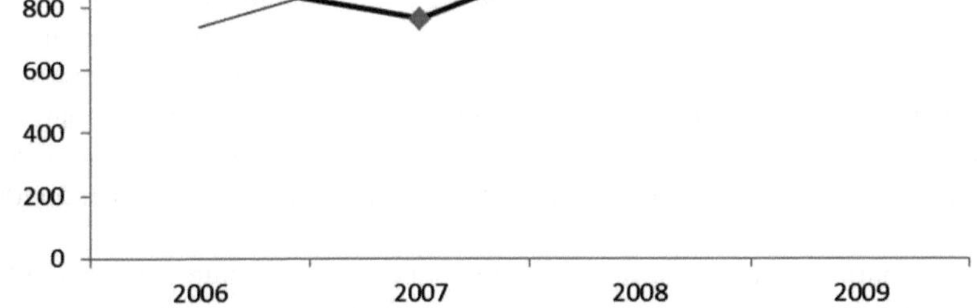

Fig. 5.2 Trend of hate crime in Canada

This study focuses on refugees and immigrants who are HIV sufferers. However, it does not assume that all refugees or all HIV sufferers are victims of xenophobic violence. Rather, even in places where xenophobic violence is not apparent, refugees with HIV positive are still extremely vulnerable. Interestingly, although there is substantial emphasis on xenophobic violence occurring in South Africa, there is not much data available on xenophobia in the Western world. It can be argued that xenophobia exists in Canada, but it is expressed under the guise of social chaos blamed on the presence of refugees and migrants. Countries across the OSCE region are also experiencing racist incidents of an increasingly violent nature. Physical assaults, arson attacks and murders have become the sad reality of progressively more diverse societies (OSCE 2011). OSCE countries are concerned about the growing number of hate crimes and have called on political leaders to speak out against all forms of violence motivated by racial hatred or xenophobia and to act responsibly and refrain from providing simplistic explanations (with racist, xenophobic or anti-Semitic connotations) for complex social, political and economic problems or phenomena (OSCE 2011). The following excerpt is a good example of hate crime.

> When my friend called me for a tour of the harbor, I happily agreed. It has been a long time since we saw each other. After I quit my job, I saw him once in the past two years, and was looking forward to seeing him. We were joined by three more people on the way, and I did not know them. When we got to the harbor they began to ridicule me. I kept silent, but became angry when they crossed the limit. One of them kicked me hard and uttered obscenities. I later realized that my friend had set this up to ridicule me.

Asked about the motivation behind this kind of behaviour, the respondent added 'it might be due to my colour. I remember my initial days with him at my work place. He declined to exchange simple pleasantries. We became friends later on. This is not just discrimination or stigma. I believe they do this because we were not born in this country'. Clearly, the respondent was not able to define this violence as xenophobia; however, the treatment he received was an example of xenophobic violence. Such cases are generally under-reported. When asked if he reported the above incident to police, the respondent replied, 'No. There was no point reporting it to police. I would rather not augment his anger. I was also ashamed to report' (Fig. 5.3).

Under-reporting of xenophobic violence and hate crime remains a problem everywhere. Victims often do not report crimes against the perpetrators for a number of reasons, including fear of the police or a lack of conviction that the authorities will take their cases seriously. In some instances, victims may not identify the crime against them as a hate crime, either because the experience is so common among people in such circumstances or because they are unaware that a crime with a hate motive is more serious than the same crime without such a motive. 'A hate crime that is associated to one's sexual orientation is an incident that is often not reported due to the degradation associated with being ostracized based on an individual's sexual preference' (Espiritu 2004).

Discrimination and stigma against foreigners often emanate from xenophobia which is an attitudinal orientation of hostility against and strong fear of people who came from a different country, is spreading worldwide and is primarily being

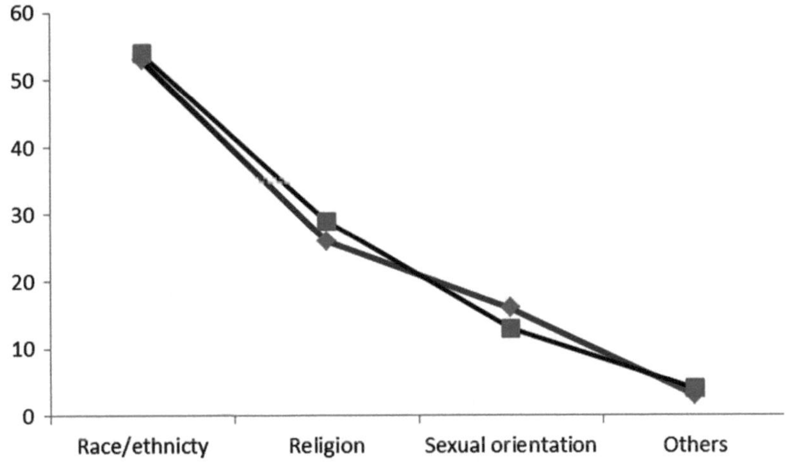

Fig. 5.3 Hate crimes, by type of motivation, 2008 and 2009

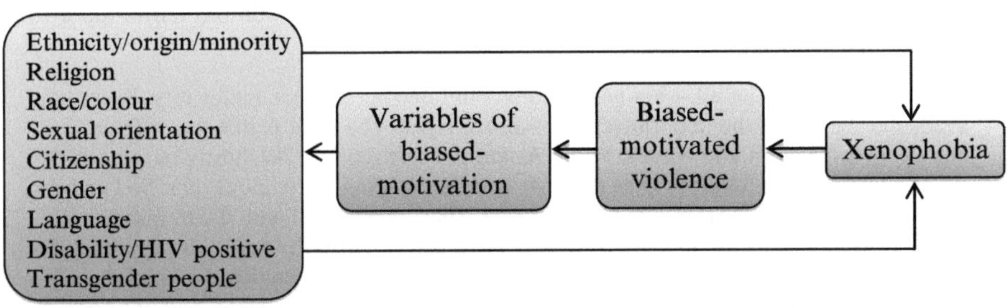

Fig. 5.4 Xenophobic violence dynamics (Source: Compiled from OSCE 2011)

directed towards migrants and refugees (WCAR 2001). This is particularly important because xenophobic orientations add further trauma to the existing burden facing PLWHA. Migrants and refugees are frequently subjected to unequal treatment, unequal opportunities, discriminatory behaviour and racism (Grant 2010). PLWHA generally tend to be highly defensive, to be overly protective of themselves and to harbour a desire to stay hidden.

The connection between xenophobia and HIV-related stigma, and discrimination-related violence cannot be readily demonstrated. A deeper analysis is required to demonstrate the connections. Absolute HIV-related stigma is different from a mix of HIV-related stigma and hate-induced violence. Hutton (2009) argues that hate crime is tantamount to bias motivation, that is, a distinct crime. The expressions of violence towards a native and a non-native HIV-infected person are different from one case to the other. Obviously, non-natives are treated worse than the natives. The differential treatment between natives and non-natives would be the outcome of xenophobia. Hence, xenophobia is highly relevant for studying HIV-related stigma and discrimination (Fig. 5.4).

There is no evidence of any research that treats physical assault resulting from HIV infection, stigmatization and discrimination separately. Although some research on physical assault towards PLWHA was conducted in the African context, it is rare in the North American context. However, some studies were conducted in the 1990s, and these can be used as points of reference for the Canadian case. Violence or physical assault towards PLWHA, especially gender-based violence, has serious implications for the physical health of those who were weakened by the virus and sought treatment. Researchers confirm that violence may occur any time during the entire HIV trajectory; however, a diagnosis of HIV infection may trigger violence at the time of disclosure. Abbott and colleagues (1995) added that women may not wish to know the results of HIV test due to their perceived fear that disclosing their status may result in physical violence and expulsion from their home. They further found that 54 % of women with HIV infection had been assaulted, threatened or made to feel afraid by male partners at some time in their lives. This situation may have changed somewhat over the years, but more in-depth study is required to confirm this assertion. Zierler and colleagues (2000) found that in 1994, an estimated 6.6 million men and 5 million women were assaulted annually due to HIV status. They further revealed that most of these incidents of HIV-related violence come from their partners and spouses.

> I am not stupid. Not at all. I am not hated by only one person, one nationality. Everyone avails themselves of the opportunity to insult us, right? The truth is that the difference is clear between Asians and whites. While Asians ridicule us, they do mostly because it is, they think, related to religion. They think we were not abiding by religious rites. So I understand, Asians blame us from that point of view. They sympathize with us. In many cases, they pray to God for us, ask forgiveness to God on our behalf. I mean by 'our' those are infected. The case is different for the natives. They hate us because they consider us as importers of this infection. They hate us because they think we (immigrants, refugees) are adding burden to their economy and health services. We are taking up their jobs. I understand this. When Asians ridicule us, we feel some affection, but when natives ridicule us, I can sense their anger and hatred.

It is important to articulate the fact that there may be hatred towards the disease, but there may be love for the patients. Interestingly, they [PLWHA from Asian] consider 'scolding' from Asians as blessings. When they meet some elderly relatives, they ask the patients to seek help and forgiveness from God. Although this is painful for the patients, they understand that there is love beneath the surface. Some participants believed that these people have the right to ridicule and scold them.

It is widely recognized that destination countries have experienced rising antiforeigner hostility and racism, which have compounded discrimination based on HIV status. Crush and Ramachandran (2009) argue that as migration increases, many developing countries institute restrictive and anti-migrant policies influenced by xenophobia (Crush and Ramachandran 2009; WCAR 2001).

Generally, there are two distinct camps of scholarly opinion on xenophobia. The first group draws on sociobiological approaches, in which xenophobia is seen as a natural reaction to outsiders. The second group, exemplified by Allport's 'nature of contact' approach, argues that contact can result in greater harmony and understanding if four broad conditions are met. The conditions are that (a) groups in question should have or be perceived to have equal status, (b) contact should be effective to make groups work together, (c) the need for intergroup cooperation rather than competition must be emphasized and (d) authorities must support intergroup contact (Allport 2004:41). Pettigrew (1998) goes further, arguing that not all of Allport's conditions must be met for contact to have positive outcomes, and Legge (1995) states that variations in contact matter. McLaren (2002) suggests that contact between native and migrant populations can substantially ease levels of perceived threat (Allport 2004:42).

In many cases, hate crime is not considered criminal offence, and therefore, perpetrators cannot be punished (Perry 2003). In the city of Montreal in Canada in January 1993, 10 synagogues were attacked and defaced with swastikas and a Nazi slogan. At the time, the attacks were described as the worst acts of anti-Semitic vandalism in Quebec (Peritz 1993). In June of the same year, a Tamil who had left Sri Lanka to escape the ethnic conflict was attacked by three men. He was on his way home from work at a Toronto restaurant. Police confirmed that it was a racially motivated attack (Gilmour 1994; DiManno 1993). These events endorse our earlier argument that xenophobic violence in the Western world is not a rare phenomenon. It is not difficult to conjecture how badly an HIV patient could be treated.

The demographics of Canada have changed over decades; for example, the proportion of Asians in Canada has increased to outnumber Europeans. In order to recognize this reality, Canada has taken constitutional action and other legal steps. In 1988, the federal government passed the Canadian Multiculturalism Act, setting out a policy to promote the multicultural heritage of Canada (Gilmour 1994; Semenak 1989a; Rahman and Ullah 2012). However, despite having the legal protection in place, attacks against immigrants and refugees based on sexuality, race and religion continue. Petersen (1991) noted one Canadian legal commentator stated that queer-bashing is a social phenomenon of epidemic proportions (Petersen 1991).

Refugees and migrants from underdeveloped or low-income countries face more incidences of xenophobic violence than those from developed countries. However, this does not necessarily mean that xenophobia is less prevalent in developed countries. Xenophobia in developed or high-income countries may be more prevalent than in low-income countries. The particular religion or minority group to which one belongs has an impact on the level of xenophobic violence. Figure 5.5 describes how xenophobia and xenophobic violence play out at different levels. Statistics Canada (2012) presented some alarming data on racially motivated incidents in Canada. Afro-Canadians are the most commonly targeted racial group, while more than half of all hate crimes in Canada motivated by sexual orientation are violent. In 2006, about six in ten police-reported hate crimes were motivated by race/ethnicity, including colour and nationality (Statistics Canada 2012). Although xenophobia and related violence have increased, these are not evenly spread among victim groups.

A useful definition of AIDS-related stigma comes from the field of sociology:

> In conceptualization, stigma exists when the following interrelated components converge. In the first component, people distinguish and label human differences. In the second, dominant cultural beliefs link labeled persons to undesirable characteristics - to negative

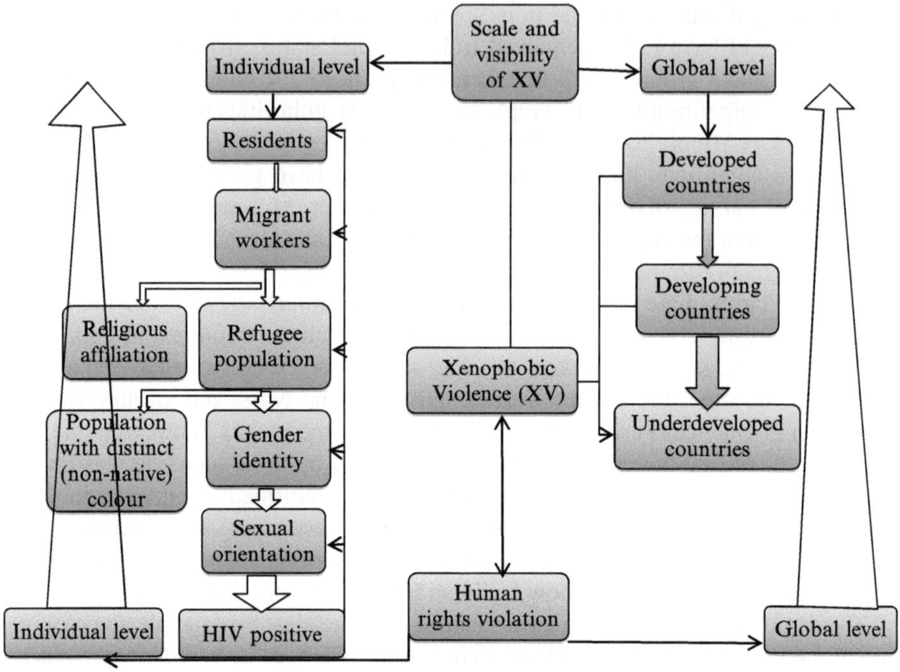

Fig. 5.5 Linkage between xenophobia and HIV positive and human rights

> stereotypes. In the third, labeled persons are placed in distinct categories so as to accomplish some degree of separation of "us" from "them." In the fourth, labeled persons experience status loss and discrimination that lead to unequal outcomes. Finally, stigmatization is entirely contingent on access to social, economic, and political power that allows the identification of differentness, the construction of stereotypes, the separation of labeled persons into distinct categories, and the full execution of disapproval, rejection, exclusion, and discrimination. (Link and Phelan 2001:367)

Human rights and stigma seem to be intertwined. Due to stigma, human rights of the PLWHA are often found to be violated in many spheres of life such as employment, housing and health and social services. According to AIDS CHAIC (2005), for instance, one-third of respondents of a research on HIV sufferers in Alberta reported being treated unfairly by employers or co-workers as a result of their HIV status. Their jobs were terminated, they were asked to quit or their hours of work were reduced. Some suggest that recent shootings (e.g. 2 June 2012 at Eaton Centre and 11 July 2012 at Danzig Street) in the Toronto area could be construed as race-related violence. In her article 'Racism in Canada', Douglas (2008) describes her frustration with the level of race-related violence by citing Mohanty (2003): 'global economic and political processes have become more brutal, exacerbating economic, racial, and gender inequalities' (Mohanty 2003:509). Hall suggests that renewed attention is necessary to minimize gendered racialization because in its myriad forms, 'racism enacts a violence which is psychological, physical and cultural' (1996:41).

An understanding of violence in any given society must be attained in the context of the historical relations. There is no denying that violence is a function of prejudicial relations that recall not only recent history but also the events related to nation-building.

It is relevant to describe Allport's (2004) analysis of the concept of scapegoating. Native people tend to vent their frustrations on a convenient target, such as migrants and refugee populations that produce negative and biased stereotypes. While it is well-known that xenophobia stems from fears of migrants being criminals and stealing jobs. The perceived danger posed by immigrants to cultural identity far outweighs other concerns related to safety and economic well-being. Some scholars see xenophobia as the direct consequence of uneven globalization; for example, materialist analysis proposes that xenophobic sentiments derive from real competition over limited resources (Sniderman and Hagendoorn 2007:53).

The current fragmented process of international migration and refugee status determination processes, and irregular migration status that may result from gaps in the two systems, can also lead to xenophobia. As argued in the World Conference Against Racism (WCAR 2001), irregular and unauthorized migration leads to exploitation and discrimination. Refugees are reluctant to seek or be provided police protection to address xenophobia or access to justice, which also impedes the ability of authorities to respond to xenophobia. Without comprehensive, human-centred and rights-based responses to refugee issues, xenophobia continues unabated (Fig. 5.6).

Xenophobia and treatment generated from it have grave and negative effects on the overall well-being of migrants and refugees. Crush and Ramachandran (2009) argued that xenophobia weakens the international human rights framework and threatens social order and social justice, thus decreasing protection for refugee populations. It also increases social inequality and creates an underclass of individuals facing discrimination. On a personal level, xenophobic treatment has long-term implications and erodes dignity, opportunities and the ability to live a normal life.

In discussing xenophobia, there is a tendency to discuss the case that particularly exemplifies its rise in South Africa in 2008. Xenophobic violence lasted for months and featured horrific, large-scale attacks on migrants (Crush and Ramachandran 2009),

Fig. 5.6 Interlink of xenophobia, racism and hate crime

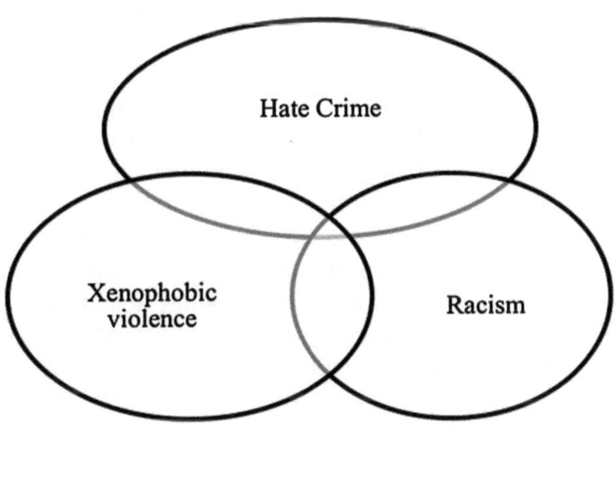

such as murder, rape, injury, robbery and theft. The violence was characterized by 'brutality, and flagrant disregard for the law or for the basic humanity of the victims and survivors of the violence' (Nyar 2011:18) displacing approximately 100,000 people and killing 62 (Hlatshwayo 2011). Incidents of violence in Canada may be no fewer in number, although more varied in form.

'We may very well be a tolerant nation, but this is hardly an admirable quality in and of itself because it does not indicate an unconditional embrace of difference; rather it suggests disingenuousness on the part of the dominant' (Douglas 2008:42). Douglas describes a number of examples of the brutal xenophobic violence in Canada, including the assault and drowning of South Asian teenager Reena Virk on 14 November 1997 in British Columbia and the 15 May 2006 arson death of Congolese refugee, Adela Etibako. Another example involves Laibar Singh, a Sikh man who suffered an aneurysm following his journey to attain refugee status. Singh's efforts to challenge deportation orders have produced a vitriol expressed on blogs that is supported by an indifferent dominant media. The second example relates to the 27 November 2007 remarks about immigrants by Bruce Allen, a member of Vancouver's Olympic Committee (VANOC). On CKNW, a local radio show, Allen told immigrants that if they do not like the 'rules', they should 'shut up and fit in or leave the country'. 'All of these articulations of racism and anti-immigrant violence expose the atmosphere of our everyday lives as one that contradicts claims that Canada is a nation that lives comfortably with its racial difference' (Douglas 2008:44).

Along with others, Nyar (2011) also attempted to link xenophobic attacks with poverty, unemployment, inequality and struggle for economic survival and their attendant consequences (Nyar 2011; Amisi et al. 2011; McConnell 2009). The South African incident is a reminder of how inequality could trigger xenophobia. Chapter 3 attempted to identify the pockets of poverty in Canada and discussed how it contributes to stigma, xenophobia and discrimination.

Crush and Ramachandran (2009) found that during the 2008 crisis in South Africa, the civil society offered short-term responses to suppressing violence. The fact that civil society organizations lost ground and returned to the status quo in their activities eventually, however, demonstrates the need for more comprehensive, planned and collaborative initiatives. Long-term programmes to alleviate social conditions such as poverty and unemployment must also be devised (Sinwell 2011; Everatt 2011). However, in Canada no such initiative has played any role in mitigating the suffering of PLWHA. One respondent stated: 'I am an infected person. Is it not a sufficient element do taunt me? Why am I asked about my origin? As if I have brought my disease from my origin country. It sounds like my disease is not a problem; rather my origin is a problem to them.'

Many scholars concluded that violence against HIV sufferer refugees and migrants will continue unless 'profound socio-economic and attitudinal changes occur' (Everatt 2011:17) and approaches to addressing xenophobia are pioneered. Xenophobia presents strong and deeply rooted challenges to refugees, and several approaches are recommended by scholars for addressing it. Policies that promote multiculturalism, respect for diversity and the rights and dignity of migrants can be the first step for reducing such hostility (WCAR 2001).

Canada is gradually losing its good image as a country of tolerance; for instance, recently a design for a new banknote depicting Canada's medical advancement was rejected by focus groups, who were dissatisfied with the ethnicity of the Asian-looking woman depicted in the design (Beeby 2012). The concerns expressed dumbfounded many people. Canada claims to be a tolerant and multicultural country. However, many people are concerned about the ethnic representation of an image on the banknote. Some people think the image shows a stereotype of Asians excelling in technology. Others feel that an Asian should not be the only ethnicity represented on banknotes. Some other people think that the banknotes reinforced the perception that the woman was Asian and 'racialized' (Beeby 2012). Bank of Canada immediately ordered the image redrawn, imposing what a spokesman called a 'neutral ethnicity' for the woman scientist who, now stripped of her 'Asian' features, appears on the circulating note. Her light features suggest her to be a Caucasian. There were several justifications for the modifications. But it may be fair to observe that the Bank replaced one 'racial image' with another.

Reaction to the proposed design for a banknote varied from focus groups varied by region. The Toronto groups were positive about the image of an Asian woman because 'it is seen to represent diversity or multiculturalism'. In Quebec, however, 'the inclusion of an Asian without representing any other ethnicities was seen to be contentious'. One person in Fredericton commented: 'The person on it appears to be of Asian descent which doesn't represent Canada. It is fairly ugly' (Beeby 2012). The 2006 census found that Canada's population included more than five million people from visible minority groups, of which 1.2 million were Chinese and another 240,000 with ancestry from Southeast Asia, including Vietnam, Cambodia, Malaysia and Laos. Now two important issues come to the fore. First, who decides that a Caucasian image is neutral? Secondly, why should other people of Asian origin accept this image as neutral?

Management of Stigma and Discrimination

Management of stigma and xenophobia is not possible in isolation; rather, it requires concerted efforts from government, civil society organizations, non-profit organizations and affected individuals. A human rights-based approach to protecting migrants and refugees from xenophobia through comprehensive anti-discrimination legislation should be devised at the local, national and international levels. Global, regional and national monitoring of the treatment of refugee population; national political leadership and the will to acknowledge and condemn xenophobia; public education; identification and critical analysis of xenophobic discourse in the media; and legislative solutions such as criminalization of xenophobia as hate speech (Crush and Ramachandran 2009) are some initiatives that can be considered (McConnell 2009).

Ross and colleagues (1994) found that issues of livelihood emerge continuously among PLWHA in the face of threats to physical and psychological well-being. They go on to argue that existential isolation—a fear of being rejected—may lead to anxiety and depression. The existential issues may involve spirituality and religious belief, which could be a major source of psychosocial support that may come from various sources. Traditionally, such support was provided by counsellors, social workers, healthcare workers, volunteers, friends and family. In particular, individual and supportive counselling can help patients come to terms with their HIV diagnosis and its impact on all aspects of their lives.

Similar to virus transmission, psychological effects also pass on from one generation to another. For example, families can be labelled as 'HIV family'. When HIV infects one partner in a relationship, both partners are affected. Cultural, social, biological and economic pressures make women more vulnerable to HIV infection than men. In some areas, the high prevalence of rape puts women or children at greater risk of acquiring HIV (Schweitzer et al. 2009). Many rape victims are subsequently forced to leave their village, or even the country, if possible, because of the social stigma of rape, leading them to seek refuge in Canada or other countries that accept refugees.

Within the family, females play the primary role of caregivers. However, when a female in the family is infected, she still appears as a caregiver, though she should be a care-receiver.

> We have been a nice family, with strong bond. It seems this disease has shattered the bond. I am often blamed by my brother for bringing shame to the family. I am blamed for the stress my parents are going through. My father sometimes stops talking to my mum and other siblings. Regardless of the reason for his sudden change in mood, I am held responsible.

Strong family bonds are an important factor for facing such high level of stress. However, family structure could be affected by this disease, and individual families may face changes in their political, cultural and religious contexts. This can contribute to social instability, including growing frustration within families, while of course the lack of social services and increased poverty may trigger social unrest and crime.

The experience of stigma and discrimination results in a confluence of physical, psychosocial, economic and health outcomes. Self-isolation, poverty and social exclusion are powerful obstacles to accessing healthcare services. They contribute to poor interactions with health providers, increased risk of infections and lower quality of life (Phelan et al. 2008). Once stereotypes and stigma are recognized, they can result in individuals being avoided, regarded as deviant and even blamed for engaging in immoral behaviour. This type of social environment can be devastating to vulnerable populations who suffer from stigmatized conditions. The implication is far-reaching for them because it can result in the internalization of self-blame:

> The first disclosure was made to one of my close friends, a member of my community i.e. he is also a gay. I did it in a good faith that he would understand my distressed situation. Unfortunately, he rejected me outright. It was also a new experience for me to know that homosexuals could also be homophobic. That was a more harmful thing in my life than I could have thought of. My self-esteem was dismantled. It has gone to a level that I cannot trust and recognize myself anymore. The experience may be different for other infected individuals.

Moral and religious condemnations against homosexuality were revealed in most respondents' narratives. Some respondents thought that their situation would be better once religion accepted multi-sexual orientation. This suggests that they expect religion to play a role in managing social stigma.

> I am a religious person but I am a gay. Religion finds it contradictory. Sexuality is a social issue, religion is divine. Is society and divinity far from each other? I respect religion and get much consolation and hope from it. But when it comes to sexuality and HIV, no matter how I was infected, it is assumed that I got it from homosexual activity.

Research participants engage in stigma management strategies such as hiding themselves during social interactions; engaging in victim behaviours, isolation or denial; and blaming and devaluing themselves. These are not healthy strategies for managing stigma; rather this is something that undermines social, mental and physical well-being of the individual. The attempt to avoid social situations often increases stress, owing to the fear and anxiety of being found out. Rather than recommending macro-level strategies, it might be productive to focus on interventions in the local contexts related to the perceived moral status of HIV sufferers (Corrigan et al. 2005; Thornicroft 2006).

> I was at a family party; I noticed people were not shaking hands with me. They just said hello from a 'safe' distance. One boy of around 15 approached me and asked how I was and why I was keeping aloof. When I attempted to reply, he was dragged away by his mother who whispered something in his ear. I never found him around me anymore during the party. My parents spent time with me in the party. I realize they noticed I was being shunned. They are nice. I am grateful to them.

Emotional responses of anger, shame, humiliation and psychological distress are common when coping with gossip, teasing, rejection, exclusion and differential and poorer treatment in institutional and community settings. The coping processes for managing stigma are influenced by the distress associated with their status, prejudicial attitudes and discriminatory actions, as well as personal characteristics and the social context of their lives.

Herek (1999) noted that 'the widespread expectation of stigma, combined with actual experiences with prejudice and discrimination, exerts a considerable impact on people with HIV, their loved ones, and caregivers'. He further goes on to say that it affects many of the choices about being tested. 'I understand this would not happen to my life had I not been tested. I disclosed my status in good faith. However, I did not expect to have such experience.'

Parker and Aggleton (2003:22) suggest that together with an emphasis on community mobilization aimed at unleashing resistance to stigmatization and discrimination, a rights-based approach to reducing stigma should be a high priority in order to create a social climate in which stigmatization and discrimination will not exist. The problem for stigma reduction is that the negative behaviours of some individuals, due to their internalized stigma, become generalized to, and associated with, all members of the group. Contemporary commentators on the stigma associated with race provide compelling evidence that over the years, only the manner in which racial prejudice is expressed has changed, but racist ideologies continue to prevail.

Role and Responsibility

Along with self-management strategies, the degree of vulnerability and resilience may largely depend on the roles and responsibilities undertaken by loved ones such as parents, wives or husbands and children. Familial support, acceptance and endurance are very important for PLWHA. The attitudes of family members play a key role in shaping an individual's response to their infection. If discouraged by their family, PLWHA may begin to think that the rest of society will treat them the same way and contribute to the build-up of a defeatist attitude at the outset.

According to our respondents, the roles and responsibilities of family members have become important disease management mechanisms. In the Asian context, being a mother or wife of a PLWHA means accepting the role of caregiver. While their roles are voluntary, continuous and spontaneous, they are also expected to take up these responsibilities by the society. Their roles could be temporary or permanent, and the level of responsibility could vary. Mothers, in particular, are seen as permanent and most passionate caregivers. However, wives could respond differently to the condition of their husbands, depending on their personal strength, values and resilience. Wives' roles often depend on the financial well-being of their husbands and the age of the wives. In some cases, women terminate their existing roles and responsibilities once the husbands disclosed their status. Those wives who continue as caregivers felt strongly that wives should be loyal to their husbands (Fig. 5.7).

Virtue means behaviours, opinions and feelings associated with high moral standards. This connotes both positive and negative attitudes and individual actions. The individual's virtue can be communicated to other family members, the community or society. Weak virtue, characterized by engaging in risk-taking behaviours, is associated with an increased risk of HIV/AIDS transmission.

The magnitude, frequency and duration of support and care provided to a PLWHA were determined by the level of HIV infection and the extent of concern felt by the family and the community. Respondents placed significant value on voluntary care provided by family and community members, and many suggested

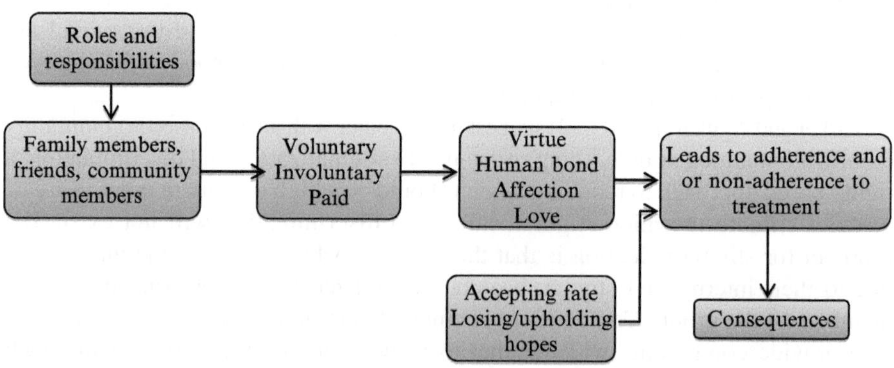

Fig. 5.7 Role and responsibility

that such care is invaluable. The majority of participants receive financial and psychosocial support as well as care from the family and the community. The degree of concern between the caregivers and their patients is generally associated with the level of risk of exposure to HIV. They believe this actually generates hope in them and adds discipline to their treatment regimen.

A general belief among South Asians is that they should accept God's will. This tenet drives people to avoid taking action to address their health issues. Accepting 'fate' could increase the risk of transmission. Patients, caregivers and members of the community often expressed sentiments such as 'let it be' and 'whatever will be will be' to reflect their acceptance of fate. Some participants believe that their fate was an early death, and they could do nothing but accept this. Such beliefs have a significant impact on respondents' adherence or non-adherence to treatment regimens. The most commonly perceived adherent behaviours for preventing HIV transmission are associated with dining behaviours and eating habits. These included isolation during dining, use of separate utensils and dishwashing arrangements, as well as restriction from consuming certain food items.

> I studied human rights also in my courses. In any case, nobody can violate human rights of anyone. But, in this case of HIV/AIDS, I see only a few people care about human rights. A person who has tested positive for HIV has just as much of a right as any other person to decide what's best for her health and her life, and to be treated with respect and dignity, Canada may be making great strides forward in the economic sphere, but economic development and respect for human rights do not necessarily go hand in hand.

With the advent of highly effective antiretroviral therapy (HAART), HIV sufferers are living much longer than they did in the 1980s and early 1990s, when the time between diagnosis and death was measured in months. But living for many years with an infectious disease takes an immense toll on people's health, quality of life, finances, independence and self-esteem (PHAC 2005:7). Therefore, efforts should be made to ensure the lives of PLWHA as stress-free as possible between the onset of infection and death. As human beings, PLWHA deserve this. As an employee who is an HIV sufferer, an individual may be concerned with the way their employer and co-workers respond should they learn of their status. Fortunately, HIV sufferer employees are granted protection from discrimination under both provincial and federal laws.

Chapter 6
Managing the Crisis and Policy Directions

Geographically, HIV/AIDS is not confined to a specific region, and topically, it is not isolated to a single discipline. Debates about HIV/AIDS have numerous dimensions, and researchers and policymakers are paying increasing attention to these nuances. Overall, since the onset of the pandemic, the world has witnessed a paradigmatic shift in traditional thinking about health politics, the social determinants of health, funding policies and directions, as well as migration flows in relation to public health. In order to fully explore and understand the issues, the analysis in this book covered a range of factors: social, psychosocial, economic, political and cultural.

These issues have not been fully explored in contemporary HIV and stigma literature. This book expects to generate new knowledge, assist with formulation of policy recommendations on HIV sufferers of South Asian refugees and immigrants in Canada and disseminate findings to a wider audience. This information will be useful to health service providers to ensure better access to the services for immigrants and refugees living with HIV/AIDS. The overall impact is expected to fill a vacuum in the literature on the experience of immigrants and refugees in handling stigma, discrimination and treatment regimens.

The findings of this research have policy implications, both regionally and globally. It is necessary to examine the role and impact of existing policies that protect the rights of the refugees and immigrants living with HIV/AIDS. This should help formulate a set of recommendations for policymakers, researchers, medical professionals and service providers. Policy recommendations for Canada, in particular, will include bringing together various institutions and authorities, as well as health service providers, to develop a unified approach to minimize the impact of stigmatization and discrimination.

This disease is considered to be the fourth major cause of death worldwide (UNAIDS 2012; Lopez and Mathers 2006). According to UNAIDS, the number of people who live with HIV/AIDS reached 47.5 million in 2011. While cases of HIV/AIDS have been reported in all regions of the world, almost all those living with HIV (97 %) reside in low- and middle-income countries, particularly in sub-Saharan Africa. Most people living with HIV or at risk of HIV infection have very limited

A.A. Ullah, A.S. Huque, *Asian Immigrants in North America with HIV/AIDS*,
DOI 10.1007/978-981-287-119-0_6

Table 6.1 HIV prevalence and incidence by region

Region	Total no. (%) living with HIV end of 2010	Newly infected in 2010	Adult prevalence rate 2010
Global total	**34 million (100 %)**	**2.7 million**	**0.8 %**
Sub-Saharan Africa	22.9 million (67 %)	1.9 million	5.0 %
South/Southeast Asia	4.0 million (12 %)	270,000	0.3 %
Eastern Europe/Central Asia	1.5 million (4 %)	160,000	0.9 %
Latin America	1.5 million (4 %)	100,000	0.4 %
North America	1.3 million (4 %)	58,000	0.6 %
Western/Central Europe	840,000 (2 %)	30,000	0.2 %
East Asia	790,000 (2 %)	88,000	0.1 %
Middle East/North Africa	470,000 (1 %)	59,000	0.2 %
Caribbean	200,000 (0.6 %)	12,000	0.9 %
Oceania	54,000 (0.2 %)	3,300	0.3 %

Source: The Kaiser Family Foundation (2011)

access to prevention, care or treatment, and worse, there is still no cure. HIV primarily affects those in their most productive years; about half of new infections are found among those under the age of 25. This not only affects the health of individuals but impacts households, communities and the development and economic growth of nations. Many of the countries hardest hit by HIV also suffer from other infectious diseases, food insecurity and other serious problems (The Kaiser Family Foundation 2011). Its impact is also highly gendered in terms of those infected and those affected, as the task of caring shifts additional burden of labour onto women (Table 6.1).

The global prevalence rate—that is, the per cent of people aged 15–49 who are infected—has stabilized since 2001. Various sources confirm that in 2010, 1.8 million people died of AIDS, a 21 % decrease since 2005. Deaths have declined due in part to greater availability of, and access to, antiretroviral treatment (ART) and increased awareness. However, HIV remains a leading cause of death worldwide and the number one cause of death in Africa. Most new infections are transmitted through heterosexual contact, although risk factors vary. In some countries, men who have sex with men (MSM), injection drug users (IDUs) and sex workers (SW) are at significant risk. Since a majority of people with HIV are unaware of their status, it makes little difference, although the testing capacity has increased over time.

Women represent approximately half of all people living with HIV worldwide and more than half (59 %) in sub-Saharan Africa. Gender inequalities, differential access to services and sexual violence increase women's vulnerability to HIV. Young people aged 15–24 account for 42 % of new HIV infections among those aged 15 and over, and within this age group women are impacted at a greater frequency than men in sub-Saharan Africa. For instance, in Southern Africa, young women are up to 5 times more likely to become infected with HIV than their male counterparts.

In 2010, there were 3.4 million children living with HIV in the world, 390,000 new infections among children, and 250,000 AIDS-related deaths among children (UNAIDS 2012). In 2009, there were approximately 16.6 million AIDS orphans, that is, children who have lost one or both parents to HIV, 89 % of whom live in sub-Saharan Africa. Nearly five million people are living with HIV across Southeast and East Asia (Kaiser Family Foundation 2011). While most national epidemics appear to have stabilized, HIV prevalence is increasing in some countries in Asia such as Bangladesh, Pakistan and the Philippines. The Southeast Asian region is also home to the two of the most populous nations in the world —China and India— where even relatively low prevalence rates translate into very large numbers of infections (Kutikuppala 2012).

A specific group that is more affected than any other by the HIV/AIDS pandemic is refugee population. Despite the misconception that HIV/AIDS is a refugee problem and thus vulnerability to HIV is high, research has demonstrated that HIV/AIDS is not common among refugees. The more pressing dilemmas facing refugees are noticeable hostility from the host community and obstacles in accessing medication and other healthcare services. Refugees lack livelihood tools and social networks and are deprived of health and educational opportunities.

Stigma, Discrimination and Xenophobia

Both generally and in relation to refugees in particular, HIV/AIDS is associated with three significant issues: stigma, discrimination and xenophobia. Stigma encompasses negative characteristics associated with various features of a society, including ethnicity, race, religion and so on. Stigmatization against PLWHA is often more severe for women because of their relatively vulnerable position in the society. Stigmatization leads to violations of human rights, which negatively affect the well-being of PLWHA.

There are particular behaviour patterns that aggravate discrimination and stigmatization towards specific groups. For instance, homosexual behaviour is stigmatized almost everywhere in the world as it is considered to be antireligious, deviant and unnatural. Although the perception about homosexuality as a disease has been removed from the Diagnostic and Statistical Manual (DSM), it remains embedded in many minds that it is a disease. This behaviour is a risk factor linked to HIV/AIDS, leading to discrimination, violence and stigmatization towards PLWHA. In developing countries, many members of the society are sympathetic towards infected people, but this has not translated into a more compassionate approach to them. People usually blame those who are infected as they see PLWHA as responsible for bringing HIV/AIDS into the community. Thus, migrants and refugees are subject to discrimination due to their diverse origins and for being members of particular communities. In such cases, discrimination is intensified by its multimodal nature.

Stigma is a social label that negatively shapes a person's life, as well as the lives of their families, partners and friends. Stigma can be viewed in two typologies: internal and/or external, and felt and/or acted. External stigmatization exists where people reject individuals who have psychological and physical attributes that are different from prevailing norms, preventing stigmatized people from full participation in the surrounding environment. HIV sufferers may be stigmatized based on their physical appearance, as HIV/AIDS can manifest in noticeable physical markers, as well as based on knowledge of their HIV status.

Internal stigmatization occurs when stigmatization is internalized, and victims often blame themselves for causing it. This can lead PLWHA to refrain from seeking or accepting treatment due to feelings of guilt and the belief that they deserve to be infected. Internal stigma is highly dependent on an individual's self-perception. The indicator of internal stigma is self-exclusion, which refers to excluding oneself from social events, contact with friends and relatives and even the use of counselling resources. Indicators of internal stigmatization also include engaging in deception or overcompensation. Among PLWHA, deception means HIV sufferer who admit to having 'lied about their status to their family or friends for fear of the withdrawal of others' (USAID 2006:13).

Social factors are significant in the development of internal stigma. For example, the level of internal stigma depends, in part, on the perception of the avenue through which the virus was acquired. Women are considered responsible for the vertical transmission of HIV/AIDS to their children (often known as 'mother to child' transmission, even if it was the father who was originally HIV sufferer), while children born HIV positive are considered innocent. Contextual factors refer to the environment in which the infected person lives, whether it is supportive or hostile (USAID 2006). Internal factors, such as an individual's health and acceptance of their infection, can either contribute to an individual's ability to cope with internal stigma or exacerbate it.

In addition, stigmatization can be either felt or acted out. As Goffman suggests, 'enacted stigma refers to actual discrimination or unacceptability, whereas felt stigma refers to the fear of such discrimination' (1963:12). The analysis in the previous chapters presented various dimensions of stigma and its prevalence and ramifications in social life. The International Center for Research on Women (ICRW) expanded the concept of stigma and described it by producing and reproducing social structures of hierarchy and exclusion and by transforming difference into inequality (International Center for Research on Women 2002). Hierarchy refers to power structure and class, and difference refers to class, race, ethnicity, health status, sexual orientation and gender. In aiming for a more nuanced understanding of the functioning of stigma, it is important to note that the nature, consequences, frequency and severity of stigma varies widely when yielded by and upon different social classes and professional groups. This results in widely different implications for stigma occurring from different people, depending upon their social positioning. For instance, when practitioners such as doctors or nurses or social workers fail to overcome stigmatization, a patient may become far more demoralized than being stigmatized by a friend or a neighbour. Therefore, this has to be taken into account in conceptualizing stigma.

Refugees are faced with intense discrimination due to racial and ethnic factors, as well as discrimination based on their unique modes of migration, in addition to discrimination based on their HIV status. Xenophobia in relation to HIV/AIDS appears when people blame foreigners for the spread of the virus. Discrimination and xenophobia prompt governments to impose harsh rules and selective criteria on migrants and or refugees, as they are perceived as carriers of the infection. For example, migrants and refugees may face restrictions on entry, mobility and residence in a foreign country because of their serostatus. The length of time to be spent in the country typically determines whether an HIV test is required, with entry prohibitions generally affecting persons who want to stay in a country for longer periods of time. HIV-positive test results generally lead to refusal of entry or to being forced to leave if one is already in the country. Such regulations limit the choices available to PLWHA in their opportunities for employment and education.

Countries impose specific controls at the borders to regulate entry of foreigners. There are restrictions in relation to health of those seeking to enter, and immigration officials require information about an applicant's general health history and/or specific diseases on the entry visa application form. If HIV sufferer applicants do not state the truth in responding to this question, they will also have to hide medications which they carry with them, and pretend to be healthy in front of the entry control officials, and this may be impossible in many cases. Those who disclose their positive status may be refused entry by some countries. Visitors may be required to present evidence of regular health examinations, which could include an HIV test. The costs for all these tests must be borne by the applicant, putting financially weak applicants at a disadvantage (Wiessner and Lemmen 2013).

Xenophobia, in particular, originates from distrust of outsiders. It can be perpetrated by either majority or minority groups depending on the context (Soyombo 2008). The xenophobic behaviour of the apartheid regime in South Africa is a reminder of the majority suffering from xenophobic oppression by the minority. Xenophobia, however, is different from racism: while racism usually entails notions of racial superiority by one group over another, xenophobia is related to feelings of fear or hatred. But both result from the multigroup/multicultural nature of contemporary society. The multicultural composition of societies has been accentuated by globalization and the increasing removal of barriers to the free movement of people across national borders (Soyombo 2008).

The build-up of xenophobia often leads to violent clashes between dominant and minority groups. Often times, many individuals, including victims, bystanders and perpetrators of xenophobia, risk losing their lives as a result of xenophobic violence, while many others suffer various degrees and forms of injury. If uncontrolled, xenophobia may lead to a dramatic increase in the incidence of 'hate' crimes and other atrocities in a community or society. It may also lead to retaliatory attacks that could result in a cyclical and intractable retributive process.

Discrimination and xenophobia can translate into a variety of social outcomes that negatively impact immigrants and refugees, particularly those who are HIV positive. For example, prejudice is a predetermined bias that one group of people usually have about others before they get to know them, or before they have information or knowledge about the other group, situation or event (Soyombo 2008). Prejudice is attitudinal—an expression of a state of mind—and is usually negative. In terms of relationship sequence, prejudice usually proceeds, and often leads, to xenophobia. Thus, people are usually prejudiced before they exhibit xenophobia.

Prejudice is closely related to, but different from, discrimination. It is attitudinal, while discrimination is behavioural. Kornblum (1997:395) clarified the difference between prejudice and discrimination noting that 'prejudice is an attitude that pre-judges a person, either positively or negatively, on the basis of real or imagined characteristics (stereotypes) of a group to which that person belongs'. Discrimination refers to the differential treatment of people based on particular social categories. This usually entails coexistence (on unequal terms), while xenophobia emphasizes a willingness or desire to extinguish or eliminate the other group.

Similarly, racism, according to Marshall (1998:548), refers to 'the unequal treatment of a population group purely because of its possession of physical or other characteristics socially defined as denoting a particular race'. Race is anchored in histories of prejudice, exclusion and poverty. According to Goffman (1968), racism can be seen as synonymous to stigma. Howarth (2006) reports that this poses a threat to the esteem of an individual and offered a number of justifications for equating racism with stigmatization. One of his arguments highlight the fact that race is often evident in the appearance of a person such as colour of skin. Howarth argues that the origin of 'stigma' can be traced back to Ancient Greece, when a stigma was considered as a mark 'burnt or cut into the skin to symbolize the threat or danger of the stigmatized person' (2006:443). As with the original stigma, race is read as a marker of belonging to a stigmatized group in the eyes of the racist.

In addition, stereotyping, scapegoating and 'hate crimes' illustrate the variety of forms that discrimination, xenophobia and prejudice can take. Stereotyping is the act of 'attributing to all group members qualities observed in a few of them' (Goffman 1963:13). Scapegoating refers to the idea of identifying a weaker—and usually innocent—object upon which blame for one's predicament can be put (Soyombo 2008). This is usually associated with the frustration–aggression theory and is a form of displaced aggression as opposed to direct aggression. Scapegoats are usually picked because the agent or cause of frustration is too powerful to be confronted. The anger of frustration is thus vented on other people, groups or objects (scapegoats). Hate crimes are those that are committed against people because of their membership of certain groups or categories (such as race, ethnic background, nationality, political affiliation, religion, gender, sexual orientation, etc.). Hate crimes can take many forms, including physical assault, pelting with dangerous or offensive objects, verbal assault, taunting, damage to property, bullying, harassment, offensive graffiti or letters and so on.

Stigma, prejudice and discrimination are often used interchangeably, but they need to be conceptualized separately to highlight their impact on one another. Discrimination is considered an important component of stigma, and prejudice and stereotyping can lead to discrimination. Additionally, prejudice is viewed as a negative evaluation or conceptualization of a particular group of people. A clear and specific contextualization of these and other key concepts is needed for understanding, analyzing and suggesting appropriate strategies for solving health issues driven primarily by inequality.

An Approach to the HIV Epidemic

Poverty and HIV/AIDS are closely connected. The AIDS pandemic does not differentiate between rich and poor; however, it does the most damage among the poorest groups. For example, the antiretroviral treatment is too expensive to be purchased by the poor and is therefore structurally restricted to those who can afford to pay for treatment. The relationship between poverty and HIV results in a dangerous, vicious cycle. For instance, HIV/AIDS is related to bad economic conditions since, in poor countries, many people choose sex work for a livelihood that puts them at risk of infection. Additionally, the virus itself affects the economic condition of infected individuals, as those people become incapacitated to work normally, leading to loss of employment and income. Maintaining good health while living with HIV/AIDS is also dependent to a great extent on nutrition, which is difficult to attain for those under economic hardship.

In addressing HIV from an economic perspective, there are three factors that deserve consideration: risk environment, susceptibility and vulnerability. A risk environment develops through a process that may take years and is formed by any number of factors that act together to increase risk, such as gender inequalities (Barnett and Whiteside 2002). Susceptibility refers to 'an increase in social predisposition to virus transmission, as occurs in a risk environment' (Barnett and Whiteside 2002:6). Vulnerability is determined by the coping mechanisms that are available within the society, such as healthcare facilities.

Sufficient information about the virus and its means of transmission are critical, and an increased level of awareness and knowledge can decrease the possibility of infection. Such information and availability of protection tools are not easily accessible in cases when individuals struggle to attain the basic necessities of life. For example, in order to prevent infection in poor areas, a government must support (in terms of subsidizing) the cost of purchasing condoms (or if possible distribution for free of charge), because generally poor people compare the costs of having safe versus unsafe sex in terms of the costs of protection. Gender-related factors exacerbate these challenges, as women in many societies lack the power to negotiate safe sex.

Poverty is not only the inability to meet basic needs. It is rather a deprivation of knowledge, education and communication. Poverty lines are either restrictive or inclusive. Restrictive poverty is defined as 'the point at which people's physical/medical survival is at risk', and inclusive poverty, on the other hand, is defined as 'the cost of meeting the physical, emotional, social and spiritual needs of individuals and families' (deGroot-Maggetti 2002:4–5). In Canada, newly arrived refugees and immigrants face both restrictive and inclusive poverty because they are not included in the economic cycle in Canada, which puts them at risk of living in poor socioeconomic and physical environments, increasing the potential for contracting HIV/AIDS.

Most HIV sufferers come from specific ethnic or cultural minority groups and generally face greater stigma and discrimination. In addition, refugees and newcomers to Canada do not have access to the healthcare system for the first 90 days after their arrival, and this policy places them at greater risk of HIV/AIDS infection. In cases where newcomers are allowed to gain access to healthcare services, they are faced with other obstacles that prevent them from maximizing the benefits. These obstacles include cultural and language barriers.

The migrants and refugees who live in very poor conditions in Canada are at high risk of infection. Along with inadequate access to health services, they are at risk of homelessness, because many face difficulties in finding employment. Along with housing, education is also affected by poverty. Poor students lack study space and access to computers, which has an adverse impact on attaining education. Poverty has a gendered dimension as well. While poverty among men is related to low wages, poverty among women is related to their social status as single mothers, separated wives, divorced women and caregivers (deGroot-Maggetti 2002:8).

HIV discrimination is fuelled by practical constraints related to resource scarcity and limited choices. It is interesting to question how society perceives infected individuals from different backgrounds, and how this perception intersects with HIV/AIDS-related stigma. Are there different manifestations of stigma and discrimination between a rural and urban PLWHA? Would perceptions of an infected individual be different if the PLWHA is wealthy or poor? The answers are related to the politics of resource hierarchies. Decisions in the context of poverty are often the results of discriminatory actions (Ullah 2010b, c). The decisions themselves are not always an outcome of stigma per se, but the actions are experienced as stigmatization. For example, orphans feel stigmatized by being forced to remain out of school, with bleak prospect of succeeding in life. Further, decisions are voiced through a language of attribution and blame.

The intersections between poverty and stigma related to HIV/AIDS reinforce the fact that stigma cannot be isolated from other social processes and that it must be understood in the larger sociopolitical context and in relation to hunger, deprivation and limited coping capacities (Wallman 1988; Bond 1998). Most societies in the global South are suffering from economic hardship, the impact of HIV, poor education and health services, and widening inequality. The outcomes are reflected in rising incidences of violence, alcohol abuse and family breakdown. de Waal and Whiteside (2003) (see also Barnett and Whiteside 2002) highlighted the argument of 'new variant famine' to argue that the prevalence of HIV in Southern Africa in particular and globally in general has been aggravated by other attendant problems, such as poverty and hunger. The food crisis could be attributed largely to the HIV/AIDS epidemic.

These stresses lend themselves to the process of stigmatization. As a consequence, stigma is 'allowed' to unfold within the context of inequitable power relations (Link and Phelan 2001), where it plays a role in separating 'us' from 'them' and reinforces social stereotypes. The relationship between 'diverse forms of inequality and stigma' (Parker and Aggleton 2003:182) is evident in the additional vulnerability of the poor, women and orphans to stigma. Castro and Farmer (2005:55) pointed out that 'poverty, already representing an almost universal stigma, will be the primary reason that poor people living with HIV suffer from greater AIDS-related stigma' and that 'social forces determine not only the risk of HIV infection but also risk of AIDS-related stigma'.

Discrimination Within Refugee Communities and Beyond

Knowledge of the variety of means of transmission and their outcomes is not given adequate consideration when dealing with PLWHA. The result is that others within refugee communities avoid contact with PLWHA regardless of the means by which they were infected. People believe that the infected individuals deserve this condition because the means of transmission are considered immoral behaviour in many societies. For example, HIV is linked to homosexuality, and therefore, in societies where homosexuality is forbidden on religious, social or cultural norms, stigmatization of PLWHA is more intense.

Stigma towards PLWHA is also related to a fear of infection. Hostile reactions towards PLWHA may be extended to family, friends, healthcare providers and families of healthcare workers as well. Manifestations of this stigma towards PLWHA can be seen in the form of avoidance and exclusion, which contribute to low self-esteem, isolation and hopelessness.

The decision to conceal or not disclose one's HIV status is significantly affected by the impact of stigma towards HIV. PLWHA conceal their status in order to avoid losing family support or employment and to circumvent being subjected to avoidance. However, in the process of concealing their status, PLWHA become reluctant to seek medical attention and find it difficult to justify their practice of unsafe sex. Nevertheless, this state cannot be sustained, since symptoms of the infection manifest themselves over time.

There are several factors that act as barriers to the process of disclosure. Rejection by sexual partners, family members, peers, friends and colleagues is one of the most significant barriers to disclosure of the status (Mahajan et al. 2008). The well-being of PLWHA is affected by stigma, since it leads to severe violations of human rights. Adherence to HIV medication is affected by stigma as well, since persons who reveal their status are faced with diverse challenges, along with the perceived stigma towards HIV/AIDS. Criminalization of purposeful HIV transmission can also hinder disclosure of status by the infected person. The mindset of a PLWHA as part of an individualist or collectivist culture can also impact their willingness to disclose their status. In collectivist societies, such as those in Southeast Asia, an individual's infection is perceived to be a reflection on their family, community and society at large. Typically, the family is informed first of their HIV status. In individualistic societies, PLWHA generally disclose first to physicians and healthcare providers. Legally, HIV sufferers must inform their partners about their infection before engaging in sexual activity. Determinants of who is informed include the relationship between the PLWHA and the informant, and how sympathetic and trustworthy the PLWHA believe the informant to be.

Multimodal Discrimination

When refugees become infected with HIV, the level of isolation and discrimination increases significantly. In order to avert the consequences of these attitudes, coping strategies are considered temporary but important solutions for adaptation.

Resilience, often referred to as adaptive capacity (Bajek and Okada 2007), is the ability to endure and withstand external shocks and to recover from them (UNCTAD 2013). When dealing with HIV/AIDS, resilience is addressed through two dimensions: emotional or psychological, and material or economic. While the emotional or psychological dimension represents positive thinking, acceptance of HIV status and coping with pain, the material perspective characterizes responses that are adopted by individuals in the process of avoidance of the negative consequences of HIV/AIDS. Resilient persons are those who have self-confidence, trust, self-esteem and communication skills which are acquired from the environment in which a person grows up. Social support could play a role in helping people cope with the stress of living with HIV/AIDS, and interestingly, there is an association between social support and immune functions (Malgas 2005).

The percentage of respondents in this research who showed resilience and self-acceptance was very small. Nevertheless, some respondents expressed a desire to live longer, which helped them fight against stigma and discrimination. Refugees face several forms of discrimination and poverty in the host country, which put them at increased risk of infection and a decline in their economic, social, mental and physical well-being. It has been demonstrated that a degree of systematic discrimination against minorities exists in Canada (Beck et al. 2002). Migrants and refugees face xenophobia, in addition to violence motivated by race, ethnicity and religion. Xenophobia may work as the source of discrimination and stigma. Fear of people from other countries and dislike of foreigners cause resentments towards migrants and refugees. Although HIV sufferers are stigmatized and discriminated against due to their status, the burden of being from another country and carrying the status of refugee or migrant makes it worse. Yet, members of these communities usually do not report attacks or discrimination against them because they are apprehensive of the treatment by law enforcement officials and do not trust the authorities. They may also be unaware of the fact that they have the right to seek redress. The role of family members in providing support contributes to determining an individual's level of vulnerability or resilience. For example, parents or partners can provide support, acceptance and endurance; in cases where parents or partners withhold support, acceptance and endurance, a PLWHA's quality of life is severely impacted. Fundamentally, the family is considered a major coping mechanism.

Psychological strength, as well as physical strength, is an important factor for making an individual resilient. HIV/AIDS weakens those infected physically as well as psychologically. The weaker an individual is, the less resilient they are. Therefore, PLWHA are more vulnerable to the effects of discriminatory attacks and stigma. Although it is medically recognized that HIV/AIDS can be transmitted in a number of ways, the primary assumption is that it is acquired through immoral or deviant behaviour, and the stigma emanates from such a perception. Based on this erroneous notion, people begin to act negatively towards PLWHA. The misconception that this virus has specific geographic origins, such as Africa, leads many people to perceive immigrants and Afro-Canadians negatively. Thus, infected persons from these categories face multimodal discrimination and unequal treatment. This sets up a dividing line between 'innocent' HIV/AIDS patients (infected through a blood transfusion) and 'guilty/deserving' HIV/AIDS patients (injecting drug users, sex workers or MSM). It should be reiterated that everyone deserves to be treated with dignity and respect and to remain free from stigma. The sympathy should not be reserved only for those who are socially considered as 'innocent victims' of the disease.

Any ailment should be treated regardless of the social status, gender or ethnic background of an infected person. Canadian citizens, immigrants and refugees should receive equal support in medical care from the government. Although the Canadian government has taken important steps in ensuring equal treatment for individuals from different ethnic backgrounds, regardless of their place of origin, there is a need to do much more. When an individual contracts HIV/AIDS, they continue to be entitled to their rights and freedoms that cannot be taken away on grounds of the infection. Protecting human rights is the responsibility of the state. According to Canadian Charter of Rights and Freedom, 'Every individual is equal before and under the law and has the right to the equal protection and equal benefit of the law without discrimination and, in particular, without discrimination based on race, national or ethnic origin, colour, religion, sex, age or mental or physical disability' (Canadian Charter of Rights and Freedom, Section 15- Equality Rights 2013:1). Canada is committed to international human rights standards. This should be reflected in state policies, and the government needs to ensure that they are effectively implemented. This will have a positive, long-term impact on the care available to PLWHA. Equal and fair treatment from the government has the potential to contribute to recalibrate the attitudes of citizens towards this group.

Canada accepts a large number of immigrants and refugees, and public policies influence the lives of these people, especially those who suffer from HIV/AIDS. At the same time, policies are driven by the experience, voice and actions of the public. People with HIV/AIDS who would like to get a temporary Canadian visa do not face much difficulty, as they are not required to take HIV tests. However, those who seek permanent residence have to meet more stringent requirements. The *Immigration and Refugee Protection Act* does not consider HIV or AIDS as a prohibitive factor for staying in Canada, but it contends that 'foreign nationals can be deemed medically inadmissible to Canada and denied a visa if they are likely to be a danger to public health or public safety; or they might reasonably be expected to cause excessive demand on health or social services' (Canadian HIV/AIDS Legal Network 2012:1).

Although the government of Canada has taken several steps to cope with the demographic changes brought by a significant number of immigrants and refugees, discrimination against them continues. Xenophobia threatens social justice and erodes human rights standards. It increases inequalities within Canadian society and degrades people, stripping away their dignity, and hinders social cohesion. Collective efforts are needed to manage stigma and xenophobia, and these should ideally be initiated by the state, with support from civil society, nonprofit organizations, the private sector and individuals.

Policies in Countries of Origin

In South Asia, legal policy, case law and legislation are the three key elements that help understand the methods used by governments to deal with the HIV/AIDS crisis. Information on the pandemic is transmitted mostly through NGOs, media and popular culture rather than through legal channels. A specific legislation that deals with HIV/AIDS has not yet developed within the legal system in South Asia. In most countries of the region, the legal system encompasses a set of penal provisions to deal with drug use, sex work and sex between men. These have significant impact on the spread of HIV and the rights of PLWHA (UNAIDS 2011:13). For example, although India has specific provisions for dealing with privacy and health issues, it allows detaining an HIV sufferer on the grounds of public interest and public health, although this is in contravention of the policies on privacy and health provisions. India is the only country in South Asia that has specific legislation on people with disabilities, but it does not include PLWHA.

Privacy and confidentiality are major issues in dealing with HIV in order to encourage voluntary testing and reduction of discrimination and stigma. Forcing an individual to take an HIV test is a violation of rights to privacy; however, in many cases, this violation is justified on the basis of preserving public health (UNAIDS 2009:16). Employment is another area affected by HIV status. Some countries, such as South Africa, Australia and Canada, have legal arrangements for preventing discrimination in the workplace, yet termination based on HIV status remains a common phenomenon (see Gerntholtz 2004; Magnusson 1996; de Bruyn 1998). The UN Chronicle often reports cases in which individuals suffer from this type of discrimination and states that 'employers knew that firing people for having HIV was illegal, but with little enforcement, some people always managed to find ways to do so, without repercussions' (Altaf and Lovelace 2011). This is not only a matter of discrimination but also a violation of labour code and rights. It also shows the lack of workplace prevention and protection programmes that work to prevent the spread of the virus and make workers aware of their conditions and rights.[1]

Mitigating Stigma and Discrimination in Canada

Stigma and discrimination present significant barriers to limiting the spread and impact of HIV (Pan Caribbean Partnership Against HIV & AIDS—PANCAP 2010:16). The existing international guidelines[2] were adopted by UNAIDS following calls for

[1] http://www.thebody.com/content/art30954.html. See also http://www.voanews.com/content/hiv-positive-liberians-fight-workplace-discrimination-91713094/154192.html

[2] UNAIDS in collaboration with the Office of the High Commissioner for Human Rights (OHCHR) and other partners has developed guidelines advancing human rights in the context of HIV/AIDS. In February 1998, UNAIDS and OHCHR jointly published the International Guidelines on HIV/AIDS and Human Rights. These guidelines set the standards for upholding HIV/AIDS-related human rights at the national, regional and international levels (UNAIDS 2003).

an international framework that governs HIV/AIDS issues in relation to human rights on the national, regional and international level (OHCHR and UNAIDS 2006:9).

The main principles of the guidelines suggest that:

(a) States are responsible for establishing a framework on the national level to respond to HIV/AIDS, and this responsibility applies to all branches of the government.
(b) It is the state that should ensure community consultation occurs at all phases of HIV/AIDS policy design.
(c) Public health laws should be reformed and reviewed by states in order to make sure that issues of HIV/AIDS are adequately addressed and consistent with international human rights law.
(d) Criminal laws and correctional systems should be reformed so as to make sure they are consistent with international obligations and are not used against vulnerable groups.
(e) Anti-discrimination and protective laws should be enacted by states to protect the HIV/AIDS-infected population.
(f) States should enact legislation that deals with preventive measures, HIV-related services and effective medication.
(g) People affected by HIV/AIDS need to be educated about their rights and other legal services.
(h) States should promote a supportive and enabling environment for women, children and other vulnerable groups by addressing underlying prejudice and inequalities through community dialogue.
(i) States should promote the wide and ongoing distribution of creative education, training and media programmes explicitly designed to change attitudes of discrimination and stigmatization associated with HIV/AIDS to understanding and acceptance.
(j) States should ensure that government and the private sector develop codes of conduct regarding HIV/AIDS issues that translate human rights principles into codes of professional responsibility and practice, with accompanying mechanisms to implement and enforce these codes.
(k) States should ensure monitoring and enforcement mechanisms to guarantee the protection of HIV-related human rights.
(l) States should cooperate through all relevant programmes and agencies of the United Nations system, including UNAIDS, to share knowledge and experience concerning HIV-related human rights issues and should ensure effective mechanisms to protect human rights in the context of HIV/AIDS at international level (OHCHR and UNAIDS 2006:12).

The sixth guideline, in particular, is related to national legislation which targets the accessibility of HIV/AIDS treatment, medication, medical care and support, and the sustainability of access for ensuring equitable care and support based on the right to health (OHCHR and UNAIDS 2006:13). The Caribbean states adopted a useful model described as the 'three E's': empowerment, education and an enabling environment (UNAIDS 2003). Empowerment is instrumental in strengthening resilience among stigmatized and marginalized groups. The more empowered a person, the better their response to stigma, discrimination and oppression (PANCAP 2010:23). Education as a policy tool helps to effectively educate people and organizations against the perceived stigma targeting PLWHA. Stigma can be reduced through direct strategies such as counselling, improving access to information and educating both PLWHA and their allies about coping strategies. The main theme of the strategic framework for the Caribbean states is the creation of an enabling environment through 'the development of policies, programmes and legislation that affirm human rights and counter deep underlying social barriers' (PANCAP 2010:27).

There is significant correlations between human rights and stigma (see Chap. 2). According to Amnesty International (2011), human rights are fundamental to addressing the HIV/AIDS epidemic. Human rights violations fuel the epidemic by increasing people's vulnerability to infection. In addition, human rights violations often follow infection. Ensuring equality before the law and compliance with international obligations are effective legal measures in tackling discrimination and stigma. This requires a solid legal foundation along with effective implementation to avoid any violation of the laws (PANCAP 2010:29). Confidentiality is also effective in reducing stigma. This is important in working with PLWHA since in many cases they are reluctant to proceed for healthcare service because of a lack of confidentiality. South Asian people, in particular, are extremely concerned about the confidentiality issue due to its sensitive nature.

HIV/AIDS Governance

The United Nations has recognized that good governance is a critical element in the reduction of HIV vulnerability and that development alone is not a sufficient condition to reduce HIV prevalence (United Nations 2002). The UN has introduced elements of good governance into strategies aimed at combating HIV/AIDS epidemics and encouraged several national AIDS programmes to strengthen it. In many cases, the promotion of good governance was spearheaded by NGOs, CBOs or international agencies. However, the state needs to be the guiding force for designing and implementing anti-HIV/AIDS policies and strategies.

As the leading global agency on public health, the World Health Organization (WHO) took the lead in combating HIV/AIDS until 1986. Since the mid-1990s, the devastating impact of the epidemic on human lives and on social and economic development has required extensive collective efforts by the various United Nations agencies. The United Nations brought together seven UN organizations[3] and the World Bank in a co-sponsored programme to determine strategies to effectively address the epidemic on a global scale.

At present, UNAIDS is the only dedicated HIV/AIDS agency that has been tackling diverse issues of the epidemic globally. There are some other organizations such as

[3] UNAIDS, UNICEF, UNDP, UNFPA, UNESCO, UN Women and WHO.

the World Bank and various INGOs that have been instrumental in responding to the HIV endemic. The World Bank offers long-term financial and specialized technical support and knowledge to countries for the effective prevention of new HIV infections, care and treatment for PLWHA. One of the key Millennium Development Goals is to combat HIV/AIDS, malaria and other diseases. The World Bank has provided funding for HIV/AIDS programmes and contributed a total of approximately US$4.6 billion since 1989 (World Bank 2012).

The International Association of Providers of AIDS Care (IAPAC) delivers pre-ART era education about nutrition, pain management, opportunistic infections (OIs) and other complications of HIV disease. PAAC publicly confronted the American Medical Association (AMA) and the American Dental Association (ADA) in 1991 on the proposed sanctions against HIV-infected healthcare workers after reports were published that an HIV sufferer dentist had likely transmitted HIV to three of his patients.

The battle against HIV/AIDS lies squarely at the intersection between 'emergency response' and 'development intervention', and this has placed it among the most difficult policy and programme issues facing national and local governments and the international development community (Poku 2007). The biennial International AIDS Conference, attended by approximately 25,000 participants from 196 countries, is the premier gathering event for those working in the field of HIV, as well as policymakers, people living with HIV and others committed to eliminating the epidemic.

Women and children are more prone than men to abandonment and violence as a result of their HIV status. MSM, injecting drug users, sex workers and prisoners often face greater discrimination when diagnosed with HIV. At the same time, these people are most likely to have the resources required to cope with the consequences. Stigma and discrimination and other factors prevent people from seeking HIV information, adopting preventive behaviour, getting tested, disclosing their serostatus and accessing treatment. In some cases, stigma prevents families from giving or accepting care. These factors need to be taken into consideration in designing HIV governance structures and strategies.

There appears to be progress in the fight against this disease. It is claimed that there has been a decline of 19 % in the number of people newly infected with HIV in the last decade (International HIV/AIDS Alliance 2013). WHO confirmed that an infant HIV sufferer treated with triple antiretroviral drugs in the first 30 h of life appeared to be functionally cured of the virus after taking treatment for 18 months (WHO 2013). With effective dissemination, such developments will contribute to a sense of optimism among the infected population and strengthen their resolve to face the challenges.

Canada's Response to HIV/AIDS Stigma

The HIV/AIDS epidemic is significant for [im]migration policies due to its propensity to generate controversies. Because of the fact that HIV/AIDS is associated with marginalized populations, policies regarding migration and immigration are increasingly becoming restrictive. The Canadian government appears to impose a double standard by stating that HIV/AIDS is not considered a dangerous and infectious disease, but rather a chronic disease like cancer or heart disease, and that Canada has strict regulations regarding the protection of HIV/AIDS patients. However, noncitizens residing in Canada are excluded from this protection (Nirman 2004:3). In 2001 the Immigration and Refugee Protection Act came into effect, replacing the 1985 Immigration Act. Section 38(1) of the new Immigration and Refugee Act reads:

> A foreign national is inadmissible on health grounds if their health condition (a) is likely to be a danger to public health; (b) is likely to be a danger to public safety; or (c) might reasonably be expected to cause excessive demand on health or social services. (Immigration and Refugee Protection Act)

Penner strongly criticized Canada's exclusionary immigration policies and points to Canada's historical practices of migration governance, arguing that the 'history of migration in Canada has been accompanied by a history of exclusion; in which certain groups of immigrants have been categorized as undesirable' (2012:1). Canada excludes refugees and migrants from healthcare services based on the assumption that offering them access would create excessive demand on the healthcare system (Nirman 2004:5).

At the same time, Canada has a sound legal foundation for protection against HIV/AIDS-based discrimination. Federal law assures equality and non-discrimination towards people with HIV/AIDs in both governmental and private sectors. This is obvious in the constitutional protection framework provided in the equal rights clause in *Charter of Rights* (Charter). It guarantees equal rights, including the rights of PLWHA. There are additional tools for protection of rights in the *Canadian Human Rights Act* (CHRA), jurisprudence and policy (Weait and Azad 2005:24). Unlike the Canadian Charter, the CHRA is applied to governmental and private sector organizations and institutions. Under the CHRA, jurisprudence represented in 'courts and tribunals have recognized HIV/AIDS as a disability within the meaning of the CHRS'. The CHRA established the Canadian Human Rights Commission to investigate complaints of discriminatory practices that are contrary to its principles and legal stipulations (Weait and Azad 2005:25).

Additionally, each province and territory in Canada has its own statute that deals with discrimination. However, 'there is no explicit reference to HIV/AIDS in the various anti-discrimination statutes'; they refer instead to 'disability', and interpretations of the concept may vary from one jurisdiction to another (Weait and Azad 2005:25). For example, the Ontario Human Rights Code (OHRC) includes a specialized non-discrimination policy towards handicapped groups. It is not clear whether PLWHA are included in this category.

In addition to non-discrimination, the legal framework for human rights in Canada deals with a number of issues relevant to PLWHA. For instance, under the OHRC, discrimination on the basis of sexual orientation is unlawful. In terms of equality and non-discrimination in employment, the most important consideration lies in determining whether HIV testing is a legitimate hiring practice and whether

HIV disease is a barrier to performing the tasks required in the position. Hiring procedures and medical tests should comply with the OHRC. This means that medical tests should be done after the selection of the employee. Any test to determine a person's HIV status, which is not related to the nature of the job, is a violation of the OHRC (Ontario Human Rights Commission 2000:4).

Privacy and confidentiality should be ensured as much as possible when dealing with PLWHA. Not only does the OHRC prohibit any sort of discrimination, it also provides measures for dealing with violations of the code. The OHRC provides monetary compensation and other remedies such as 'implementation of a formal institutional policy expressing a commitment to the equal treatment of persons that have or have tested positive for HIV infection; educational programmes for others in the environment; other accommodation required by the person with HIV infection' (Ontario Human Rights Commission 2000:154).

The strength of the existing polices is reflected in legal advancement and gains made in enacting laws, undertaking constitutional reform and establishment of special tribunals. Through these developments, PLWHA will have increased channels of protection. Today, most countries in the world do not have specific laws to deal with HIV/AIDS. Human rights related to HIV/AIDS are specific in terms of the way that violations manifest. HIV-infected people are more vulnerable to particular types of stigma and discrimination than other people with chronic diseases. Therefore, specific policies should be tailored to protect PLWHA from human rights violations. This remains a huge challenge, and even though such polices exist in certain countries, there are considerable barriers to enforcing them.

Many states are reluctant to follow international standards on rights to health and privacy, which are closely associated with the HIV epidemic in terms of providing health services and respecting the personal life and privacy of PLWHA. Furthermore, most states refuse international cooperation in managing this crisis. The World Health Organization (WHO) advocates international cooperation for advancing positive policies towards HIV/AIDS and PLWHA in terms of testing and other initiatives. It reports that one of the recent approaches to HIV testing is:

> …health care workers should offer counseling to all those who might benefit, and then benefit from advances in the treatment and prevention of HIV infection and related diseases. Services and benefits cannot be accessed unless the status is disclosed. Once people know of the status they can plan for the future, prevent further transmission of HIV, better cope with the infection and gain early access to care and treatment. (WHO 2003:1)

Other relevant strategies proposed by the WHO are related to testing and the engagement of healthcare providers within local communities. It is worth noting that WHO suggests that HIV testing should be voluntary rather than mandatory (WHO 2003:2). At the same time, HIV testing services should not be restricted to specific groups. In order to have positive engagement with communities, healthcare teams can be strengthened by employing PLWHA who can work to support other patients (WHO 2003:4), and peer support groups in the community could be helpful. Any strategic directions should be guided by human rights-based approaches, gender-based analysis, anti-oppression frameworks and population-specific approaches (Patten 2003: 34).

To sum up, laws need to be amended to respond to the HIV pandemic, and this will entail significant changes. At the same time, current penal codes could be reviewed and revised in light of existing challenges to governments and PLWHA. The importance of effective implementation of human rights standards and anti-discrimination protection must be emphasized as well as the need to provide affordable legal assistance to PLWHA. Public awareness about the pandemic and the plight of the infected need to be developed with adequate information and guidance. The global nature of the epidemic renders cooperation among states and international bodies critical. More research is required to determine measures to strengthen the resilience of PLWHA. Community-based, participatory research and rigorous evaluations of prevention, care and treatment interventions, especially aimed at reducing stigma and discrimination, are necessary, and this might require substantial financial commitments from the government (MacIntosh 2007:8). Continued research on the epidemic should have a positive impact in monitoring the spread of this disease, contribute to global efforts to manage the crisis, maintain support for people with HIV, implement effective care and treatment programmes, articulate necessary policy and ensure maximum benefit from limited resources (CPHA 2005:17).

Criminalization of HIV/AIDS has a significant negative impact on PLWHA, who would become less likely to seek treatment, and other citizens, who would have less information in relation to the HIV status of those around them. People who do not disclose their HIV status are liable to be subjected to criminal charges in Canada. It is worth mentioning that the number of new charges has increased significantly since 2004, and consequently serious criminal offences and imprisonment resulted for not disclosing HIV status before sexual encounters (CATIE 2010:23). Although criminalization of HIV has the potential to be effective, the approach is open to criticism. For example, people who are imprisoned for this infraction will be in a risky environment for transmission, such as sexual encounters with other men and potentially intravenous drug use. Also, criminalization will prevent people from accessing testing services, as it will increase stigma among the general population towards PLWHA. It may affect the privacy and confidentiality of PLWHA, which further increases stigma and discrimination. Criminalization is also gendered, as women may face violence after revealing their HIV status, or are unable to negotiate safe sex (CATIE 2010:24).

Many respondents agree that the level of stigmatization and discrimination has not decreased over time since they first became infected. One respondent suggested that a person with HIV may live for several years, while those with other infections may not survive for a single year. This leads to confusion over the perception of HIV as a deadly condition. As long as Canadian society adds sexuality issues to perceptions of HIV/AIDS, it will not be possible to dissociate it from immoral behaviours and shame, and discrimination and stigma will persist. Awareness could be the most powerful tool to overcome this problem. Self-stigma is especially damaging, whereas being comfortable with their own status has the potential to propel PLWHA towards a better quality of life.

To what extent is the issue of double discrimination of HIV-positive immigrants and refugees protection being addressed in Canadian law? First, provincial governments have no constitutional authority to legislate on criminal law matters, since the making of criminal law lies within the exclusive jurisdiction of the federal government (The Nizkor Project 2013). Therefore, there is no prospect of a Canadian province legislating a crime of assault, for example, and the federal government legislating another crime of violation of one's rights protected by the Charter that would give rise to a similar 'dual sovereignty' doctrine regarding criminal offences in Canadian law (Walker 2010).

However, given that criminal law authority lies exclusively within the jurisdiction of the federal government, double jeopardy issues may arise in the context of prosecution of hate-motivated crime (The Nizkor Project 2013). For instance, if a person were to be prosecuted for a hate-motivated crime—that is, committing an assault by reason of hatred of another person's actual or perceived race, colour, religion, and ethnic origin—then upon an acquittal or conviction for that crime, a subsequent prosecution for the basic crime would be barred because the assault would be included in the hate-motivated crime.

Canada's constitutional guarantees of rights and freedoms differ from those of the USA, in that they are restricted to protect exclusively against abusive government action. Section 32 of the Charter ensures that the Charter applies to the parliament and government of Canada or to the legislature or government of a province. Under section 24, a person whose rights are denied or violated could apply to a court to obtain a remedy (Walker 2010). In those proceedings, the court may exclude evidence if established that its admission would bring the administration of justice into disrepute (The Nizkor Project 2013).

Systemic racial discrimination in employment—that is, that which is built into organizational structures and processes and often involving informal activities and cultures—is, by its nature, difficult to identify. As a result, there is no clear consensus on its prevalence, practical significance or policy remedy. Formulation of policies and enforcement responsibilities does exist exclusively at the federal level as defined by the Canadian Human Rights Act (CHRA) and the Employment Equity Act (EEA), but there is no consensus on their effectiveness. There are a number of organizations that claim to have been working for PLWHA, and it is important to understand how they perform and who their clients are. The role of support organizations needs to be calibrated carefully to align their mission and activities with the policies intended to serve migrants and refugees living with HIV/AIDS.

The need to mitigate stigma and discrimination against HIV sufferers emerges as an important issue. Stigma and discrimination emanate from multiple sources at the family, community, institutional, legal and policy levels. Practitioners can apply a common core response to stigma and discrimination with appropriate modifications across different settings. Discrimination is often ingrained in the mindset of some people. Therefore, although policies are in place, culturally or personally people are still unable to overcome their prejudices. This is evident in widespread practices that discriminate across all aspects of life. Campaigns to create awareness about stigma can be accorded priority in designing policies, and elimination of misconceptions about HIV transmission is critical. An effective regime of human rights will complete the requirements to terminate or reduce stigma and discrimination.

Appendix

Interview Questions

Department of Political Science
McMaster University

Information About the Interview Questions

This gives an idea what I would like to learn about Asian refugees and migration in North America. Interviews will be one-on-one and will be open ended (not just 'yes' and 'no'). This might require some change in the wording. I may use sub-questions to make sure I understand what you said or if I need more information when we are talking.

Some of the things I will ask you about will be very personal. I want to make sure you understand that all of your answers will be kept confidential, meaning that they are private and will not be shared with others. Your name will not be written on this survey to add more protection to your privacy. All research material will be kept in a locked file and destroyed after the research has ended. You will be assigned a number, which will be used to refer to quotations from your interview that may be used in publications or presentations. You have the right to withdraw from the study at any time or to not respond to questions you do not wish to answer.

If you have any questions, feel free to ask them at any time during the interview.

If you have questions, or things that you'd like to talk about after this interview, you can call Ahsan Ullah 905 525 9140 ext ..... or you may contact my supervisor *Professor Ahmed Shafiqul Huque* 905 525 9140 *ext* ...... I would like to thank you for allowing me the opportunity to get to know a little about you and of your experiences and views about living with HIV in Canada.

A.A. Ullah, A.S. Huque, *Asian Immigrants in North America with HIV/AIDS*,
DOI 10.1007/978-981-287-119-0

1. I am interested in your migration experience. How many years have you lived in Canada?
2. Where did you apply for immigration/refugee/asylum? Would you please describe the circumstances under which you made your decision to immigrate or seek refuge in Canada? (Probes: relatives already in Canada, economic hardships, political problems, conflict)
3. When did you first learn about your HIV status – was it before or after you moved here? Can you remember your immediate feelings and reaction after learning your status? Can you tell me why you felt that way?
4. What were your experiences like with the IRB officials/members during your immigration/refuge or asylum application processing? (Probes: effect of positive status on application experiences, possible discrimination, stress, perceived fairness/unfairness)
5. Please tell me how has money or your financial situation influenced your life experiences in relation to your status? What has been your experience with the cost of various categories of support and treatment?
6. Please describe how have you changed your life style because of your status (Probes: eating habits, work life, sexual practices, spiritual state of mind, mobility etc.)?
7. How did your family members learn about your status, I mean how was your status disclosed? Can you describe how they reacted to this knowledge? How did their behaviours towards you change, if at all? And if their behaviours did change, why do you think so?

   7a. How did your friends learn about your status, I mean how was your status disclosed? Can you describe how they reacted to this information? How did their behaviour and attitude towards you change, if at all? And if their behavior and attitude did change, why do you think so?
   7b. How did your neighbours learn about your status, I mean how was your status disclosed? Can you describe how they reacted to this knowledge? How did their behavior and attitude towards you change, if at all? And if their behavior and attitude did change, why do you think so?

8. I'd like to know a little bit now about your work experience here in Canada. What kinds of jobs have you had since arriving? For how long did you have these jobs? Would you say these jobs paid you enough to keep healthy and contribute to your household expenditure? (experience of how HIV has impacted their work/jobs and financial stability)
9. I'd also like to know a little about whether you experienced anything different from other workers in your jobs because of your HIV positive status. (Probes: did/do colleagues know your status, any discrimination, any lost salary due to health-related absences, etc).
10. Would you please describe the neighborhood, community you live in? Are there any particular reasons why you chose to live there? What do you find to be the most encouraging and helpful and assistance from your community and neighbors? (how many neighbours/community members know your status etc.)

(Can you describe how people in your neighbourhood act (negative and positive) towards you? If they don't know your status, do you think their behavior would be different if they did?)

11. Would you please tell me about the medical or health care services you have received over this time? (Probes: attitudes of health care providers, longer waiting time, feeling about the care etc.).
12. Children whose parents have HIV or other diseases are sometimes treated differently by classmates or teachers at school or when they play in the community. Have your children experienced any different treatment from others that might be related to your HIV positive status?
13. Would you please describe what kind of support you are receiving? (who provides support, nature and range of support – financial support, social, housing, transportation, emotional etc.; who is providing the most support). What kinds of support do you receive from neighbourhood community, or from your ethnic community? How adequate do you find the level of support? Are any of these supports (or their inadequate levels) related to your HIV positive status?
14. You might have a range of experiences (good and bad) about how you have been treated by others because of your HIV positive status. Would you tell me what have been the best and worst aspects of your treatment experiences from you family members? (Probes: avoid eating together or avoid cooked food (cooked by you) etc.).
15. If you could go back to when you first knew your status, what would you do differently? What can others learn from your experiences? What advice would you share with others?
16. Would you describe the differences in the comfort level between here and in your own country? (what way is that different, most difficult challenges being a positive etc.)
17. Would you please share some of your demographic information such as your family; i.e. your family members, your age, your civil status and your nationality (current and previous).
18. Finally, is there anything else or any experiences, observations or thoughts you think we should know?

Bibliography

Abbott, J. R., Koziol-McLain, J., & Lowenstein, S. (1995). Domestic violence against women: Incidence and prevalence in an emergency department population. *JAMA, 273*(22), 1763–1767.

Adamczyk, A., & Pitt, C. (2009). Shaping attitudes about homosexuality: The role of religion and cultural context. *Social Science Research, 38*(2), 338–351.

Adam, B. D. (2011). Epistemic fault lines in biomedical and social approaches to HIV prevention. *Journal of the International AIDS Society, 14*(Supplement 2), S2.

Adams, J. S. (1965). Inequity in social exchange. In L. Berkowitz (Ed.), *Advances in experimental social psychology*. New York: Academic Press.

Adetunji, J., & Meekers, D. (2001). Consistency in condom use in the context of HIV/AIDS in Zimbabwe. *Journal of Biosocial Science, 33*(1), 121–138.

Adger, W. (2000). Social and ecological resilience: Are they related? *Progress in Human Geography, 24*(3), 347–364.

Ahlburg, D. A., & Jensen, E. R. (1998). The economics of the commercial sex industry. In M. Ainsworth, L. Fransen, & M. Over (Eds.), *Confronting AIDS: Evidence from the developing world*. Luxembourg: European Commission.

Aidslaw. (1999). *Criminal law and HIV/AIDS: The Cuerrier case*. Toronto: Aidslaw. Download on 21 August 2013. http://www.aidslaw.ca/newsite/wp-content/uploads/2013/04/Criminal+Law+-+ENG.pdf

Aidslaw. (2005). *Recent changes to visitor visa process affecting entry into Canada for people living with HIV/AIDS*. XVI international AIDS conference, AIDS 2006, Toronto.

Ainsworth, M., Fransen, L., & Over, M. (Eds.). (1998). *Confronting AIDS: Evidence from the developing world*. Brussels: The World Bank and the European Commission, Official Publications of the European Communities.

Allport, A. (2004). *Immigration policy*. New York: Chelsea House.

Alonzo, A. A., & Reynolds, N. R. (1995). Stigma, HIV and AIDS: An exploration and elaboration of a stigma trajectory. *Social Science and Medicine, 41*(3), 303–315.

Altaf, S. A., & Lovelace, R. E. (2011). *Labour, HIV & the workplace: Working to get the job done*. New York: United Nations.

Amisi, B., Bond, P., Cele, N., & Ngwane, T. (2011). Xenophobia and civil society: Durban's structured social divisions. *Politikon, 38*(1), 59–83.

Amnesty International. (2011). *Annual report 2011*. New York: Amnesty International.

Andersen, M. L., & Hill Collins, P. (2010). Why race, class, and gender still matter. In M. L. Andersen & P. Hill Collins (Eds.), *Race, class, and gender: An anthology* (7th ed., pp. 1–16). Belmont: Wadsworth.

A.A. Ullah, A.S. Huque, *Asian Immigrants in North America with HIV/AIDS*,
DOI 10.1007/978-981-287-119-0

Anderson, K., & Jack, D. C. (1991). Learning to listen: Interview techniques and analyses. In S. B. Gluck & D. Patai (Eds.), *Women's words: The feminist practice of oral history*. London: Routledge.

André, P. (2004, November 8–9). *Stigma and discrimination against persons living with HIV/AIDS in the workplace, in health care facilities, in accessing treatment, and in society*, The Hague. www.nuigalway.ie/sites/eu-china.../seminars/.../andre%20pereira-eng.doc

APIAHF. (2006). *Asian and Pacific Islander American Health Forum, health brief: South Asians in the United States*. Revised 2 August.

Archavanitkul, K., & Guest, P. (1994). Migration and the commercial sex sector in Thailand. *Health Transition Review, 4*, 273–295.

ASAAP. (2007). *South Asian women living with HIV/AIDS. Report*. Toronto: ASAAP.

Avert. (2012). *Living with HIV*. West Sussex: Avert. http://www.avert.org/living-hiv.htm. Accessed 23 June 2013.

Bajek, R., & Okada, N. (2007). Examining definitions of resilience and adjusting a resilience model to the Japanese cultural context: A preliminary study. *Annuals of Disaster Prevention Research Institute*, Kyoto University, No. 50B.

Ball, D. P. (2012, June 19). *Conservatives' refugee health cuts rile doctors. 'Groundswell' of anger by MDs, other health providers, against hit to Interim Federal Health program*. TheTyee.ca. Accessed on 19 Apr 2013.

Barnett, T., & Whiteside, A. (1999). HIV/AIDS and development: Case studies and a conceptual framework. *European Journal of Development Research, 11*(2), 200–234.

Barnett, T., & Whiteside, A. (2002). *AIDS in the twenty-first century: Disease and globalisation*. Basingstoke: Palgrave.

Basnett, I. (2001). Health care professionals and their attitudes toward decisions affecting disabled people. In G. L. Albrecht, K. D. Seelman, & M. Bury (Eds.), *Handbook of disability studies*. Thousand Oaks: Sage.

Batson, D. C., Chang, J., Orr, R., & Rowland, J. (2002). Empathy, attitudes, and action: Can feeling for a member of a stigmatized group motivate one to help the group? *The Society for Personality and Social Psychology, 28*(12), 1656–1666.

Baumeister, R. F., Smart, L., & Boden, J. M. (1996). Relation of threatened egotism to violence and aggression: The dark side of high self-esteem. *Psychological Review, 103*(1), 5–33.

Bayer, R. (2008a). Stigma and the ethics of public health: Not can we but should we. *Social Science and Medicine, 67*(3), 463–472.

Bayer, R. (2008b). What means this thing called stigma? A response to Burris. *Social Science and Medicine, 67*, 476–477.

Beck, H. J., Reitz, J. G., & Nan, W. (2002, March). *Addressing systemic racial discrimination in employment: The health Canada case and implications of legislative change*. This paper was presented at the Canadian Human Rights Commission case against Health Canada. Ottawa.

Becker, G. (1976). *The economic approach to human behavior*. Chicago: University of Chicago Press.

Becker, G. S., & Kilburn, M. R. (1994). *The economics of misery*. Chicago: Department of Economics, University of Chicago.

Beeby, D. (2012, August 17). Bank of Canada bans image of Asian-looking woman from new $100 banknotes. *The Canadian Press*.

Berger, B. E., Ferrans, C. E., & Lashley, F. R. (2001). Measuring stigma in people with HIV: Psychometric assessment of the HIV stigma scale. *Research in Nursing & Health, 24*(6), 518–529.

Bharat, S., Aggleton, P., & Tyer, P. (2001). *India: HIV and AIDS – Related discrimination, stigmatization and denial, Joint United Nations Program on HIV/AIDS (UNAIDS)* (pp. 1–66), Switzerland, Geneva.

Bilsborrow, R. E. (Ed.). (1998). *Migration, urbanization, and development: New directions and issues*. New York: United Nations Population Fund/Kluwer Academic Publishers.

Bird, J. (2002). *The heart's narrative: Therapy and navigating life's contradictions* (2nd ed.). Auckland: Publishing Press Ltd.

Blank, R. M. (2001). An overview of trends in social and economic wellbeing, by race. In N. J. Smelser, W. J. Wilson, & F. Mitchell (Eds.), *Racial trends and their consequences*. Washington, DC: National Academy Press.

Blank, R. M., Dabady, M., & Citro, C. F. (Eds.). (2004). *Measuring racial discrimination*. Washington, DC: National Academy of Sciences/National Academies Press.

Bless, C., Higson-Smith, C., & Kagee, A. (2006). *Fundamentals of social research methods: An African perspective* (4th ed.). Cape Town: Juta & Co.

Block, J. (1971). *Lives through time*. Berkeley: Bancroft Books.

Block, J. H., & Block, J. (1980). The role of ego-control and ego-resiliency in the organization of behavior. In W. A. Collins (Ed.), *Minnesota symposia on child psychology* (Vol. 13, pp. 39–101). Hillsdale: Erlbaum.

Blumberg, H. M. (2000). Tuberculosis infection control. In L. B. Riechman & E. S. Hershfield (Eds.), *Tuberculosis: A comprehensive international approach* (2nd ed.). New York: Marcel Dekker.

Bobo, L. (2001). Racial attitudes and relations at the close of the twentieth century. In N. Smelser, W. J. Wilson, & F. Mitchell (Eds.), *America becoming: Racial trends and their consequences* (pp. 262–299). Washington, DC: National Academy Press. http://www.wjh.harvard.edu/soc/faculty/bobo/pdf%20documents/RacialAt.pdf

Bond, V. (1998). *Household capacity and "coping up" in rural Zambia: Dealing with AIDS, other illness and adversity in Chiawa*. Doctorate thesis, University of Hull.

Bonnel, R. (2000). *HIV AIDS: Does it increase or decrease growth? What makes an economy HIV-resistant?* Paper presented at the IAEN symposium, Durban.

Botnick, M. R. (2000). Part 1: HIV as 'the line in the sand'. *Journal of Homosexuality, 38*(4), 39–76.

Brennan, R. J. (2010, March 30). Canada's failed asylum seekers will be shown the door. *The Star*. Ottawa Bureau.

Brodkin, A. M., & Coleman, M. (1996). Kids in crisis: Helping a foster child heal. *Instructor, 105*(5), 34–35.

Brouard, P. (2006). A closer look: The internalization of stigma related to HIV. United States Agency for International Development (USAID). Center for the Study of AIDS/University of Pretoria, and Caroline Wills, POLICY.

Buehler, S. (2013). *What every mental health professional needs to know about sex*. New York: Springer.

Cameron, E. (2007). *Legislating an epidemic: The challenge of HIV/AIDS in the workplace*. Geneva: ILO Headquarters.

Canada Without Poverty. (2012). *Yukon poverty progress profile*. Ottawa: CWP.

Canadian Council for Refugees-CCR. (2005, March). *The refugee appeal: Is no one listening? Report*. Montreal: CCR.

Canadian HIV/AIDS Legal Network. (2007). Legislation contagion: The spread of problematic new HIV laws in Western Africa. *HIV/AIDS Policy and Law Review, 12*(2–3), 1–77.

Canadian HIV/AIDS Legal Network. (2012, May). *Questions and answers, Canada's immigration policy as it affects people living with HIV*.

Cardol, M., de Haan, R. J., van den Bos, G. A. M., de Jong, B. A., & de Groot, I. J. (1999). The development of a handicap assessment questionnaire: The Impact on Participation and Autonomy (IPA). *Clinical Rehabilitation, 13*(5), 411–419.

Care India. (2011, October). *Vulnerability to HIV & AIDS: A social research on cross border mobile populations from Nepal to India* (p. 1). New Delhi.

Carey, M., & Russell, S. (2003). Outsider-witness practices: Some answers to commonly asked questions. *The International Journal of Narrative Therapy and Community Work, 3*, 3–16.

Carlisle, C. (2000). The search for meaning in HIV and AIDS: The carers' experience. *Qualitative Health Research, 10*(6), 750–765.

Carpenter, S. R., & Brock, W. A. (2004). Spatial complexity, resilience and policy diversity: Fishing on lake-rich landscapes. *Ecology and Society, 9*(1), 8.

Castells, M. (1996). *The Network Society*. Oxford: Blackwell Publishers Inc.

Castells, M. (1998). *End of millennium*. Oxford: Blackwell Publishers Inc.

Castro, A., & Farmer, P. (2005). Understanding and addressing AIDS-related stigma: From anthropological theory to clinical practice in Haiti. *American Journal of Public Health, 95*(1), 53–59.

CATIE (Canadian AIDS Treatment Information Exchange). (2010). *HIV in Canada, trends and issues that affect HIV prevention, CARE, treatment and support*. Toronto: CATIE.

Census. (2006). *Statistics Canada 2006*. Census Canada.

CHAIC (Canadian HIV/AIDS Information Centre). (2005). *Leading together: Canada takes action on HIV/AIDS, (2005–2010)*. http://www.leadingtogether.ca/pdf/Leading_Together.pdf. Accessed 12 May 2013.

Chandra, P. S., Deepthivarma, S., & Manjula, V. (2003). Disclosure of HIV infection in South India: Patterns, reasons and reactions. *AIDS Care, 15*(2), 207–215.

Charmaz, K. (2000). Grounded theory: Objectivist and constructivist methods. In N. K. Denzin & Y. S. Lincoln (Eds.), *Handbook of qualitative research*. Thousand Oaks: Sage Publications.

Charmaz, K. (2003). Grounded theory: Objectivist and constructivist methods. In N. K. Denzin & Y. S. Lincoln (Eds.), *Strategies of qualitative inquiry* (2nd ed.). Thousand Oaks: Sage Publications.

Cheru, F. (1999). Effects of structural adjustment policies on the full enjoyment of human rights (E/CN.4/1999/50). In *Report by the Independent Expert, Mr. Fantu Cheru, submitted in accordance with Commission decisions 1998/102 and 1997/103*. United Nations Economic and Social Council. Ottawa.

Chesney, M. A., & Smith, A. W. (1999). Critical delays in HIV testing and care: The potential role of stigma. *American Behavioral Scientist, 42*(7), 1162–1174.

CIC. (2007). *Facts and figures: Immigration overview-permanent and temporary residents*. Ottawa: CIC.

CIC. (2011). *Applying as a member of the Family Class. Government of Canada*. CIC: Ottawa. Downloaded 14 April 2013. http://www.cic.gc.ca/english/information/applications/3998-temp.asp

CIC. (2013). *Report on plans and priorities 2013–2014*. http://www.cic.gc.ca/english/resources/publications/rpp/2013-2014/

Clark, R., Anderson, N. B., Clark, V. R., & Williams, D. R. (1999). Racism as a stressor for African Americans: A biopsychosocial model. *American Psychologist, 54*(10), 805–816.

Clay, S., Bond, V., & Nyblade, L. (2003). *"We can tell them: AIDS is not spread by being together" children's experiences of HIV-related stigma and discrimination in Zambia* (Working Report). Lusaka: Associated Press. Retrieved from http://www.icrw.org.

Cochran, W. G. (1963). *Sampling techniques* (2nd ed.). New York: Wiley.

Collins, P. Y., Unger, H., & Armbrister, A. (2008). Church ladies, good girls, and locas: Stigma and the intersection of gender, ethnicity, mental illness, and sexuality in relation to HIV risk. *Social Science and Medicine, 67*(3), 389–397.

Conrad, P. (1985). The meaning of medications: Another look at compliance. *Social Science and Medicine, 20*(1), 29–37.

Corr, C. A., Doka, K. J., & Kastenbaum, R. (1999). Dying and its interpreters: A review of selected literature and some comments on the state of the field. *Omega: The Journal of Death and Dying, 39*, 239–259.

Corrigan, P. W., & Kleinlein, P. (2007). The impact of mental illness stigma. In P. W. Corrigan (Ed.), *On the stigma of mental illness*. Washington, DC: American Psychological Association.

Corrigan, P., Glomm, G., & Mendez, F. (2005). AIDS crisis and growth. *Journal of Development Economics, 77*(1), 107–124.

Courtenay-Quirk, C., Wolitski, R. J., Parsons, J. T., Gómez, C. A., & Seropositive Urban Men's Study Team. (2006). Is HIV/AIDS stigma dividing the gay community? Perceptions of HIV-positive men who have sex with men. *AIDS Education and Prevention, 18*(1), 56–67.

CPHA. (2005). *Leading together: Canada takes action on HIV/AIDS (2005–2010)*. Ottawa: Canadian Public Health Association.

CPHA. (2006). *The Canadian HIV vaccines plan towards a world without AIDS*. Ottawa: Canadian Public Health Association.

Crenshaw, K. W. (1996). Mapping the margins: Intersectionality, identity politics, and violence against women of color. In K. W. Crenshaw, N. Gotanda, G. Peller, & K. Thoma (Eds.), *Critical race theory: The key writings that formed the movement* (pp. 357–383). New York: New Press.

Creswell, J. W. (1998). *Qualitative inquiry and research design: Choosing among five traditions*. Thousand Oaks: Sage.

Creswell, J. W. (2003). *Research design: Qualitative, quantitative and mixed method approaches* (2nd ed.). Thousand Oaks: Sage.

Cresswell, M. (2005). Psychiatric "survivors" and testimonies of self-harm. *Social Science & Medicine, 61*(8), 1668–1677.

Crocker, J. (2011). Safety in numbers: Shifting from egosystem to ecosystem. *Psychological Inquiry: An International Journal for the Advancement of Psychological Theory, 22*(4), 259–264.

Crocker, J., & Garcia, J. A. (2006). Stigma and the social basis of the self: A synthesis. In S. Levin & C. Van Laar (Eds.), *Stigma and group inequality*. Mahwah: Erlbaum.

Crocker, J., Major, B., & Steele, C. (1998). Social stigma. In D. Gilbert, S. T. Fiske, & G. Lindzey (Eds.), *Handbook of social psychology*. Boston: McGraw Hill.

Crush, J., & Ramachandran, S. (2009, September). *Xenophobia international migration and human development* (Human Development Research Paper 2009/47). New York: United Nations.

Cullinan, K. (2001, September 6). Health minister promotes nutiritional alternative to ARV roll-out. *Health System Trust South Africa*.

Dasgupta, P. (2001). *Human well-being and the natural environment*. Oxford: Oxford University Press.

Davies, S. (1996). *Adaptable livelihoods: Coping with food insecurity in the Malian Sahel*. London: Macmillan.

de Bruyn, T. (1998). *HIV/AIDS and discrimination: A discussion paper*. Montréal: Canadian HIV/AIDS Legal Network and Canadian AIDS Society.

de Waal, A., & Whiteside, A. (2003). New variant famine: AIDS and food crisis in southern Africa. *Lancet, 362*(9391), 1234–1237.

Deacon, H., Prosalendis, S., & Stephney, I. (2004). *Understanding HIV/AIDS stigma: A theoretical and methodological analysis*. Cape Town: HSRC Press.

deGroot-Maggetti, G. (2002, March). *A measure of poverty in Canada: A guide to the debate about poverty lines*. Ottawa: Citizens for Public Justice.

Derlega, V. J., Metts, S., Petronio, S., & Margulis, S. T. (1993). *Self-disclosure*. Newbury Park: Sage.

DeVoretz, D., Pivnenko, S., & Coulombe, D. S. (2003). *The immigration triangle: Quebec, Canada and the rest of the world* (RIIM Working Paper No. 03-11). Vancouver: Simon Fraser University, Centre of Excellence, Immigration.

DeVoretz, D., Pivneko, S., & Beiser, M. (2004). *The economic experiences of refugees in Canada* (pp. 1–31). The Institute of Study of Labor (IZA). Ottawa.

Dewar, P. (2012). *Report from the hill: Full reversal of refugee health cuts essential*. Ottawa: Ottawa Centre.

DHHS (Department of Health Services Human). (2003). *New freedom commission on mental health: Achieving the promise: Transforming mental health care in America* (DHHS Publication No. SMA-03-0832). Virginia: DHHS.

DiManno R. (1993, June 16). The quiet dignity of a Tamil beaten by racists. *The Toronto Star*, pp. A7.

Dion, K. L. (2001). The social psychology of perceived prejudice and discrimination. *Canadian Psychology, 43*(1), 1–10.

Dodds, C., et al. (2001). *The cost of HIV/AIDS in Canada*. Nova Scotia: GPI Atlantic, Genuine Progress Index for Atlantic Canada.

Doka, K. J., & Martin, T. L. (2010). *Grieving beyond gender: Understanding the ways men and women mourn*. New York: Routledge.

Donald, A., & Mottershaw, E. (2009). *Poverty, inequality and human rights: Do human rights make a difference?* York, UK: Josephine Rowntree Foundation.

Dorais, L.-J. (2003, September). *From refugees to transmigrants: The Vietnamese in Canada*. Paper presented at the 8th international metropolis conference, Vienna, Université Laval, Québec, Canada.

Douglas, D. D. (2008, April). Racism in Canada: The evidence of things not seen. *The Ardent Review, 1*, 41–44.

Dovidio, J. F., Louis, A., Penner, T. L., Albrecht, W. E., Norton, S. L., Gaertner, J., & Shelton, N. (2008). Disparities and distrust: The implications of psychological processes for understanding racial disparities in health and health care. *Social Science and Medicine, 67*(3), 478–486.

Dunkle, K. L., Jewkes, R. K., Brown, H. C., Gray, G. E., McIntryre, J. A., & Harlow, S. D. (2004). Transactional sex among women in Soweto, South Africa: Prevalence, risk factors and association with HIV infection. *Social Science and Medicine, 59*(8), 1581–1592.

Eastwood, S. V., & Hill, P. C. (2004). A gender-focused qualitative study of barriers to accessing tuberculosis treatment in The Gambia, West Africa. *International Journal of Tuberculosis and Lung Disease, 83*, 198–242.

Eaton, L. A., Kalichman, S. C., O'Connell, D. A., & Karchner, W. D. (2009). A strategy for selecting sexual partners believed to pose little/no risks for HIV: Serosorting and its implications for HIV transmission. *AIDS Care, 21*(10), 1279–1288.

Edward, K., & Warelow, P. (2005). Resilience: When coping is emotionally intelligent. *Journal of the American Psychiatric Nurses Association, 11*(2), 101–102.

Ellis, F. (2003). *Human vulnerability and food insecurity: Policy implications. Forum for Food Security in Southern Africa*. London: Overseas Development Institute.

Emlet, C. A., Tozay, S., & Raveis, V. H. (2011). "I'm not going to die from the AIDS": Resilience in aging with HIV disease. *The Gerontologist, 51*(1), 101–111.

Erica, R, Katie, D, & Malika, S. (2012, May 17). *Refugee health cuts are bad for all of us: Reducing coverage endangers them – And public health*. http://www.thespec.com/opinion/columns/article/72582--efugee-health-cuts-are-bad-for-all-of-us

Espiritu, A. (2004). Racial diversity and hate crime incidents. *The Social Science Journal, 41*(2), 197–208.

Everatt, D. (2011). Xenophobia, state and society in South Africa, 2008–2010. *Politikon, 38*(1), 7–36.

Eysenbach, G., & Till, J. E. (2001). Ethical issues in qualitative research on internet communities. *British Medical Journal, 323*, 1103–1105.

Farmer, P. (1997). On suffering and structural violence: A view from below. In A. Kleinman, V. Das, & M. Lock (Eds.), *Social suffering*. Berkeley: University of California Press.

Fennell, R. S., Foulkes, L. M., & Boggs, S. R. (1994). Family-based program to promote medication compliance in renal transplant children. *Transplantation Proceedings, 26*(1), 102–103.

Fenton, L. (2004). Preventing HIV/AIDS through poverty reduction: The only sustainable solution? *The Lancet, 364*(9440), 1186–1187.

Fenton, K. A. (2007). Changing epidemiology of HIV/AIDS in the United States: Implications for enhancing and promoting HIV testing strategies. *Clinical Infectious Disease, 45*(4), 213–s220.

Fernandes, A. P., Sanches, R. S., Mill, J., Lucy, D., Palha, P. F., & Dalri, M. C. (2007). Lipodystrophy syndrome associated with antiretroviral therapy in HIV patients: Considerations for psychosocial aspects. *Revista Latino-Americana de Enfermagem, 15*(5), 1041–1045.

Ford, N. J., & Kittisuksathit, S. (1996). *Youth sexuality: The sexual awareness, lifestyles and related-health service needs of young, single, factory workers in Thailand*. Nakhon Pathom: Institute for Population and Social Research, Mahidol University.

Fox, A. M. (2010). The social determinants of HIV serostatus in Sub-Saharan Africa: An inverse relationship between poverty and HIV? *Public Health Reports, 124*(4), 16–24.

Friedli, L. (2009). *Mental health, resilience and inequalities – A report for WHO Europe and the Mental Health Foundation*. London/Copenhagen: Mental Health Foundation and WHO Europe. http://www.euro.who.int/mentalhealth/topics/20090309_1

Friis, H. (1998). The possible role of micronutrients in HIV infection. *SCN News, 17*, 11–12.

Frist, T. F. (1996). *Don't treat me like I have leprosy* (1st ed.). London: TALMILEP.

Froman, R. D., & Owen, S. V. (2001). Measuring attitudes toward persons with AIDS: The AAS-G as an alternate form of the AAS. *Scholarly Inquiry for Nursing Practice, 15*(2), 161–174.

Froman, R. D., Owen, S. V., & Daisy, C. (1992). Development of a measure of attitudes toward persons with AIDS. *Image - The Journal of Nursing Scholarship, 24*(2), 149–152.

Frost, D. M., Parsons, J. T., & Nanín, J. E. (2007). Stigma, concealment and symptoms of depression as explanations for sexually transmitted infections among gay men. *Journal of Health Psychology, 12*(4), 636–640.

Fuller, K. L. (1993). Refugee mental health in Aalborg, Denmark. Traumatic stress and cross-cultural treatment issues. *Nordic Journal of Psychiatry, 47*(4), 251–256.

Fullilove, M. T., & Fullilove, R. E. (1999). Stigma as an obstacle to AIDS action. *American Behavioral Scientist, 42*(7), 1117–1129.

Furnham, A., & Shiekh, S. (1993). Gender, generational and social support correlates of mental health in Asian immigrants. *International Journal of Social Psychiatry, 39*(1), 22–33.

Gaffeo, E. (2003). The economics of HIV/AIDS: A survey. *Development Policy Review, 21*(1), 27–49.

Galabuzi, G.-E. (2005). *The racialization of poverty in Canada: Implications for Section 15 Charter Protection*. The National Anti-Racism Council of Canada national conference, Ottawa, pp. 1–39.

Ganong, L., & Coleman, M. (2002). Family resilience in multiple contexts. *Journal of Marriage and the Family, 64*(2), 346–348.

Ganyaza-Twalo, T., & Seager, J. (2005). *Literature review on poverty and HIV/AIDS measuring the social and economic impacts on households*. Cape Town: Human Sciences Research Council (HSRC).

Garmezy, N. (1991). Resiliency and vulnerability to adverse developmental outcomes associated with poverty. *American Behavioral Scientist, 34*(4), 416–430.

Garmezy, N., Masten, A. S., & Tellegen, A. (1984). The study of stress and competence in children: A building block for developmental psychopathology. *Child Development, 55*(1), 97–111.

Gerntholtz, L. (2004). An overview of some of the key legal developments in HIV/AIDS and the law – 2003. *Southern African Journal of HIV Medicine, 5*(1), 40–43.

Gersovitz, M. (2000). A preface to the economic analysis of disease transmission. *Australian Economic Papers, 39*(1), 68–83.

Gertler, P., Shah, M., & Bertozzi, S. M. (2005). Risky business: The market for unprotected commercial sex. *Journal of Political Economy, 113*(3), 518–550.

Gilmour, G. A. (1994, May). *Hate-motivated violence* (Working Document). Research and Statistics Division, Department of Justice, Canada. WD1994-6e.

Glaser, B. G., & Strauss, A. S. (1967). *The discoverer of grounded theory*. Chicago: Aldine.

Goffman, E. (1963). *Stigma: Notes on management of spoiled identity*. Englewood Cliffs: Prentice-Hall.

Goffman, E. (1968). *Stigma: Notes on the management of spoiled identity*. Harmondsworth: Penguin.

Gordon, D. (1972). *Theories of poverty and underemployment*. Lexington: Lexington Books.

Gordon, P., & Crehan, K. (1995). *Gender, sexual violence and the HIV epidemic, SEPED conference paper series 1*. New York: United Nations.

Government of Canada. (2011). Regulations amending the immigration and refugee protection regulations. *Archived* — Part I: Vol. 145.

Grant, S. (2010). *International migration and human rights*. Geneva: GCIM (Global Commission on International Migration).

Grant, I. (2011). The prosecution of non-disclosure of HIV in Canada: Time to rethink Cuerrier. *McGill Journal of Law and Health, 5*(1), 7–59.

Gray, A., Punpuing, S., Yoddumnern-Attig, B., Chongsatitmun, C., Thongkrajai, E., & Singsungchai, P. (1999). *Gender, sexuality and reproductive health in Thailand*. Nakhom Pathom: Institute for Population and Social Research, Mahidol University.

Greeff, M. (2005). Information collection: Interviewing. In A. S. De Vos, H. Strydom, C. B. Fouché, & C. S. L. Delport (Eds.), *Research at grass roots for the social sciences and human service professions* (3rd ed., pp. 286–313). Pretoria: Van Schaik Publishers.

Greeff, M., Phetihu, R., Makoae, L. N., Diamini, P. S., Holzemer, W. L., Naidoo, J. R., & Chirwa, M. (2008). Disclosure of HIV status: Experience and perceptions of persons living with HIV/AIDS and nurses involved in their care in Africa. *Qualitative Health Research, 18*(3), 311–324.

Greene, R. R., & Conrad, A. P. (2002). Basic assumptions and terms. In R. R. Greene (Ed.), *Resiliency: An integrated approach to practice, policy, and research* (pp. 29–62). Washington, DC: NASW Press.

Haag, D., & Gilbert, M. (2007, December). *Trends in HIV positive immigrants and reporting by Citizenship and Immigration Canada (CIC) 2000–2007*. Vancouver: Center for Disease Control (CDC).

Hall, S. (1996). *Race, the floating signifier* [Video]. Northampton: Media Education Foundation.

Hargrave, C. (1999, April). Homelessness in Canada from housing to shelters to blankets. *Share International*.

Hargreaves, J. R., Morrison, L. A., Chege, J., Rutenburg, N., Kahindo, M., Weiss, H. A., Hayes, R., & Buve, A. (2002). Socioeconomic status and risk of HIV infection in an urban population in Kenya. *Tropical Medicine and International Health, 7*(9), 793–802.

Harris, B. (2002). Xenophobia: A new pathology for a new South Africa? In D. Hook & G. Eagle (Eds.), *Psychopathology and social prejudice* (pp. 169–184). Cape Town: University of Cape Town Press.

Hashemi, S. (2001). *Linking microfinance and safety net programmes to include the poorest: The case of IGVGD in Bangladesh'* (CGAP Focus Note 21). Washington, DC: World Bank.

Hawley, D. R. (2000). Clinical implications of family resilience. *American Journal of Family Therapy, 28*(2), 101–116.

Heijnders, M. L. (2004). Experiencing leprosy: Perceiving and coping with leprosy and its treatment. A qualitative study conducted in Nepal. *Leprosy Review, 75*, 327–337.

Helie, A. (2004). Holy hatred. *Reproductive Health Matters, 12*(23), 120.

Herek, G. M. (1999). AIDS and stigma. *American Behavioral Scientist, 42*(7), 1106–1116.

Herek, G., & Glunt, E. (1998). An epidemic of stigma: Public reactions to AIDS. *American Psychologist, 43*(11), 886–891.

Hermansson, A.-C., et al. (1996). The mental health of war-wounded refugees: An 8-year follow-up. *The Journal of Nervous and Mental Disease, 190*(6), 374.

Hesketh, T., Duo, L., Li, H., & Tomkins, A. M. (2005). Attitudes to HIV and HIV testing in high prevalence areas of China: Informing the introduction of voluntary counseling and testing programmes. *Sexually Transmitted Infections, 81*(2), 108–112.

HIV/AIDS News. (2007. March 26). HIV-infected Canada woman charged with sex assault.

Hlatshwayo, M. (2011). Is there room for international solidarity within South African borders? COSATU's responses to the xenophobic attacks of May 2008. *Politikon, 38*(1), 169–189.

Holmqvist, G. (2009). *HIV and income inequality* (IPC Working Paper 54, pp. 19). Magadi: Brasilia, International Policy Centre for Inclusive Growth.

Howarth, C. (2006). Race as stigma: Positioning the stigmatized as agents, not objects. *Journal of Community and Applied Social Psychology, 16*(6), 442–451.

Hsin Yang, L., & Kleinman, A. (2008). "Face" and the embodiment of stigma in China: The cases of schizophrenia and AIDS. *Social Science and Medicine, 67*(3), 398–408.

Hulme, D. (2000). Is micro-debt good for poor people? *Small Enterprise Development, 11*(1), 26–28.

Human Resources Skills Development Canada. (2012). *Indicators of well-being in Canada*. Ottawa: Employment and Social Development Canada.

Human Rights First. (2011). *Combating xenophobic violence: A framework for action*. New York: Human Rights First.

Hunter, M. (2007). The changing political economy of sex in South Africa: The significance of unemployment and inequalities to the scale of the AIDS pandemic. *Social Science and Medicine, 64*(3), 689–700.

Hutton, E. (2009). Bias motivation in crime: A theoretical examination. *Internet Journal of Criminology*.

ILO. (2005). *HIV/AIDS and poverty: The critical connection*. Geneva: ILO Programme on HIV/AIDS and the World of Work.

Imrie, J., & Macdonald, N. (2009). HIV testing in men who have sex with men: Are we ready to take the next HIV testing test? *Sex Transmitted Infections, 85*, 487–488.

Institute of Medicine (IOM). (2002). *Unequal treatment: Confronting racial and ethnic disparities in health care*. Washington, DC: National Academy Press.

Institute of Medicine (IOM). (2003). In B. D. Smedley, A. Y. Stith, & A. R. Nelson (Eds.), *Unequal treatment: Confronting racial and ethnic disparities in health care*. Washington, DC: National Academies Press.

Interagency Coalition on AIDS and Development (ICAD). (2008). *HIV, AIDS and housing issues*. Ottawa: ICAD.

International AIDS Society. (2002). *On vaccine production and equitable distribution*. The XIV international AIDS conference, Barcelona.

International Center for Research on Women (ICRW). (2002). *Addressing HIV-related stigma and resulting discrimination in Africa: a three country study in Ethiopia, Tanzania, and Zambia*. Washington, DC: ICRW.

International HIV/AIDS Alliance. (2013). Report. Paris.

Israel, G. D. (1992, October). *Sampling the evidence of extension program impact*. Program Evaluation and Organizational Development, IFAS, University of Florida. PEOD-5

Jackman, M. R. (1994). *The velvet glove: Paternalism and conflict in gender, class, and race relations*. Berkeley: University of California Press.

Jaramillo, E. (1998). Pulmonary tuberculosis and health-seeking behaviour: How to get a delayed diagnosis in Cali, Colombia. *Tropical Medicine and International Health, 3*(2), 138–144.

Jing, J. (2006). Fear and stigma: An exploratory study of AIDS patient narratives in China. In J. Kaufman, A. Kleinman, & T. Saich (Eds.), *AIDS and social policy in China*. Cambridge: Harvard University Press.

Jürgens, R., et al. (2009). Ten reasons to oppose the criminalization of HIV exposure or transmission. *Reproductive Health Matters, 17*(34), 163–172.

Kellerman, S. E., Lehman, J. S., Lansky, A., Stevens, M. R., Hecht, F. M., Bindman, A. B., & Wortley, P. M. (2002). HIV testing within at-risk populations in the United States and the reasons for seeking or avoiding HIV testing. *Journal of Acquired Immune Deficiency Syndromes, 31*(2), 202–210.

Kennedy, D. P., Cowgill, B. O., Laura, M., Bogart, L. M., Corona, R., Ryan, G. W., Murphy, D. A., Nguyen, T., & Schuster, M. A. (2010). Parents' disclosure of their HIV infection to their children in the context of the family. *AIDS and Behavior, 14*(5), 1095–1105.

Kessler, R. C., et al. (1999). The prevalence, distribution, and mental health correlates of perceived discrimination in the United States. *Journal of Health and Social Behavior, 40*, 208–230.

Khawaja, M. (2003). The fertility of Palestinian women in Gaza, the West Bank, Jordan, and Lebanon. *Population, 58*(3), 273–302.

Kitsuse, J. (1962). Societal reactions to deviant behavior: Problems of theory and method. *Social Problems, 9*(3), 247–256.

Kleinman, A., & Hall-Clifford, R. (2013). Stigma: A social, cultural, and moral process. *Journal of Epidemiology and Community Health, 63*(6), 418–419.

Klovdahl, A. S., Graviss, E. A., Yaganehdoost, A., Ross, M. W., Wanger, A., Adams, G. J., & Musser, J. M. (2001). Networks and tuberculosis: An undetected community outbreak involving public places. *Social Science and Medicine, 52*(5), 681–694.

Knipscheer, J. W., & Kleber, R. J. (2007). Acculturation and mental health among Ghanaians in The Netherlands. *International Journal of Social Psychiatry, 53*(4), 369–383.

Kollapan, J. (1999, October 7). *Xenophobia in South Africa: The challenge to forced migration*. Unpublished Seminar. Graduate School: University of the Witwatersrand.

Kornblum, W. (1997). *Sociology in a changing world* (4th ed.). Fort Worth: Harcourt Brace.

Kotoh, A. M. (2008). Social health insurance in Ghana: Conceptualizing resilience in the context of a social health insurance scheme. Paper presented at the International CERES/EADI summer school, Amsterdam (9–12 June). 276 *Medische Antropologie, 20*(2).

Kremer, M. (1996). Integrating behavioral choice into epidemiological models of AIDS. *Quarterly Journal of Economics, 111*(2), 549–573.

Kremer, M., & Morcom, C. (1998). The effect of changing sexual activity on HIV prevalence. *Mathematical Biosciences, 51*(1), 99–122.

Kübler-Ross, E. (1969). *On death and dying*. London: Routledge.

Kutikuppala, S. R. (2012). Changing face of AIDS: Hope to infected millions. *The Health, 3*(4), 86–87.

Lachaud, J. P. (2007). HIV prevalence and poverty in Africa, micro- and macro-econometric evidences applied to Burkina Faso. *Journal of Health Economics, 26*(3), 483–504.

Lawson, E., Gardezi, F., Calzavara, L., Husbands, W., Myers, T., & Tharao, W. (2006). *HIV/AIDS stigma, denial, fear and discrimination experiences and responses of people from African and*

Caribbean communities in Toronto. Toronto: The African and Caribbean Council on HIV/AIDS in Ontario (ACCHO) and The HIV Social, Behavioural and Epidemiological Studies Unit, University of Toronto.

Lee, J. D., & Craft, E. A. (2002). Protecting one's self from a stigmatized disease…once one has it. *Deviant Behavior, 23*(3), 267–299.

Lee, M. B., Lester, P., & Rotheram-Borus, M. J. (2002). The relationship between adjustment of mothers with HIV and their adolescent daughters. *Clinical Child Psychology and Psychiatry, 7*, 71–84.

Leedy, P. D., & Ormrod, J. E. (2005). *Practical research* (8th ed.). Columbus: Pearson Merrill Prentice Hall.

Legge, K. (1995). *HRM: Rhetorics and realities*. Basingstoke: Macmillan Business.

Lemert, E. (1967). *Human deviance, social problems and social control*. Upper Saddle River: Prentice Hall.

Levin, S., & Van Laar, C. (Eds.). (2006). *Stigma and group inequality*. Mahwah: Erlbaum.

Levy, A. (2001). *A lifetime Portfolio of risky and risk-free sexual behaviour and the prevalence of AIDS* (Working Paper 01-04). Department of Economics, University of Wollongong.

Levy, A. (2002). A lifetime portfolio of risky and risk-free sexual behaviour and the prevalence of AIDS. *Journal of Health Economics, 21*(6), 993–1007.

Lewis, S. (1992). *Report to the Ontario Government on Race Relations, Toronto* (pp. 2–3). Toronto: Government of Ontario.

Lincoln, Y. S., & Guba, E. G. (1985). *Naturalistic inquiry*. Beverly Hills: Sage Publications, Inc.

Link, B. G., & Phelan, J. C. (2001). Conceptualizing stigma. *Annual Review of Sociology, 27*(1), 363–385.

Link, B. G., Struening, E., Dohrenwend, B. P., Cullen, F. T., & Shrout, P. E. (1989). A modified labeling theory approach to mental disorders: An empirical assessment. *American Sociological Review, 54*(3), 400–423.

Link, B. G., Struening, E. L., Rahav, M., Phelan, J. C., & Nuttbrock, L. (1997). On stigma and its consequences: Evidence from a longitudinal study of men with dual diagnoses of mental illness and substance abuse. *Journal of Health and Social Behavior, 38*(2), 177–190.

Lloyd, P. J. (1991). AIDS: An economic approach to the choice of policies. *The Economic Record, 7*(197), 126–138.

Loevinsohn, M., & Gillespie, S. (2003). *HIV/AIDS, food security and rural livelihoods: Understanding and responding* (Working Paper No. 2). Washington, DC: International Food Policy Research Institute.

Long, P. M. (2010, March). *Reducing health inequities: A health system approach to chronic disease prevention*. Vancouver: Project Steering Committee, Provincial Health Service Authority.

Lopez, A. D., & Mathers, C. D. (2006). Measuring the global burden of disease and epidemiological transitions: 2002–2030. *Annals of Tropical Medicine & Parasitology, 100*(5 and 6), 481–499.

MacIntosh, J. M. (2007). HIV/AIDS stigma and discrimination: A Canadian perspective and call to action. *Inter-American Journal of Psychology, 41*(1), 93–102.

Magnusson, R. (1996). Australian HIV/AIDS legislation: A review for doctors. *Australian & New Zealand Journal of Medicine, 26*(3), 396–406.

Mahajan, A. P., Sayles, J. N., Patel, V. A., Remien, R. H., Sawires, S. R., Ortiz, D. J., Szekeres, G., & Coates, T. J. (2008, August). Stigma in the HIV/AIDS epidemic: A review of the literature and recommendations for the way forward. *AIDS, 22*(Suppl 2), S67–S79.

Mak, W. W., Mo, P. K., Cheung, R. Y., Woo, J., Cheung, F. M., & Lee, D. (2006). Comparative stigma of HIV/AIDS, SARS, and tuberculosis in Hong Kong. *Social Science & Medicine, 63*(7), 1912–1922.

Malgas, H. A. (2005). *Stress, coping and the role of social support in living with HIV/AIDS: A literature review*. Unpublished master's thesis, University of Stellenbosch.

Mann, C., & Stewart, F. (2000). *Internet communication and qualitative research: A handbook for researching online*. London: Sage.

Mao, L., Kidd, M. R., Rogers, G., Andrews, G., Newman, C. E., Booth, A., Saltman, D. C., & Kippax, S. C. (2009). Social factors associated with major depressive disorder in homosexually

active, gay men attending general practices in urban Australia. *Australian and New Zealand Journal of Public Health, 33*(1), 83–86.
Marks, G., Richardson, J. L., & Maldonado, N. (1991). Self-disclosure of HIV infection to sexual partners. *American Journal of Public Health, 81*, 1321–1322.
Marshall, G. (1998). *Oxford dictionary of sociology*. Oxford/New York: Oxford University Press.
Marvasti, A. M. (2004). *Qualitative research in sociology*. London: Sage.
Masanjala, W. (2007). The poverty HIV/AIDS nexus in Africa: A livelihood approach. *Social Science and Medicine, 64*(5), 1032–1041.
Matsuoka, J. (1993). Demographic characteristics as determinants in qualitative differences in the adjustment of Vietnamese refugees. *Journal of Social Service Research, 17*(3/4), 1–21.
Matthews, G., Zeidner, M., & Roberts, R. (2002). *Emotional intelligence: Science and myth*. Cambridge, MA: MIT Press.
Maxwell, J. (1998). *Positive perspectives: A qualitative examination of issues facing HIV positive gay men in Toronto. Gay Men's Health Promotion*. Available from: http://www.actoronto.org/research.nsf/Pages/positive+perspectives. Accessed 26 Aug 2010.
Mayank, K. S. (2012). Understanding the gender disparity in HIV testing in India. In *Conference paper for the population association of America 2012*. Princeton: PAA. Downloaded on April 2014 http://paa2012.princeton.edu/papers/122798
Meyer, I. H. (2008). Social patterning of stress and coping: Does disadvantaged social status confer more stress and fewer coping resources? *Social Science and Medicine, 67*(3), 368–379.
McConnell, C. (2009). Migration and xenophobia in South Africa. *Conflict Trends, 11*(1), 34–40.
McCubbin, L. (2001, August 24–28). *Challenges to the definition of resilience*. In Paper presented at the annual meeting of the American psychological association, 109th, San Francisco, CA.
McLaren, L. M. (2002). Public support for the European Union: Cost/benefit analysis or perceived cultural threat? *The Journal of Politics, 64*, 551–566.
Mian, A. Q. (1999). *Applied statistics*. Pathum Thani: Asian Institute of Technology (AIT).
Miaoulis, G., & Michener, R. D. (1976). *An introduction to sampling*. Dubuque: Kendall Hunt Publishing.
Miller, S., McDaniel, S., Rolland, J., & Feetham, S. (2006). *Individuals, families and the new era of genetics: Biopsychosocial perspectives*. New York: Norton.
Mills, J., Bonner, A., & Francis, K. (2006). Adopting a constructivist approach to grounded theory: Implications for research design. *International Journal of Nursing Practice, 12*(1), 8–13.
Ministry of Education – British Columbia. (2009). *Students from refugees backgrounds – A guide for teachers and schools* (pp. 1–45). Victoria: Ministry of Education.
Mishra, V., Assche, S. B., Greener, R., Vaessen, M., Hong, R., Ghys, P. D., Boerma, J. T., Van Assche, A., Khan, S., & Rutstein, S. (2007). HIV infection does not disproportionately affect the poorer in sub-Saharan Africa. *AIDS, 7*(Suppl), S17–S28.
Mohanty, C. T. (2003). "Under western eyes" revisited: Feminist solidarity through anti-capitalist struggles. *Signs, 28*(2), 499–535.
Moller, V. (1998). Quality of life in South Africa: Post apartheid trends. *Social Indicators Research, 43*(1–2), 27–68.
Moriya, T. M., Gir, E., & Hayashida, M. (1994). A scale of attitudes towards AIDS: A psychometric analysis. *Revista Latino-Americana de Enfermagem, 2*(2), 37–53.
Morris, A. (1998). 'Our fellow Africans make our lives hell': The lives of Congolese and Nigerians living in Johannesburg. *Ethnic and Racial Studies, 21*(6), 1116–1136.
Moser, C. (1996). *Confronting crisis: A summary of household responses to poverty and vulnerability in four poor urban communities*. Washington, DC: World Bank.
Mutangadura, G., Mukurazita, D., & Jackson, H. (1999). *A review of household and community responses to the HIV/AIDS epidemic in the rural areas of Sub-Saharan Africa*. Geneva: UNAIDS.
Nasreen, H. (2005). *BRAC HIV and AIDS programme: The mid-term evaluation*. Dhaka: BRAC, RED.
National Center for Health Statistics Center for Disease Control and Prevention. (2004). *U.S. Department of Health and Human Services, mortality tables*. Washington, DC: U.S. Department of Health and Human Services.

Neal, R. (2004). *Voices: Women, poverty and homelessness in Canada*. Ottawa: The National Anti – Poverty Organization (NAPO).

Neuman, W. L. (2000). *Social research methods: Qualitative and quantitative approaches*. Boston: Allyn & Bacon.

Nicholls, P. G., Wiens, C., & Smith, W. C. (2003). Delay in presentation in the context of local knowledge and attitude towards leprosy – The results of qualitative fieldwork in Paraguay. *International Journal of Leprosy and Other Mycobacterial Diseases, 71*(3), 198–209.

Nirman, D. (2004). Immigration and HIV/AIDS – Issues of medical testing, exclusion and discrimination. *Ontario Bar Journal (OBA) Citizenship and Immigration Section, 7*(3), 1–8.

Noii-Van. (2007). *The Canadian refugee process. Flowchart*. http://noii-van.resist.ca/wp-content/uploads/2007/05/refugee-process-flowchart.pdf. Accessed 10 Apr 2013.

Nyar, A. (2011). 'Business as usual': The response of the corporate sector to the May 2008 xenophobic violence. *Politikon, 38*(1), 149–167.

Nyblade, L., Pande, R., Mathur, S., MacQuarrie, K., Kidd, R., Banteyerga, H., Kidanu, A., Kilonzo, G., Mbwambo, J., & Bond, V. (2003). *Disentangling HIV and AIDS stigma in Ethiopia, Tanzania and Zambia*. Washington, DC: International Center for Research on Women.

OCASI (Ontario Council of Agencies Serving Newcomers). (2005). *When services are not enough: The role of immigrant and newcomer service organizations in fostering community leadership development*. A report prepared for Ontario Council of Agencies Serving Immigrants. Toronto: OCASI.

OHCHR, & UNAIDS. (2006). *International guidelines on HIV/AIDS and human rights. 2006 consolidated version 7*. Geneva: UNAIDS.

Ojteg, K. (2009). *Socio-economic determinants of HIV in Zambia: A district-level analysis*. Sweden: Department of Economics, The University of Lund.

Olson, R. R., Cadge, W., & Harrison, J. T. (2006). Religion and public opinion about same-sex marriage. *Social Science Quarterly, 87*(2), 340–360.

Ontario Human Rights Commission. (2000). *Human rights policy in Ontario*. Ontario: CCH Canadian Limited.

Orley, J., & Kuyken, W. (Eds.). (1994). *Quality of life: International perspectives*. Berlin: Springer.

OSCE. (2011). *Hate crimes in the OSCE region – Incidents and responses. Annual report for 2010*. Warsaw: OSCE Office for Democratic Institutions and Human Rights.

PANCAP. (2010). *Regional policy on HIV related stigma and discrimination*. Georgetown: PANCAP.

Paradies, Y. (2006). A systematic review of empirical research on self-reported racism and health. *International Journal of Epidemiology, 35*(4), 888–901.

Parker, R., & Aggleton, P. (2002, May). *HIV/AIDS-related stigma and discrimination: A conceptual framework and agenda for action*. Report prepared by the Population Council. Available from: www.popcouncil.org/pdfs/horizons/sdcncptlfrmwrk.pdf. Accessed 26 Aug 2010.

Parker, R., & Aggleton, P. (2003). HIV and AIDS-related stigma and discrimination: A conceptual framework and implications for action. *Social Science and Medicine, 57*(1), 13–24.

Patten, S. (2003). *HIV/AIDS impacts within the African and Black Diaspora. Policy paper. African and Black Diaspora Global Network on HIV and AIDS*. New Brunswick: San Patten Associates.

Patterson, J. M. (2002). Integrating family resilience and family stress theory. *Journal of Marriage and the Family, 64*(2), 349–360.

Pennebaker, J. W., Colder, M., & Sharp, L. K. (1990). Accelerating the coping process. *Journal of Personality and Social Psychology, 58*(3), 528–537.

Penner, A. (2012). *An excessive demand: Immigrants with disabilities and medical admissibility in Canada's immigration system*. Theses and dissertations. Paper 803.

Peretti-Watel, P., Spire, B., Pierret, J., Lert, F., Obadia, Y., & VESPA Group. (2006). Management of HIV-related stigma and adherence to HAART: Evidence from a large representative sample of outpatients attending French hospitals (ANRS-EN12-VESPA 2003). *AIDS Care, 18*(3), 254–261.

Peritz, I. (1993, January 5). Vandals deface seven synagogues with swastikas, anti-Semitic slogan. *The [Montreal] Gazette*, Tuesday, p. A1.

Perry, B. (2003). *Hate and bias crime: A reader*. New York: Routledge.

Person, B., Bartholomew, L. K., Gyapong, M., Addiss, D. G., & van den Borne, B. (2009). Health-related stigma among women with lymphatic filariasis from the Dominican Republic and Ghana. *Social Science and Medicine, 68*(1), 30–38.

Persson, A. (2005). Facing HIV: Body shape change and the (in)visibility of illness. *Medical Anthropology, 24*(3), 237–264.

Pescosolido, B. A., Martin, J. K., Lang, A., & Olafsdottir, S. (2008). Rethinking theoretical approaches to stigma: A Framework Integrating Normative Influences on Stigma (FINIS). *Social Science and Medicine, 67*(3), 431–440.

Peter, W., & Karl, L. (2013). *Entry and residence regulations for people living with HIV*. Berlin: Deutsche AIDS-Hilfe e.V.

Petersen, C. (1991). A Queer response to Bashing: Legislating against hate. *Queen's Law Journal, 15*, 237.

Pettaway, C. A. (1999). Racial differences in the androgen/androgen receptor pathway in prostate cancer. *Journal of the National Medical Association, 91*(12), 653–660.

Pettigrew, T. F. (1998). Intergroup contact theory. *Annual Review of Psychology, 49*, 65–85.

PHAC (Public Health Agency of Canada). (2005). *HIV/AIDS epi update: HIV in Canada among persons from countries where HIV is endemic*. Ottawa: Surveillance and Risk Assessment Division (SRAD), Public Health Agency of Canada (PHAC).

PHAC. (2005a). *HIV/AIDS. Epi*. Ottawa: Centre for Infectious Disease Prevention and Control/ Public Health Agency of Canada.

PHAC. (2008). *Summary: Estimates of HIV prevalence and incidence in Canada*. Ottawa: Surveillance and Risk Assessment Division, Centre for Communicable Diseases and Infection Control.

PHAC (Public Health Agency of Canada). (2009, May). *Population health: What determines health?* Ottawa: Public Health Agency of Canada [website]. Available from: http://www.ohtn.on.ca/Pg.s/Publications/Default.aspx

PHAC. (2010). *HIV/AIDS among aboriginal people in Canada*. Downloaded on 12 April 2013 http://www.phac-aspc.gc.ca/aids-sida/publication/epi/2010/pdf/EN_Chapter8_Web.pdf

PHAC. (2011). *Ministerial Council on HIV/AIDS. Annual Report 2009–2010*. Ottawa: Ministerial Council on HIV/AIDS, Public Health Agency of Canada.

PHAC to Address HIV/AIDS in Canada, Strengthening Federal Action in the Canadian Response to HIV/AIDS. (2004). Minister of Public Works and Government Services Canada.

Phelan, J. C., et al. (2008). Stigma and prejudice: One animal or two? *Social Science & Medicine, 67*, 358–367

Philip, S. S., Yu, X., Donnell, D., Vittinghoff, E., & Buchbinder, S. (2010). Serosorting is associated with a decreased risk of HIV seroconversion in the EXPLORE study cohort. *PLoS ONE, 5*(9), e12662.

Philipson, T. J., & Posner, R. A. (1993). *Private choices and public health: The AIDS epidemic in an economic perspective*. Cambridge: Harvard University Press.

Phoenix, A., & Pamela, P. (2006). Intersectionality. *European Journal of Women's Studies, 13*, 187–192.

Piot, P., & Coll Seck, A. M. (2001). International response to the HIV/AIDS epidemic: Planning for success. *Bulletin of the World Health Organization, 79*(12), 1106–1112.

Pitkin, K., et al. (2007). Immigrants and health care: Sources of vulnerability. *Health Affairs, 26*, 1258–1268.

Poku, N. K. (2007). *HIV/AIDS and Governance in Africa. Population, health, environment, and conflict* (ECSP Report 12). Wilson Center.

Pottie, K., Vissandjée, B., Grant, J., Logie, C., Ullah, A. K. M. A., Murangira, F., & Welch, V. (2011). Evidence-based clinical guidelines for immigrants and refugees. *Canadian Medical Association Journal, 183*(12), E824–E925.

Pruyser, P. W. (1986). Maintaining hope in adversity. *Pastoral Psychology, 35*(2), 120–131.

Rahlenbeck, S. I. (2004). Knowledge, attitude, and practice about AIDS and condom utilization among health workers in Rwanda. *Journal of the Association of Nurses in AIDS Care, 15*(3), 56–61.

Rahman, M., & Ullah, A. K. M. A. (Eds.). (2012). *Migration policies in Asia: South, South East and East Asia*. New York: Nova Science.

Ramana, P. V. (2011). India's Maoist insurgency: Evolution, current trends, and responses. In K. Michael (Ed.), *India's contemporary security challenges*. Washington, DC: Woodrow Wilson International Center for Scholars.

Ralston, K. M. (2012). An intersectional approach to understanding stigma associated with male sexual assault victimization. *Sociology Compass, 6*(4), 283–292.

Raymond, H. F., & McFarland, W. (2009). Racial mixing and HIV risk among men who have sex with men. *AIDS and Behavior, 13*(4), 630–637.

Reidy, D. (1993). Stigma is social death: Mental health consumers/survivors talk about their lives. *Education for Community Initiatives*.

Ren, X. S., Amick, B., & Williams, D. R. (1999). Racial/ethnic disparities in health: The interplay between discrimination and socioeconomic status. *Ethnicity and Disease, 9*(2), 151–165.

Rintamaki, L. S., Davis, T. C., Skripkauskas, S., Bennett, C. L., & Wolf, M. S. (2006). Social stigma concerns and HIV medication adherence. *AIDS Patient Care and STDs, 20*, 359–368.

Rodriguez, W. R., Christodoulides, N., Floriano, P. N., Graham, S., Mohanty, S., Dixon, M., Hsiang, M., Peter, T., Zavahir, S., Thior, I., Romanovicz, D., Bernard, B., Goodey, A. P., Walker, B. D., & McDevitt, J. T. (2005). A Microchip CD4 counting method for HIV monitoring in resource-poor settings. *PLoS Medicine, 2*(7), E182.

Rollason, K. (2009, October 22). *Refugees immigrants in poverty: Report: Problem could grow as more arrive here*. Winnipeg Free Press – Printed edition. Ottawa.

Ross, M., et al. (1994). Prison: Shield from threat or threat to survival? *British Medical Journal, 308*, 1092–1095.

Sahadevan, P. (1999). *Ethnic conflict in South Asia*. Notre Dame: Joan B. Kroc Institute of International Peace Studies, University of Notre Dame.

Salthouse, S. M. (2010). *Downward spirals: Disability and health costs as contributors to poverty and imagining ways forward*. Australia: Women with Disabilities Australia.

Sandelowski, M., Lambe, C., & Barroso, J. (2004). Stigma in HIV-positive women. *Journal of Nursing Scholarship, 36*(2), 122–128.

Scambler, G. (1998). Stigma and disease: Changing paradigms. *The Lancet, 352*, 1054–1055.

Scheff, T. J. (1966). *Being mentally ill: A sociological theory*. Chicago: Aldine.

Scheff, T. J. (1984). *Being mentally ill: A sociological theory* (2nd ed.). Chicago: Aldine.

Scheier, M. F., & Carver, C. S. (1987). Dispositional optimism and physical well-being: The influence of generalized expectancies on health. *Journal of Personality, 55*(2), 169–210.

Schuman, H., Steeh, C., Bobo, L., & Krysan, M. (1997). *Racial attitudes in America: Trends and interpretations*. Cambridge: Harvard University Press.

Schweitzer, A., Mizwa, M. B., & Ross, M. W. (2009). *Psychosocial aspects of HIV/AIDS: Adults*. Romania: Baylor Black Sea Foundation.

Seager, J, Ganyaza-Twalo, T, & Tamasane, T. (2005, December 12–14). *Development of a conceptual framework to help understand the interactions between poverty and HIV/AIDS at the household level*. Paper presented at the IUSSP seminar, Cape Town, South Africa.

Seidman, G. (1999). Is South Africa different? Sociological comparisons and theoretical contributions from the Land of Apartheid. *Annual Review of Sociology, 25*, 419–440.

Seligman, M. E. P., & Csikszentmihalyi, M. (2000). Positive psychology: An introduction. *American Psychologist, 55*(1), 5–14.

Semenak, S. (1989, March 21). Stabbing victim was dying of AIDS: Friends say killing was part of recent wave of attacks on gays. *The [Montreal] Gazette*, Tuesday, pp. A1–A2.

Semenak, S. (1989, March 27). Gay Bashing: Montreal gays say it's getting worse as gangs cruise streets for trouble. *The [Montreal] Gazette*, Monday, pp. A5.

Sentell, T. L., & Halpin, H. A. (2006). Importance of adult literacy in understanding health disparities. *Journal of General Internal Medicine, 21*(8), 862–866.

Serovich, J. M. A. (2001). Test of two HIV disclosure theories. *AIDS Education and Prevention, 13*(4), 355–364.

Shamoo, A., & Resnik, D. (2009). *Responsible conduct of research* (2nd ed.). New York: Oxford University Press.

Shelton, J. D., Cassell, M. M., & Adetunji, J. (2005). Is poverty or wealth at the root of HIV? *The Lancet, 366*(9491), 1057–1058.

Sherrell, K. M. (2011). *Finding a home: The housing experiences of government assisted refugees and refugee claimants in Winnipeg and Vancouver* (pp. 1–250). Thesis, The University of British Columbia.

Sheth, L. (2001, August). *First national meeting on HIV/AIDS prevention in the South Asian Population in the U.S.*, Los Angeles.

Sidhu, M., Gill, P., & Poonia, P. (2003. November/December). Step 1: Facing HIV in the South Asian community. *Living+ Magazine, 8*.

Sinclair, M. R. (1998). Community, identity and gender in migrant societies of southern Africa: Emerging epistemological challenges. *International Affairs, 74*(2), 339–353.

Sinclair, M. R. (1999). 'I know a place that is softer than this …' emerging migrant communities in South Africa. *International Migration, 37*(2), 465–481.

Sinwell, L. (2011). Obtaining 'Peace', searching for justice: evaluating civil society and local government responses to xenophobia in Alexandra. *Politikon, 38*(1), 131–148.

Smit, P. J., Brady, M., Carter, M., Fernandes, R., Lamore, L., Meulbroek, M., Ohayon, M., Platteau, T., Rehberg, P., Rockstroh, J. K., & Thompson, M. (2012). HIV-related stigma within communities of gay men: A literature review. *AIDS Care, 24*(3–4), 405–412.

Smith, M. F. (1983). *Sampling considerations in evaluating cooperative extension programs* (Florida Cooperative Extension Service Bulletin PE-1). Gainesville: Institute of Food and Agricultural Sciences, University of Florida.

Smith, J. A., & Osborn, M. (2003). Interpretative phenomenological analysis. In J. A. Smith (Ed.), *Qualitative psychology: A practical guide to methods*. London: Sage.

Smith, M. J. (2011). Violence, xenophobia and the media: A review of the South African media's coverage of xenophobia and the xenophobic violence prior to and including the events of 2008. *Politikon, 38*(1), 111–129.

Sniderman, P., & Hagendoorn, L. (2007). *When ways of life collide. Multiculturalism and its discontents in the Netherlands*. Princeton: Princeton University Press.

Snyder, C. R., Harris, C., Anderson, J. R., Holleran, S. A., Irving, L. M., Sigmon, S. T., Yoshinobu, L., Langelle, C., & Harney, P. (1991). The will and the ways: Development and validation of an individual-differences measure of hope. *Journal of Personality and Social Psychology, 60*(4), 570–585.

Soyombo, O. (2008). Xenophobia in contemporary society: A sociological analysis. *IFE Psychologia – Special Issue: Xenophobia, 16*(2), 85–104.

Srinivasula, S., Lempicki, R. A., Adelsberger, J. W., Huang, C., Roark, J., Lee, P. I., Rupert, A., Stevens, R., Sereti, I., Lane, H. C., Di Mascio, M., & Kovacs, J. A. (2011). Differential effects of HIV viral load and CD4 count on proliferation of naive and memory CD4 and CD8 T lymphocytes. *The Journal of the medical Society of the Hematology, 118*(2), 262–270.

Statistics Canada. (2003). *Ethnic diversity survey: Portrait of a multicultural society*. Canada: Statistics Canada.

Statistics Canada. (2006). *Population by selected ethnic origins, by province and territory*. Ottawa: Statistics Canada.

Statistics Canada. (2009). *Population by selected ethnic origins, by census metropolitan areas (2006 Census)*. Ottawa: Stat Canada. http://www.statcan.gc.ca/tables-tableaux/sum-som/l01/cst01/demo27a-eng.htm. Accessed 22 Apr 2014.

Statistics Canada. (2011). *Immigration and ethnocultural diversity in Canada*. Ottawa: Statistics Canada.

Statistics Canada. (2012). *Canadian Centre for Justice Statistics Profile Series*. Ottawa: Statistics Canada.

Steel, Z., Silove, D., Phan, T., & Bauman, A. (2002). Long-term effect of psychological trauma on the mental health of Vietnamese refugees resettled in Australia: A population-based study. *Lancet, 360*(9339), 1056–1062.

Steinberg, J. (2007). *Masculinity, race and antiretroviral treatment in South Africa: A report from the old Transkei*. African Studies Centre Seminar, St Antony's College, Oxford University.

Steinfatt, T. M. (2002). *Working at the bar: Sex work and health communication in Thailand*. Westport: Ablex Publishing.

Strauss, A., & Corbin, J. (1998). *Basics of qualitative research: Techniques and procedures for developing grounded theory* (2nd ed.). Thousand Oaks: Sage.

Strydom, H. (2005). The pilot study. In A. S. De Vos, H. Strydom, C. B. Fouché, & C. B. L. Delport (Eds.), *Research at grass roots for the social sciences and human service professions* (3rd ed.). Pretoria: Van Schaik.

Stuber, J., Meyer, I., & Link, B. (2008). Introduction-stigma, prejudice, discrimination and health. *Social Science and Medicine, 67*(3), 351–357.

Stutterheim, S. E., Bos, A. E. R., & Schaalma, H. P. (2008). *HIV-related stigma in the Netherlands*. Amsterdam/Maastricht: Dutch Aids Fonds (Aids Fund).

Sudman, S. (1976). *Applied sampling*. New York: Academic Press.

Sumartojo, E. (1993). When tuberculosis treatment fails. A social behavioral account of patient adherence. *American Review of Respiratory Disease, 147*(5), 1311–1320.

Surgeon General of the United States. (2001). *Mental health: Culture, race, and ethnicity. A supplement to mental health: The report of the surgeon general*. Rockville: US Department of Health and Human Services.

Symington, A. (2010). *Women and criminalization of HIV non-disclosure in Canada from the Ontario HIV/AIDS treatment network annual conference*. Research at the front lines: Targeting the complexities of HIV held on 15th November, Toronto.

Sztompka, P. (2008). The focus on everyday life: A new turn in sociology. *European Review, 16*(1), 23–37.

Tajfel, H. (1970). Experiments in intergroup discrimination. *Scientific American, 223*, 96–102.

Taylor, S. E. (1991). *Health psychology*. Los Angeles: McGraw-Hill.

Thapa, G. (2004, April 27–28). Rural poverty reduction strategy for South Asia. In *Paper presented at an international conference on ten years of Australian South Asia research centre organized at the Australian National University*, Canberra.

The Kaiser Family Foundation. (2011, November). *The global HIV/AIDS epidemic, U.S. Global Health Policy Fact Sheet*. www.kff.org, Menlo Park

The Nizkor Project. (2013). *Hate-motivated violence: The Rodney King case possible implications for Canada*. http://www.nizkor.org/hweb/orgs/canadian/canada/justice/hate-motivated-violence/hmv-006–01.html. Accessed 10 Apr 2013.

Thornicroft, G. (2006). *Actions speak louder ... Tackling discrimination against people with mental illness*. London: Mental Health Foundation.

Topouzis, D., & du Guerny, J. (1999). *Sustainable agricultural/rural development and vulnerability to the AIDS epidemic*. Geneva: UNAIDS.

Tran, K., Kaddatz, J., & Allard, P. (2005). *South Asians in Canada: Unity through diversity*. Statistics Canada. Retrieved from http://www.statcan.gc.ca/bsolc/olc-cel/olc-cel?catno=11-008-X20050028455&lang=eng [affiliation: government].

Trochim, W. M. (2000). *Research methods knowledge base – Survey research*. http://trochim.human.cornell.edu/kb/survey.htm

Turner, R. J., & Lloyd, D. A. (1999). The stress process and the social distribution of depression. *Journal of Health and Social Behavior, 40*(4), 374–404.

Turton, W. R., & Chalmers, B. E. (1990). Apartheid, stress and illness: The demographics context of distress reported by South African Africans. *Social Science and Medicine, 31*(11), 1191–2000.

Tusaie, K., & Dyer, J. (2004). Resilience: A historical review of the construct. *Holistic Nursing Practice, 18*(1), 3–8.

Ullah, A. K. M. A. (2000). An unwanted profession: Do the women willingly choose it? *Development Review, 12*, 11–24.

Ullah, A. K. M. A. (2003). Prostitution and AIDS situation in Bangladesh: Is the ignorance not endangering us? *Asian Journal of Women's Studies, 9*(2), 95–114.

Ullah, A. K. M. A. (Ed.). (2008a). *South and Southeast Asia: Dealing with history and development*. Berlin: VDM-Verlag.

Ullah, A. K. M. A. (2008b). The price of migration from Bangladesh to distant lands: Narratives of recent tragedies. *Asian Profile, 36*(6), 639–646.

Ullah, A. K. M. A. (2010a). *Rationalizing migration decisions: Labour migrants in South and South-East Asia*. Aldershot: Ashgate.
Ullah, A. K. M. A. (2010b). *Population migration in Asia: Theories and practice*. New York: Nova Science Publishers.
Ullah, A. K. M. A. (2010c). Rohingya refugee to Bangladesh: Historical exclusions and contemporary marginalization. *Journal of Immigrant and Refugee Studies, 9*(2).
Ullah, A. K. M. A. (2011, March/April). HIV/AIDS-related stigma and discrimination: A study on health care providers in Bangladesh. *Journal of the International Association of Physicians in AIDS Care (JIAPAC), 10*, 97–104.
Ullah, A. K. M. A. (2013). Irregular migrants, human rights and securitization in Malaysia: A policy analysis. In C. Tazreiter (Ed.), *Globalization and social transformation in the Asia Pacific: The Australian and Malaysian experience* (pp. 270–295). London: Palgrave McMillan.
Ullah, A. K. M. A. (2014). *Refugee politics in the Middle East and the Africa: Human rights, safety and identity*. London: Palgrave McMillan.
Ullah, A. K. M. A., & Routray, J. K. (2003). *NGOs and development: Alleviating rural poverty in Bangladesh*. Chile: Book Mark International.
Ullah, A. K. M. A., & Routray, J. K. (2007). Rural poverty alleviation through NGO interventions in Bangladesh: How far is the achievement? *International Journal of Social Economics, 34*(4), 237–248.
Ullah, A. K. M. A., Rahman, A., & Murshed, M. (1999). *Poverty and migration- slums of Dhaka city: The realities*. Dhaka: ARDS.
UNAIDS. (2005). *HIV – Related stigma, discrimination and human rights violations: Case studies of successful programmes*. Geneva: UNAIDS.
UNAIDS. (2006). *Report on the global AIDS epidemic*. Geneva: UNAIDS.
UNAIDS. (2007). *AIDS epidemic update*. Geneva: UNAIDS/WHO.
UNAIDS. (2008). *Report on the global AIDS epidemic* (No. 08.25E/JC1510E). Geneva: UNAIDS.
UNAIDS. (2009). *Joint action for results UNAIDS outcome framework 2009–2011*. Geneva: UNAIDS.
UNAIDS. (2011a). *Global AIDS response progress reporting 2012: Guidelines, construction of core indicators for monitoring the 2011 political declaration on HIV/AIDS*. Geneva: UNAIDS.
UNAIDS. (2011b). *UNAIDS World AIDS day report*. Geneva: UNAIDS.
UNAIDS. (2012). *Report on the global AIDS epidemic*. Geneva: UN Joint Programme on HIV/AIDS.
UNCTAD. (2013, April 16–17). *Prospects for building resilience to external shocks and mitigating their impact on trade and Development*. Multi-year expert meeting on enhancing the enabling economic environment at all levels in support of inclusive and sustainable development first session, Geneva
UNFPA. (2006). Gender and HIV/AIDS resource pack. *HIV/AIDS and Gender-Based Violence (GBV) Literature Review*.
UNHCR. (2007). *The state of the world's refugees: Fifty years of humanitarian action*. Oxford: Oxford University Press.
UNHCR (United Nations High Commissioner for Refugees). (2011). *UNHCR helps Italy cope with high seas influx of thousands of Tunisians*. Geneva: UNHCR. Available at http://www.unhcr.org/4d5a92b56.html. Accessed 14 Feb 2014.
UNHCR. (2014). *2014 UNHCR country operations profile*. Geneva: UNHCR
UNICEF Canada. (2012). *Is Canada doing its job to protect children's rights?* Toronto: UNICEF Canada.
United Nations. (2001). *Discrimination. Extract from the report on the world social situation 1997, Chapter VIII presented by Larry Willmore*. New York: United Nations Department of Economic and Social Affairs.
United Nations. (2002, June). *Introducing governance into HIV/AIDS programmes: People's Republic of China, Lao PDR and Vietnam*. Bangkok: South East Asia HIV and Development Programme
United Nations. (2005). *HIV/AIDS with particular emphasis on poverty: The concise report*. New York: Department of Economic and Social Affairs: Population Division.
United Nations (UNAIDS). (2010). *Global report. Fact Sheet*. Geneva: UNAIDS.

USAID. (2000). *USAID concept paper: Combating HIV/AIDS stigma, discrimination and denial: What why forward?*, Washington, DC.

USAID. (2006). *A closer look: The internalization of stigma related to HIV*. Washington, DC: USAID.

U.S. Department of Health and Human Services. (2000). *Healthy people 2010: Understanding and improving health*. Washington, DC: Government Printing Office.

Vajpayee, M., & Mohan, T. (2011). Current practices in laboratory monitoring of HIV infection. *Indian Journal of Medical Research, 134*(6), 801–822.

Van Brakel, W. H. (2005). *Measuring health-related stigma – A literature review. Report*. Amsterdam: Royal Tropical Institute.

Van Brakel, W. H. (2006). Measuring health-related stigma: A literature review. *Psychology of Health and Medicine, 11*(3), 307–334.

Van der Straten, A., King, R., Grinstead, O., Serufilira, A., & Allen, S. (1995). Couple communication, sexual coercion and HIV risk reduction in Kigali, Rwanda. *AIDS, 9*(8), 935–944.

Van Landingham, M. J., Grandjean, N., Suprasert, S., & Sittitrai, W. (1997). Dimensions of AIDS knowledge and risky sexual practices: A study of Northern Thai males. *Archives of Sexual Behaviour, 26*(3), 269–293.

Vanable, P. A., Carey, M. P., Blair, D. C., & Littlewood, R. A. (2006). Impact of HIV-related stigma on health behaviors and psychological adjustment among HIV-positive men and women. *AIDS and Behavior, 10*(5), 473–482.

Walker, J. (2010). *Section 13 of the Canadian Human Rights Act, Anti-Hate Laws and freedom of expression*. Ottawa, Canada: Law and Legislative Affairs. Parliamentary Information and Resources Services.

Wallman, S. (1988). Sex and death: The AIDS crisis in social and cultural context. *Journal of AIDS, 1*(6), 571–578.

Walsh, F. (2003). Family resilience: A framework for clinical practice. *Family Process, 42*(1), 1–18.

WCAR. (2001, August). *International migration, racism, discrimination and xenophobia. ILO, IOM, OHCHR*. World conference against racism, racial discrimination, xenophobia and related intolerance.

Weait, M., & Azad, Y. (2005). The criminalization of HIV transmission in England and wales: Questions of law and policy, Part 1. *HIV/AIDS Policy and Law Review, 10*(2), 5–12.

Weatherburn, P., Keogh, P., Dodds, C., Bourne, A., Owuor, J., Hammond, G., & Jessup, K. (2009). *What do you need? 2007–2008: Findings from a national survey of people diagnosed with HIV*. London: Sigma Research.

Weiser, S., Wolfe, W., Bangsberg, D., Thior, I., Gilbert, P., Makhema, J., Kebaabetswe, P., Dickenson, D., Mompati, K., Essex, M., & Marlink, R. (2003). Barriers to antiretroviral adherence for patients living with HIV infection and AIDS in Botswana. *Journal of Acquired Immune Deficiency Syndromes, 34*(3), 281–288.

Weiss, M. G., Ramakrishna, J., & Somma, D. (2006). Health-related stigma: Rethinking concepts and interventions. *Psychology, Health & Medicine, 11*(3), 277–287.

Wheaton, B. (1985). Models for the stress-buffering functions of coping resources. *Journal of Health and Social Behavior, 26*(4), 352–364.

White, M. (2004). Working with people who are suffering the consequences of multiple trauma: A narrative perspective. *The International Journal of Narrative Therapy and Community Work, 1*, 45–76.

Whitzman, C. (2010). Making the invisible visible: Canadian women, homelessness, and health outside the "big city". In D. J. Hulchanski, P. Campsie, S. Chau, S. Hwang, & E. Paradis (Eds.), *Finding home: Policy options for addressing homelessness in Canada*. Toronto: University of Toronto.

WHO. (2003). *HIV self-testing among health workers*. Geneva: WHO.

WHO. (2008). *Health of migrants—Report by the Secretariat*. Available from www.who.int/gb/ebwha/pdf_files/A61/A61_12-en.pdf

WHO. (2013). *WHO welcomes news that a child born with HIV now appears "functionally cured" through early antiretroviral treatment. Report*. Geneva: WHO.

Williams, D. R., Neighbors, H. W., & Jackson, J. S. (2003). Racial/ethnic discrimination and health: Findings from community studies. *American Journal of Public Health, 93*(2), 200–208.

Willig, C. (2001). *Introducing qualitative research in psychology: Adventures in theory and method*. Buckingham: Open University Press.

Wilson, D. P., Regan, D. G., Heymer, K. J., Jin, F., Prestage, G. P., & Grulich, A. E. (2010). Serosorting may increase the risk of HIV acquisition among men who have sex with men. *Sexually Transmitted Diseases, 37*(1), 13–17.

World Bank. (1997). *Confronting AIDS: Public priorities in a global epidemic*. New York: Oxford University Press for World Bank, European Commission and UNAIDS.

World Bank. (1998). HIV/AIDS South Asia. Available from: http://go.worldbank.org/TDJQZUCEK0. (cited on 2009 Apr 5)

World Bank. (2006). *The development impact of workers remittances in Latin America* (Vol. 2. Report No. 37026). Washington, DC: World Bank.

World Bank. (2011). *World Development Indicators (WDI)*. Washington, DC: World Bank.

World Bank. (2012). *World Bank and HIV/AIDS: The facts*. Washington, DC: The World Bank.

Yang, Y., Zhang, K. L., Chan, K. Y., & Reidpath, D. D. (2005). Institutional and structural forms of HIV-related discrimination in health care: A study set in Beijing. *Aids Care, 17*(Suppl. 2), S129–S140.

Yoshioka, M. R., & Schustack, A. (2001). Disclosure of HIV status: Cultural issues of Asian patients. *AIDS Patient Care and STDs, 15*(2), 77–82.

Zablotska, I. B., Imrie, J., Prestage, G., Crawford, J., Rawstorne, P., Grulich, A., Jin, F., & Kippax, S. (2009). Gay men's current practice of HIV seroconcordant unprotected anal intercourse: Serosorting or seroguessing? *AIDS Care, 21*(4), 501–510.

Zaidi, I. F., Crepaz, N., Song, R., Wan, C. K., Lin, L. S., Hu, D. J., & Sy, F. S. (2005). Epidemiology of HIV/AIDS among Asians and Pacific Islanders in the United States. *AIDS Education and Prevention, 17*(5), 405–417.

Zea, M., et al. (2005, March). Disclosure of HIV status and psychological well-being among Latino Gay and Bisexual Men. *AIDS and Behavior, 9*(1), 15.

Zhou, J., Sirisanthana, T., Kiertiburanakul, S., Chen, Y. M., Han, N., Lim, P., Kumarasamy, N., Choi, J. Y., Merati, T. P., Yunihastuti, E., Oka, S., Kamarulzaman, A., Phanuphak, P., Lee, C. K., Li, P. C., Pujari, S., Saphonn, V., & Law, M. G. (2010). Trends in CD4 counts in HIV-infected patients with HIV viral load monitoring while on combination antiretroviral treatment: Results from The TREAT Asia HIV Observational Database. *BMC Infectious Diseases, 10*, 361.

Zierler, S., Cunningham, W. E., Andersen, R., Shapiro, M. F., Bozzette, S. A., Nakazono, T., Morton, B. S., Crystal, S., Stein, M., Turner, B. J., & St. Clair, P. A. (2000, February). Violence victimization after HIV infection in a US probability sample of adult patients in primary care. *American Journal of Public Health, 90*(2), 208–215.

Zulu, E. M., Dodoo, F. N., & Ezeh, A. C. (2002). Sexual risk-taking in the slums of Nairobi, Kenya, 1993–1998. *Population Studies, 56*(4), 311–323.

Index

A.A. Ullah, A.S. Huque, *Asian Immigrants in North America with HIV/AIDS*,
DOI 10.1007/978-981-287-119-0

C

N

O

MIX
Papier aus verantwortungsvollen Quellen
Paper from responsible sources
FSC® C105338

If you have any concerns about our products,
you can contact us on
ProductSafety@springernature.com

In case Publisher is established outside the EU,
the EU authorized representative is:
Springer Nature Customer Service Center GmbH
Europaplatz 3, 69115 Heidelberg, Germany

Printed by Libri Plureos GmbH
in Hamburg, Germany